TIGERS UNDER THE TURF

TIGERS UNDER THE TURF

✦

A life disrupted by the horrors of World
War Two: the struggle to survive and lead
a normal life.

Bert Scorgie

iUniverse, Inc.
New York Lincoln Shanghai

TIGERS UNDER THE TURF
A life disrupted by the horrors of World War Two: the struggle to survive and lead a normal life.

Copyright © 2007 by Bert Scorgie

iUniverse books may be ordered through booksellers or by contacting:

iUniverse
2021 Pine Lake Road, Suite 100
Lincoln, NE 68512
www.iuniverse.com
1-800-Authors (1-800-288-4677)

Because of the dynamic nature of the Internet, any Web addresses or links contained in this book may have changed since publication and may no longer be valid.

The views expressed in this work are solely those of the author and do not necessarily reflect the views of the publisher, and the publisher hereby disclaims any responsibility for them.

ISBN: 978-0-595-45544-7 (pbk)
ISBN: 978-0-595-89853-4 (ebk)

Printed in the United States of America

The Tunnel Tigers

In the 50s & 60s the quest for hydropower was at its peak
all over the highlands where it was remote and bleak.
A hardy breed of men battled the seasons to bring power to the nation.
There were joiners, cranemen, labourers and drivers.
Most were hard working but there were quite a few skivers!
But the tunnel tigers were the stars of the show—
the prima donnas as far as the hydro workers go.

Tunnel Tigers were a special breed,
slightly nuts, a little bit 'wrong in the heid!'
Their workplace was the bowels of the earth,
but they were a happy bunch with plenty laughter and mirth
to light up their otherwise sunless and challenging world.
From all over the world they came for a start—
Poles, Germans, Russians and Paddy's, all playing their part.
Working twelve-hour shifts, they battled every day.
The more footage they removed the bigger the pay.

As you entered the tunnel you encountered thick reek.
The fumes of the gelignite made you feel sick.
It was wet and dirty, the conditions dog rough.
To work in those tunnels one had to be mighty tough!

The tigers looked after each other,
A fellow tiger was like a brother.
(If one of the guys was down on his luck
The others would say, "You're as sound as a pound!"
Then hastily organise a whip round.)

It was a dangerous place to earn your bread,
One careless move and you could end up dead.
It happened many times to some unfortunate men,
Their concrete memorials still stand in the Scottish glen.

Contents

FOREWORD

This story is a protest against war and conflict, and incorporates how my life was turned upside down by WW2. Fortunately I have never been in a war zone and never gave it much thought until one day in the summer of 2003. I was gardening for a young lady in Contin, Ross-shire. It was a lovely hot summer day, causing me to sweat a bit. As I straightened my back to wipe away the sweat I near had a second heart attack! Unbeknown to me I was in a low flying zone, possibly in the flight path to the bombing range at Tain. Suddenly from out of nowhere two high-powered Jet Planes swooped low overhead. The noise was horrendous and very frightening. Having a cup of coffee to calm my shattered nerves, I thought what if those planes had been armed and dropped bombs on Contin? It would have been terrible! Britain and America were pounding the daylights out of Iraq at the time so my thoughts turned to the poor innocent people who had to suffer the daily bombardments. Can you imagine the stress of the children, the old people, mentally handicapped people and, of course, the women? They must have been terrified, especially when the B52's did their carpet-bombing runs—it doesn't bear thinking about. We kept getting daily figures of the American and British casualties but I don't recall reading about Iraqi civilian casualties. I'm sure the figure would be frightening.

Having suffered the tragic loss of my own father early in the last war, I have followed the daily reports of how the recent conflicts are progressing both in the papers and on the television. One report I was reading sent my memory back sixty plus years. It was the treatment meted out to a young widow whose husband had been recently killed in Iraq. It was on a par with the way my own mother had been treated by the government when she was widowed with a young family in WW 2. My mother was left homeless and penniless; she was paid a pittance of a pension that included 10/-(50 pence) per week to help with my upbringing, then left to fend for herself. She was very vulnerable. The day I was fifteen my 50 pence per week stopped! It wasn't index linked either, so it remained 10/-per week after twelve years. The article about the young widow of Iraq was about a family named Seymour, according to the Press. Mrs Seymour's husband was killed early in the Iraqi conflict of 2003 due to an administrative error. Mrs Seymour received ten days' pay after her husband had been killed—a mistake by the

Royal Navy, she received a demand that the money be paid back to the Navy. At the same time she was told she would have to vacate her married quarters at the end of three months. What a lovely surprise after her husband had made the ultimate sacrifice for his country. Due to public pressure, the Secretary of State rescinded the request, but by then the poor woman had to suffer this added worry along with the loss of her husband. We are a very caring nation! Mrs Seymour received £400 she was not entitled to—just a little statistic. Are people aware that each missile fired from the submarine *HMS SPLENDOUR* cost one million pounds? The mind boggles. If this is the way we treat the families of our war heroes, what chance have the rest of us? I hope and pray my sixteen-year-old grandson never has to go to war, or anybody else's grandson, for that matter. It is a dirty mucky business. The more sophisticated the weapons become, the more horrendous the damage inflicted. During my sixty-six years of life I doubt if we ever had one year without conflict; but as long as we have people like Bush and Blair, we will have to keep battling on at their command.

The following is an account of how my life turned out. I often wonder if things would have been different had my father survived. I will never know, but I am quite content with my lot.

My appearance on planet earth occurred on the 14/12/1937, at around 08.00. I was born in my Granny's house at No 5 South Castle Street, Cullen, Banff-shire; due to boundary changes it is now Aberdeen-shire. My father was a regular soldier with twelve years service to his credit before the war started; my mother was a domestic worker until they married in February 1937. Ten months later I was the result of their planning and hard work.

Granny's house was at the top of the hill overlooking one of the finest views on the North East coast. I still visit just to watch the waves breaking on the sandy beach. No 5 was one of the biggest houses in the town with seven rooms. We were probably one of the more modern residences as we had a sink with a cold-water tap. The cooking and lightening was done by gas. We also had a water closet out in the back yard. Many of the other houses still had dry toilets—those were pre-chemical days! We had no bathroom and no electricity. My granny and grandfather had parted company, so to make ends meet she used to take in tourists, her busiest fortnight of the year being Glasgow Fair. We still had a railway station in Cullen; the visitors would arrive by train and stay for two weeks at a time. As we had no sanitation in the house my Granny would supply a chamber pot known locally as a chanti; these pots held about a gallon and boy did they honk in the morning! Also in the bedroom there was a basin with an ewer full of cold water to allow the visitors to wash. Pretty Spartan conditions, but that was the same for everybody in those dark days. At the rear of the house was a fairly big yard where my forefathers ran a business. One half was dedicated to a coal yard while the other half was a Dairy from where they supplied milk—two very contrasting commodities. Our health and safety buffs of today would have had heart failure! The business had been wound up before my birth. Due to the recession at the end of the thirties, they had to close down. Many times as I grew up older folk would tell me that if our family had all the money they were owed due to the depression, we would be rich people. In many instances people got their goods on tick and were never able to pay.

The next two and a half years of my life are what I have picked up from other people, as I was not old enough to remember. My father was stationed at Aldershot with his Regiment, the 1st Battalion Gordon Highlanders. He had taken a posting as a Batman to an Officer so that my mother and I could join him. This we did as soon as my mother was fit to travel. We made the journey at the end of January, 1938. It would be a horror journey for my mother on her own, for the steam trains were dirty mucky brutes and they needed about twenty-four hours to get from Cullen to Aldershot. I must have slept all the way as I don't recall the journey. The next bit of info I have is being home in Cullen the summer of 1939. I am a bit vague about the reasons, but my mother and I travelled back to Aldershot alone. When my father met her at the station he helped her across the railway line from where the trains back North left. He had just had word they were moving out and dependants had to head for home. This was when my father headed for France at the start of World War 2. My parents didn't even have one night together—it was a case of 'get them home', in our case back North.

The first three years of my life are rather vague—I am sure most people will have had the same problem. I would possibly say that my first memories began when I was about three. Before that I can only work on what I have been told by others. Sadly, most of the people that could have kept me right are no longer with us. Anyhow, the day my mother and I parted from my father at Aldershot railway station, the summer of 1939 was the last time we were together. If my memory serves me correctly, my mother did have contact with my father, using what was known as field correspondence. This was possibly kept very vague in case it fell into enemy hands. It was in a sort of format where all my father could say was the he was alive and well. His final contact was a telegram dated 21/09/1939, very brief, saying 'LEAVING FRIDAY' and his forename Bert. The next telegram my mother received was from the war office telling us that he had been killed in action on 04/06/1940. The bloody awful war had only just begun! Due to my young age and various circumstances, the loss of my father didn't affect me until later on in my life, when word of his death came through. I don't recall the telegram arriving, so it didn't make a big impact on me at the time. During my lifetime I have been known to entertain a bit with jokes, songs and poetry—this is a sample of my work dedicated to my late father:

DAD

This is a word I never really said,
I was just two and a half—you were dead.
In June nineteen forty the dirty deed was done,
You were murdered by a bullet from a Nazi gun.

They laid you to rest in North West France,
Near the river Somme where the red poppies dance.
Longueval cemetery is your final resting place,
It's not unlike your home village of Fordyce.

This is what war is all about—innocent people suffering because of the actions of nutters. What did Hitler achieve? Nothing! All he did was send millions of people to their deaths, leaving hundreds of war orphans like me to face an uncertain world.

I was one of the lucky ones and lived a reasonable life, but one still had a bit of a stigma that one didn't have real father. In my later years the desire to visit my father's grave started to haunt me, so in 1989, while working in Germany, I made an effort to visit Longueval. Sadly, it turned out a disaster, as I was very unprepared and didn't even have the correct location. Our vehicle started to get low on fuel and we had no French currency, so had to abort the attempt. It was another ten years before the feeling of guilt overtook me again. I suffered a heart attack in 2000 and began to feel time might be running out for me, so I wrote to the local branch of the British Legion, asking if they could help. Their reply put me in touch with the Normandy Veterans Association. They were running a trip to the very area I wished to visit and had a spare seat on the coach—and yes, they would take me Longueval! I will forever be indebted to the chairman, Bill Loggie, for thanks to him I was able to fulfil my wish.

My father was a professional soldier with twelve years service before the war started. Most of his time was served abroad, having seen service in India, Palestine and Ireland, and now, finally, France. It was his profession, employed by the government to defend his country; but from the day he died the government did nothing to help us sort out our lives except pay my mother a pension of 10/- (50p) a week to help with my upbringing. (Her own small pension stopped when she re-married—I have no idea what that was worth.) My mother was now a widow, homeless, penniless and vulnerable. When we left Aldershot I presume we went home to my Granny's place in Cullen, as that was where the telegram telling us my father had been killed was sent. I was still too young to remember any of the happenings from that time, but my first memories at about the age of three are of living in Buckpool with an uncle of my father. My granny was a bit of a tarter so she and mother must have fallen out and we had to move. These are vague memories, though my next memory is clearer—we had moved yet again and were once again living in Aberdeen with relatives of my father. Three incidents are quite clear to me although I don't remember moving; the first is that I had a small sister, so there were actually three of us; secondly, there is the memory of me pulling a draught excluder off one of the doors and getting a severe beating from my mother for being so wicked; my third memory of Aberdeen is walking along a very dark street when suddenly there was an Air Raid. The siren was wailing and there were soldiers running about like headless chickens shouting and pushing people into shop doorways. There were a couple of explosions but they were well away from where we were.

We must have moved digs under cover of darkness as we were now staying with friends of my mother and father at Dunecht. It was winter time as there was snow on the ground, but again I have no recollection of moving. The outstanding memory of Dunecht is that the lavatory was straddled across a burn. The comical bit about it was that inside the small wooden hut there were two oval holes so that two could use it sitting side by side—a rather embarrassing situation, I would imagine, when the small burn was in spate! It would be very hygienic but otherwise rather disgusting.

Our stay at Dunecht must have been short, for before long we were on the move again. My mother must have applied for a position as a housekeeper to a crofter from Gamrie in Banff-shire, for after he interviewed her she agreed to go and keep house for him. The deal was that he would return the following Sunday and pick us up by car. My mother must have been travelling light as we all managed to travel in the one car with all her belongings.

This was the start of another adventure for me. One I can remember very well; the journey is a bit vague but it would have lasted over an hour. My mother's boss didn't have a car so he had to get someone else to drive. That meant there were five of us in a Standard Ten. I remember our arrival well as it was like an adventure playground for me. I had spent the most of my short life in towns so to land on a farmyard with all the implements and animals was just the ticket for a wee chap like me. This move was to shape my life forever; perhaps it was confusing for a little boy who had seen so much turmoil in the space of three years, but it was the beginning of possibly a more stable existence, especially for my mother.

A WHOLE NEW BALL GAME

We arrived at Wester Cross-slacks Gamrie on a Sunday afternoon. The place was a whole new world for me. In the farmyard there were all sorts of things to take up my attention—implements with seats and levers, in the byre cattle and two lovely Clydesdale horses. It was an adventure playground. It is doubtful if my mother was as enthusiastic as I was when she found out what she had let herself in for. The house was basically a shell with a corrugated iron roof. If my memory serves me correctly, the floors were hard packed earth! It was a but and ben one room used as a living room; in one corner there was a recess with a double bed in it, while at the other gable wall there was a hole with a hook hanging above a grating—this was the fireplace, the only means of heating and cooking. The lighting was a paraffin lamp. There was no water—it had to be taken from a well about half-a-mile away; this was done by means of an old whisky cask lying on its side and mounted on shafts so that it could be moved by horse. This was also the only means of watering the livestock. No sanitation to speak of—we were probably a step up from the Stone Age! The place was overrun with rats: the minute the light went out at night they would appear out of the wall in droves! How my sister and I were never bitten I will never know.

The next big event I remember—and it didn't mean a lot to me at the time—was that my mother married her boss, so our landlord now became my stepfather! We were always on first name terms from the time we met. Arthur was worse off than me regarding his parents—he had been born in Glasgow and then boarded out at a very young age. He had no idea if his parents were dead or alive. He had been shunted from pillar to post and like many other boarded out kids, used as cheap labour; some were treated dreadfully to the point that they were not even allowed to eat at the same table as their foster parents. Arthur went to his grave without being able to trace who he belonged to.

It was now 1942. The war was still raging although we were well away from the danger area. There was quite a lot of activity as there were troops billeted at the mansion house. We also had a few aerodromes close by; some mornings we would see planes arriving back from wherever they had been overnight, possibly Norway, but on a few occasions we could see damaged areas where they had been

1

hit by gunfire. Some of them would sound rather sick as they headed for Rettie Aerodrome. One particular day—it was during the haymaking season—Arthur was working in the field and I was alone with him when suddenly the normal tranquil peace of the Gamrie backwater was shattered by the sound of two aeroplanes with engines screaming, followed by the sound of gunfire. We realised it was a German and one of our own engaged in a dogfight! It lasted for a few minutes before one of them started to plunge towards the sea. At that point we had no idea who had been successful. Then we saw a tiny figure away up in the sky dangling at the end of a parachute. He was drifting over the top of us and landed quite a distance away. It was the German! He was surrounded by farm workers who held him until help arrived. I remember them saying he was just a young frightened boy who offered no resistance.

We had our share of the enemy in our area. On at least two occasions we had spies landed not too far away from where we stayed. It seemed to be an ideal place to land a seaplane—I will go into more detail later on.

The next milestone in my life was having to start school, so Easter 1943, shining like a new pin, I enrolled at Bracoden School. There was a mixture of kids, half from the fishing villages of Crovie and Gardenstown; the other half was comprised of children from the families of the farming community.

Not long into my education we were on the move again. I am sure we had Nomadic blood in us or maybe tinker blood, I don't know, but we were moving! My stepfather had successfully obtained the lease of a bigger, more modern croft about two miles away. When I say 'more modern', I mean that it had a pump in the back porch that actually produced water! The steading also had water so that the animals could help themselves when they felt like it. We still had no sanitation, bath or electricity, but a plus factor was that I attended the same school with about the same distance to walk. When the day came for us to move we loaded all our belongings on a couple of horse carts and moved—another great adventure, for this new place had trees round it and many buildings. I could now learn to climb and explore all these aspects of my new surroundings.

I forgot to mention we had another addition to the family—mother and her new husband had produced a son! Our lifestyle was very basic, probably quite Spartan as it was not an easy life trying to make a living from farming. We had no means of communication—the nearest phone was a red box about half-a-mile away. We had no wireless and possibly got a newspaper a couple of times a week, so we were most likely running a couple of weeks behind with what was happening in the world beyond Gamrie. Shortly after moving it was necessary to buy a new cow so a young heifer arrived from a cattle dealer. This move was to cause a lot of grief over the next few weeks. Two days after the cow arrived at our place it started to be unwell; the vet was called and all hell was let loose involving the police and the Ministry of Agriculture. The first examination pointed to the cow having Anthrax, causing great panic. The book of rules was produced and had to be implemented in no uncertain terms if the tests were positive. Firstly, all cloven hoofed animals were to be slaughtered, then pits of a certain depth had to be dug, the carcasses pushed into the pit and covered in quicklime—a mammoth task as there were no handy J.C.Bs in those dark days. All the digging would be by hand. This drastic measure had to include all the animals within a mile radius—quite an undertaking. My parents were worried sick, for if this went ahead they would be ruined. My mother was just getting us kids to bed when there was aloud banging on the house door. I ran to the door and opened it. On the step was the local bobby leaning against his bike, and he asked if my stepfather was in. My mother looked startled when she saw the bobby, fearing the worst, but he assured her not to worry, as he was the bearer of good news. My stepfather was out visiting about a mile down the road and it was a great relief to hear the bobby tell my mother the cow had been given a clean bill of health.

With a war on there were restrictions on what you did with eggs; they were supposed to go to the Government Pool, but my mother used to get fresh fish from the fisher folk, so she would give them eggs and butter. One old guy used to fill his flat cap with a dozen eggs, then put it on his head! It made him look a foot taller. Then he would walk straight back, all the way home. This was supposed to fool the police!

Before I continue, I would like to make a comparison between conditions today (the 10th of January 2004) and what it was like sixty years ago. On the 10th of January, 1944, I would have been seven years old. It was just ten days after Santa Claus had called! Picture the scene: it is 8 p.m. and we are all round the kitchen table playing all sorts of games—Snakes and Ladders, Ludo, Snap, or perhaps doing a jigsaw puzzle; mother is fussing about making cocoa and something to eat before we are sent to bed. We are told to get a move on and within ten minutes we are heading for the bedroom. The paraffin lamp would be burning and under the blankets there was a house builder's brick that had been in the oven most of the day being kept hot; rolled up in a towel or an old sheet, it made the perfect hot water bottle. I would be allowed to read a comic for half an hour before mother returned to extinguish the lamp, but before she did that I had to use the chantie in case I piddled in the bed.

Now fast forward to today! I know I am an adult, but most youngsters have the same as I have. I drain my glass of Glenmorngie, clean my teeth, and as I enter my room I switch on the main electric light. At either side of the bed there are bedside lamps; on the right-hand side table I have a radio with C.D and tape facilities; on the dressing table my digital camera is in the charge dock in case I decide to use the camera in a hurry. In the wardrobe I have a video camera. Moving along the room, I have a 14-inch television with video recorder. Next in the corner is my pride and joy—a Dell computer with copying and scanning facilities. On the left-hand side of my bed, yet another bedside table with possibly one hundred pounds worth of books. Am I happy with all these luxuries? Not really—I find life can get very boring, something we never experienced when we were on the bread line. Oh! I forgot to put the mobile phone on the charger in case the battery goes flat.

Zooming back to 1944, we are approaching an exciting time of year—for me, at least. The threshing mill will be due in a couple of weeks. This always used to get the adrenaline going, as the Big Steam Engine was a wonderful piece of engineering. It would arrive late afternoon and the two operators would get it all set up ready to start work at the crack of dawn next day. They had pulled a workmen's caravan behind the mill—this was their sleeping quarters. The normal practice was that they would eat at the farm they were threshing for, so they didn't need to cook for themselves. As soon as it was light enough in the morning the big Steamer would burst into life; the noise could be heard for miles around and all the neighbours would arrive just as it was getting light. It needed about a dozen men to carry out the operation and, of course, the two operators wanted to finish early afternoon so they could move on to the next croft for an early start the following day. As soon as the mill was finished the next chore was to fill the mattresses off the beds with fresh chaff. This was a yearly chore and the first night on the new bed was like lying on top of a hillock, but before the year was over it was flattened out. The one thing that annoyed me was that we had to go to school and miss all the fun.

A few weeks after the mill had gone we had a tragic incident—one of the nineteen year-old-orphans committed suicide; he had been brought up with the same people as my stepfather, so he was like a family member. He had wanted to join the army but, because he worked on the land, he was not allowed to leave. Tragically he ended his life by hanging—a very sad incident. We kids were taken into the room where he was lying in his coffin, to see the corpse; this is something I have never forgotten.

We were well into the spring again—a relief for the farmers as the past winter had been another severe one, which meant a lot of cattle feed had to be used while the beasts were inside. Now they could get on with the ploughing and then the sowing of the crops, always a busy time, especially for the one-man crofts, as the planting was only additional work to their already busy schedule. But they struggled on probably thinking that when the war is over things could only get better.

The late spring of '44 brought us more bad news. My uncle Sammy had been missing in Libya and we finally got the confirmation that he had been killed in action. My grandmother had clung to the hope that he was hiding in the desert. The galling part was that Sammy was exempt from the Army due to his job in telecommunications, but he was determined to join up and do his bit and so he had volunteered for the Tank Corps. The sad part for me personally was that I never got to know him due to this bloody awful thing called war.

Suddenly, late that spring, our normally quiet backwater burst into life with military vehicles driving like crazy all over the place—convoys driving up and down the main road. It was difficult to get across as the lorries, tanks, jeeps and motorbikes drove past in their dozens. We found out much later on that the invasion of Normandy was about to take place. The biggest mechanised invasion from the sea was to be launched in France—nothing like it had been tried out before and so it was certainly a bit of a gamble. The beaches along the Normandy coast, for anyone who has never been there, are not my idea of a battleground—they are dead flat with absolutely no cover whatsoever; then, as you get to Omaha Beach, you start to find sheer cliffs! It is like that all the way down to St Valery, so if there was ever an area where a battleground shouldn't have been, it was Normandy.

Back in Gamrie we knew very little about these preparations. As I said before, we had virtually no contact with the outside world, just our own little district. Normandy would have been history before we heard the full horror of what happened. Even then, it's only when you visit the place that you will understand, when you see the real picture, when you see all the headstones scattered throughout France, Belgium and Holland, that you get to understand the cost in human life. I often wonder how many kids like me were orphaned because of a certain madman called Adolph Hitler and his butchers.

Getting on with my life, it might be said that my childhood had in effect been on an even keel. Having not known my real father was not really a disadvantage to me. At that stage in my life we were given a reasonable upbringing, were well fed and clothed, and there was always plenty to keep us amused around the croft. My mother was an excellent cook; some of her dishes were out of this world, considering she only had basic ingredients to work with. Due to the rationing, she knitted most of our socks and jerseys, so she was kept busy. Although I never heard my parents complaining I found out in later years that it was a struggle to make ends meet as the croft was on the borderline of being self sufficient. There was no other means of employment. My stepfather did manage to get some work with the Timber Control people, dragging timber with his own horse employed by a Jewish Company.

In the late summer of '44, along with three schoolmates, we were walking home around four-thirty when suddenly we were aware of an aeroplane with a very sick sounding engine. Looking skywards, we were amazed to see this plane heading straight for us, coughing and spluttering. We turned and ran! Seconds later there was a thump as the plane crashed into the ditch at the side of the road. We were standing there, open mouthed, as the guy in the cockpit slid the canopy back and stood up and clambered down the wing and said he hoped he hadn't frightened us too much. He then asked where he could find a telephone. We pointed him towards the red box and then hurried home to tell our families our news—unnecessarily, as it happened, as my parents could see everything from the window and were aware of what was going on. I think the plane was a Mosquito. It was the first time I had been that close to one so it was quite thrilling, although it was quite frightening when it was diving towards us. In that moment of panic we didn't know which way to run, but there were at least fifty yards between the plane and us when it finally crashed. The pilot was foreign, possibly Australian, although he looked rather Latin with his black greasy hair and pencil moustache.

Our lives were never dull with plenty of intrigue and excitement. Over the next couple of days we were to learn a bit more about life as they prepared to remove the plane. We had just finished our supper when we heard a vehicle enter the farmyard. We kids were first out the door in time to see a man with a blue uniform climb out of a Military jeep. He asked us if our daddy was at home, and just then our parents arrived at the door. The man held out his hand and introduced himself as Flt Lt Ambrose. He would be in charge of the recovery operation and asked if it would be possible to park his heavy vehicles in our yard for the night as he didn't want to risk going in the field until they were sure it would support the low loaders. He was told he was welcome to leave them with us. Next to arrive was a three tonner with all the necessary camping equipment. The men in the lorry proceeded to set up a camp consisting of half a dozen tents and a small marquee for the cooking. They had a water bowser which they asked if they could fill up at our place. As the bowser was filling my mother asked the young man in charge if he would like a cup of tea. He accepted the offer and sat down at our kitchen table. While he drank the tea my mother asked about sleeping arrangements and the guy said they would be sleeping in tents but that they also had to take turns at guard duty. My mother told the lad that we had a spare room—if it got too cold they could use that—and she showed him where it was. An hour later three huge low loaders arrived and were shunted into our yard. We were a bit miffed as we had to go to bed and miss all the excitement. When we got up next morning the plane was in the middle of the field—the men must have pulled it clear of the road before they went to bed. My parents also had a tale to tell as when they wakened around 6 a.m. they heard the sound of someone in the spare room. On investigation they found half a dozen pairs of boots lined up outside the door. Even with a war going on we never thought of locking the doors day or night. As we passed the crash site there was a hive of activity as the airmen started to dismantle the plane. Of course, we again missed all the fun as we had to attend school! On arriving home that afternoon most of the plane was gone, though they were still working on one low loader gathering up the loose ends. Flt Lt Ambrose said that all would be gone except for the camp—they would dismantle it in the morning. Mother invited the four guys that were left behind to come to our house for a cup of tea that evening. Again we were ushered to bed, leaving our parents and the four R. A.F. fellows to blether into the night. They were busy dismantling the camp in the morning as we passed by, heading once again for the school. Before they left, Bill Ambrose called in at our house and gave my mother a huge cardboard box full of groceries, sugar, tea, butter, and all sorts of goodies that we normally only had as a treat due to the rationing.

It was back to the humdrum life again after the drama of the plane crash. Our teachers had a field day getting us to draw and write stories about the crash. Most Sundays after church and Sunday School our house was a meeting place for friends, neighbours and relations. There would be quite a stir with my mother making tea and everybody getting stuck into her baking scones, pancakes and cakes. She spent every Friday baking, knowing that it would be eaten on Sunday. We had a baker's van twice a week—he supplied fresh bread, but mother baked oatcakes that were as popular as bread.

After the RAF lads left with their aeroplane, the excitement for the year was over. We were beginning to hear of all the horrors that took place at Normandy with the heavy loss of life, but sadly it didn't mean a great deal to us; one reason, possibly, and maybe a very selfish reason, was that we didn't have any direct relatives involved. My uncle Dod was in the war somewhere but we had no idea where. My aunt's husband was in Burma. Many years later, after visiting the Normandy coast, it sunk in just what these young men were up against after they left the landing craft. We certainly never need anything like it again.

Another year was at an end and we children were getting excited. There was snow on the ground, heralding the approach of Father Christmas time again. We also had a Sunday School party where a great time was had by all. On that occasion we had a film show—my first Tarzan film. In the forties and fifties it was the norm to send gifts at Christmas time. We would receive a few parcels from aunts and my grandmother. We would be waiting for the postman to arrive and then, like vultures, swoop round my mother to see what we had received. She usually sat in front of the fire while she undid the string. This particular day—it was just before dinner time—she had all the pots on the open range boiling, and during the pushing and shoving to get a decent position one of us tipped the handle of the milk pan with the result that boiling milk landed on my mother's lap. She was scalded from her thighs to her toes. What a tragedy! There was nothing remotely like a paramedic in those days so she had to suffer the pain until they could get hold of the district nurse. She was out of action for three months.

One of my mother's sisters came and looked after us as my mother was unable to put her feet on the ground or get shoes on for a few weeks. My aunt turned out to be one of the hardest taskmasters I ever encountered. I would even say she would have made a good guard in one of Hitler's concentration camps! A very cruel woman, she had no children of her own at that time. Her husband was in Burma fighting the Japs. During her stay with us she got word he had been badly wounded. He recovered and went on to live until he was eighty.

The only newspapers I remember getting during the war were *The People's Journal* and the *Banff-shire Journal*, both weekly papers. I don't remember getting a daily but I can remember clearly the day the war in Europe finished. We were all standing round the horse trough at dinnertime. The horses were getting a drink when suddenly one of our neighbours who owned a wireless came running up the yard waving his arms and shouting, "The War's Finished!" There was a lot of rejoicing with parties in all the major cities and towns. They had a bit of a fête in the village of Gardenstown, but otherwise life just went on as normal. One significant difference I did notice, just as the war ended, was the amount of tractors springing up all over the place. They were replacing the faithful old horse.

One major disappointment for me that year was that the old steam engine had been replaced. When the mill arrived with the Threshing mill, it was being pulled by a shiny new Allis Chalmers tractor and, guess what, there was only one operator! So even in those early days mechanism was costing jobs. The threshing no longer held any excitement for me as there was something fascinating about the old steam engine.

One thing I was unaware of was the struggle my parents were having to keep the croft working. It was a real challenge and many weeks the only income was the few shillings the government paid my mother as a pension towards my upbringing. The North East coast could be a harsh environment to live in. We had many good summers but the winters could be very hard. We were used to it, but there were very few winters that didn't see the roads blocked and everything at a standstill. The harder the winter, the more costly it was to keep and feed the animals as they were indoors for weeks at a time.

The croft may not have been producing a lot, but my parents were making up for it as they had another addition to the family—a lovely daughter and sister for the rest of us. She recently phoned me to say they are about to become grandparents for the first time. Back to 1945: my mother had recovered from her scalding and was back on her feet, my horrible aunt had returned to her job and we were chugging along again. We had a market garden about three miles from our house; my mother would go down there to get some fresh vegetables and possibly a bit of peace. About a mile down the road there was a rise that you couldn't see over except if you stood on the strainer post at our road end. I was climbing on the post one day when I slipped and a nail caught the muscle of my leg, causing a four-inch gash about an inch wide. We couldn't get the doctor for a couple of days, but when he saw me he had one look and said the wound needed a couple of stitches. Without any freezing, he proceeded to insert two stitches. I can still feel the pain!

PEACE AT LAST

1946 and things were getting back to normal! But what is normal? We were still under quite a bit of wartime restrictions, one being food rationing. At least the blackout was gone, so gradually things were improving. Around that time, to encourage farmers to grow more crops, the Government decided to pay a subsidy for growing potatoes. I can't remember how it worked, but the crofter had to declare how many acres he had planted. A meeting was called to explain how the forms had to be filled in; one of the elder statesmen of the district appointed himself as chairman and finally, closing the meeting, he emphasised how easy it would be to cheat and the temptation was there to declare more acres than had actually been planted. His parting words were, "Be it on your own heads if you cheat and get caught!" He also pointed out that there were Government Inspectors who would be doing spot checks. As we were trooping out the door he shouted, "You have been warned!" Later on, as the potatoes were getting near time to be harvested, the Inspectors made a swoop on our area. They singled out half-a-dozen farms and carried out spot checks. Of the six places inspected, five were cleared. but the sixth one was our chairman and, lo and behold, he got his fingers burned because he told "Porkies"! I have no recollection of the punishment but he had his arse thoroughly kicked by the Government. Of course, communism states that you do not do as the boss does but you do what he tells you to do, so another chapter passed. At least it gave folks something different to talk about. Old Joe blamed the wife for getting it wrong as she had filled in the form!

I have never established whether we have the same number of lives as our feline friends, but if we have mine was reduced to eight that summer. We kids had very little in the way of toys, but one made do with what one had. Ours was an old bicycle with only a frame and two wheels. We played in a field behind the house where there was a fairly steep gradient. The idea was to push the bike to the top of the field. Once the bike had gathered speed we would jump on and run to the bottom where the main road passed. One could go out the gate and cross the road into the next field; if one gathered enough momentum, one could go quite some distance. As I said already, we had maybe four cars a week going past our house, so one of us would act as lookout to make sure it was all clear. On this occasion my brother Geordie was lookout. He waved me on so I kept going, but in the middle of the road I had an argument with one of the four cars as we met more or less head on! The bike was lying at the side of the road completely knack-ered. I was in the middle of the road with a sock torn off my leg and with some damage done to my muscle. The car was stationary, rocking from side to side, the two men occupants shouting abuse at me through the windscreen. (Anybody who would like to feel my left leg can still feel where the muscle was damaged!) The car was possibly a Standard Ten as this was a popular model around that era; anyhow, when the two occupants got over the initial shock, they demanded to know where our parents lived. We pointed them in the right direction and they marched up to our house. (Nobody enquired how I was.) When my mother answered the door she was greeted with a spray of abuse as the men ranted and raved at her for allowing her "bloody bairns to play on the road"! At first she was taken aback as she had no idea what was going on. Finally the driver calmed down and explained that he had nearly killed me and he was unhappy about the dent in his new car. After they left we were given the mother and father of all rows and threatened with murder if we played near the main road again. The rea-son I escaped lightly was that the man had just purchased the car. He had never sat a driving test so he was feeling his way and driving very slowly. Lucky me! But it was a lesson for us about playing near the road and has lived with me all my life; indeed, if I see kids walking along the pavement I am invariably a bit wary of them.

1947 was a year that changed the British way of life for ever. It was the year the Labour Government decided to let us have free National Health, the year all the lazy idle people of Britain hit the jackpot! Now, sixty years on, every leech and hanger on from around the globe enjoys the benefits that the majority of us funded so that we could enjoy a decent retirement. But do the retired people ben-efit? Not on your life! If you are a lame duck from around the globe you have a great chance of settling in Britain and never having to do a hand's turn but collect benefits on a weekly basis.

That year was a disaster for our family financially. We were too young to understand how things worked then, but as I now understand it, one of the horses that my stepfather used to work the croft belonged to someone else. Right in the busy part of the year that person required the horse back, which meant we had to buy a horse. The price would be in the region of fifty pounds (not much, I hear you say!) but that fifty pounds probably equated to two years' profit so it was quite a financial blow, more than likely putting my parents in the red with the bank. Then the next disaster and probably the death knell for my parents, was the fact that the winter of 1947 was one of the worst ever recorded. The snow was so deep it was just below the telephone wires and remained like that for twelve weeks. Everything was at a standstill. My stepfather even had to dig a hole so we could get out of the house. It is the worst I ever remember. The animals were indoors for weeks on end and by the time the thaw came food for the beasts was running low. Then, with the thaw we had floods. The fields were so wet that next year's crops could not be planted. Everything was in an uproar. Eventually things got back to normal but were running late. That spring we had a relative from Aberdeen visit us—Margaret, a real tomboy and as tough as they come. This story may sound far-fetched but I can assure you it's true! We decided to go with Margaret up to the top of the hill behind our house and as we walked across the field we came upon a hare lying asleep in its scrape. For some reason or another it never heard us, and Margaret shot out her hand and caught it by the ears. The hare suddenly was wide-awake and started to scream, just like a baby in pain! It was kicking out with its hind legs and the sound was pitiful. Margaret held on for a couple of minutes but had to let go, and a grateful hare was soon disappearing over the brow of the hill. I have never seen Margaret since that summer but heard recently that she has passed away.

Behind the scenes and possibly late into the night my parents were having deep discussions regarding the crisis they were going through regarding their survival as crofters. Some of the men were now working away from home and trying to keep the croft going on a part-time basis. The Highlands was a favourite place for employment: there were huge Hydro Schemes under construction, so this was drawing people North as the wages were much better than working the croft. It was a real dilemma and they had to make up their minds before the 28th of May, the end of the next term. It was eventually agreed that they would throw in the towel and look for a job. This would have been a great source of gossip for the local mongers. They would have plenty to talk about because the local blacksmith decided to leave at the same time. He was involved in some sort of scandal so they would have a field day. The decision taken and the letter of resignation handed in at the factor's office, we had a lot of work to get through before we left. All the stock and implements had to be sold, so a date was made to hold a roup (sale). Everything had to be numbered and catalogued. My mother had an eccentric old cousin who was a very clever old man and good with his hands; he took over the job of numbering each item, making templates so that all the numbers were uniform. Old Johnny could speak a dozen foreign languages, all self-taught, but he was quite a strange person.

I would like to dedicate a few paragraphs to the old fellow who volunteered to number all the goods for the roup. Again, I am on my high horse about the horrors of war and how people were damaged and then left to get on with it, discarded like debris. Johnny Russell was a first cousin of my granny. He was often described as being a "queer auld bugger"—even my own family said he was "queer" (queer meaning strange). I often wonder how many people took the time to find out why Johnny was queer instead of simply having a good laugh at the man's strange behaviour. I doubt that he would have told them. I never ever heard him complain—he just got on with life in his own quiet comical way. Well, the reason for Johnny's strange ways was that he had been gassed and shellshocked during the First World War—where exactly we will never find out as Johnny is long gone from this earth, having survived until he was near his eightieth birthday. There was no counselling when he came home from war. He stayed with his unmarried sister and they both remained unmarried until they passed away. His sister would have had all the trauma of getting her brother back on his feet after the damage was done on a battlefield in France. I am almost certain he never received an army pension as he worked for the old county council for some part of his life. Of course, mental injuries are invisible and unless pointed out nobody is really interested. On the outside Johnny looked just an eccentric old bloke, bald, slightly stooped—you would never have given him a second glance; but in his head was the brain of a genius! He was a part-time Coast Guard during the Second World War. If any foreign ship were in trouble, Johnny would be sent for to speak to the skipper. He had taught himself many foreign languages, one being Russian which I believe is very difficult to pick up. The last language he learned was our own native Gaelic. His reason for this was that a man from Lewis bought the local filling station and Johnny was concerned the man would miss speaking the Gaelic—so he learned it to keep the man company! Another of his skills was his ability to make models out of scrap material. One of these materials was the National Dried Milk tins the Government dished out with powdered milk to feed the babies. Anyone who remembers these tins will recall that they were about eight inches long and about four inches in diameter. He made all sorts of things. His speciality was replica fishing boats. I was given one but due to disregard for what we were given it is long gone, possibly destroyed.

Getting back to the preparation for the roup, my stepfather and Old Johnny did not see eye to eye about the numbering of the goods. Johnny was so meticulous. While our man would have slapped the number on with paint running everywhere, Johnny on the other hand had cut all the numbers from a piece of cardboard, every one symmetrical and all placed at the same height and not a drop of paint spilt anywhere. He did a wonderful job and the items were all lined up like a battalion of soldiers. Now this is where Johnny got the "queer auld bugger" tag. Unbeknown to my mother he would not eat anything made with chicken, so when he was told he would get a nice plate of chicken broth for dinner he downed tools and headed off home. He lived thirteen miles away but he would walk every inch of the way. One of his favourite ploys was if there was a railway line handy he would walk the line as he maintained that was the most direct route. Next morning, about nine-o-clock, Johnny appeared as fresh as a daisy, having completed a thirteen-mile walk I have no idea when he would have left home, possibly about 5 a.m. but he carried on with his numbering as though nothing had happened.

It was getting near roup day and my stepfather was still waiting word from a couple of prospective employers. We would have to be out of our present house before the term day 28th May. As well as getting the place ready for our leaving, my stepfather had to make sure all the crops were planted for the next tenant. This was part of the agreement so it was a busy time.

The big day arrived—roup day—which was to kick off at twelve noon. People started to arrive about half-past ten so that they could have time to browse. There was also a marquee tent where booze and food were sold. My parents got off to a bad start, for it was their first and only roup, which meant they were unfamiliar with the format. They had to hire a professional Auctioneer when he arrived he had brought his own cashier. There was a bit of a stand off as my stepfather had asked his banker to supply someone to handle the accounts. I can't remember the outcome, but my stepfather was always of the opinion that many of the goods were sold well under their value because of the cashier thing. No doubt the cashier would have been an extra cost so the Auctioneer probably lost money as he couldn't charge for someone that wasn't required. The sale began and there was a lot of activity with people bidding for goods as they were offered, but the only price that stands out in my mind was the price paid for the pair of Clydesdale horses—fifty-five pounds each, or one hundred and ten pounds for the pair. I was heartbroken when they were led out of our yard for the last time. Before we went to bed that night our place was like a ghost town as people started to move their purchases. I have a feeling there was a lot of alcohol consumed that afternoon. My stepfather must have been heartbroken, seeing all his possessions disappearing before his very eyes along with it his livelihood.

This was our second move in five years. My parents had found employment at a farm in the district of Alvah, near Banff. My stepfather was engaged to work a pair of horses. This move was a bit up-market as we moved our goods on the back of a lorry instead of the old horse and cart. The journey was less than twenty miles, so we were there in no time at all. This move was probably a step backwards for us as the house was a much smaller semi-detached. There was a sink with running cold water. The usual toilet facility was a six-by-four shed at the foot of the garden with a disgusting bucket in it. It's funny, but these so-called dry toilets always seemed to be full and a haven for blue bottles in the summer. We had no electricity so we were still using paraffin lamps. I think we were possibly using bottled gas or maybe a primus stove. The nearest bus stop was three miles away. The one plus side to this move was that we had a shop less than half-a-mile away.

The school was two miles from the house, to be walked both ways come rain, hail or shine. At this school I met another of Hitler's relatives in the shape of our Headmistress. I doubt if I ever came across a more evil woman in my life! I am sure she hated being alive and took her spite out on the kids who were terrified of her, especially the poor orphans who didn't have parents to go home to and tell of the treatment she dished out. She was definitely a devil's disciple if ever there was one. It was difficult trying to settle in a new school halfway through a term. Your classmates could make it difficult if they didn't want to accept you. I found this at Linhead School. Another problem with our new school there arose from the fact that there were four classes in one room, whereas our last school only had one class per room so our Gamrie teacher could devote her time to the one class on a one-to-one basis. Unfortunately I was not a very bright scholar, except when it came to things that interested me. The likes of ancient history about Picts and Romans did my head in!

During our stay at the farm at Itlaw we made great progress and moved into the world of modern technology. My stepfather was at a roup and he bought a second-hand wireless that cost seven pounds—probably two weeks wages. The wireless needed two accumulators to make it work, one wet and one dry. The wet one needed to be charged up, possibly once a week. This was done at the local smiddy; you needed two wets as the charging took about three days. This was a great breakthrough for us for it opened up a whole new world. I spent many happy hours listening to that old wireless. We could now keep up with the outside world. Indeed, the humble wireless was a godsend. We could listen to the news every day and find out what other people did with their lives; then there was sport, the love of my life, especially football. Once I got involved I was hooked. My life's ambition was that one day I would be a professional footballer. Unfortunately it never happened.

Back to the wireless: Saturday evening was always special with a lot of excellent entertainment. Before we got into the swing of how the accumulators worked we got caught out a few times when the wet one would run out at the most exciting part of the programme! That was the excitement over until we got a fully charged battery again. You would never know how your programme finished as we never had many repeats. We got wise in the end and would make sure we had a new battery on Saturday morning that would take us over the weekend.

We were just about getting used to our new school when our parents announced that we would be moving again! It was about a year since the last move. I have no idea what went wrong and will never find out now. I can only surmise what happened. The farm was a family-run business worked by a father and two sons along with my stepfather. Whether this had any bearing on us moving I don't know, but move we did—another ordeal having to start afresh at a new school. We were moving west this time, heading back to where I had started off. Was our old man having difficulty working for a boss?

I have no recollection of the flitting but remember our latest abode was at a farm between Whitehills and Portsoy along the coast road. My stepfather had taken on the job of foreman in charge of the other men on the farm. The farmer, a Mr Smith, was a man who didn't keep well and was often in bed ill. It was a fairly big farm with four hired men. Somewhere along the way we gained an addition to our ever-expanding family—another brother named Nigel (very posh for a farm servant's loon). The reason for the posh name? My mother had seen it in a woman's magazine!

It was now somewhere between 1948 and 1949. There were still a lot of unpleasant illnesses going about like diphtheria, scarlet, fever, mumps, measles and whooping cough. Our young Nigel ended up with a life threatening illness. I never really found out what it was but he was at death's door in the Sick Children's hospital in Aberdeen for a good number of weeks—a very anxious time for my parents. We were a bit up-market again with our accommodation: we had a bathroom and electricity, so things were looking up. Mrs Smith, the farmer's wife, was from the south. She had been a nurse before becoming a farmer's wife. She was into hens in a big way, having about thirty hen houses. When I was eleven she offered me my first job mucking out her henhouses on a Saturday. If I did five she would pay me half-a-crown. That was two and a half pence per house—big deal, but it was worth quite a bit so this was my first paid employment. It meant that with my half crown I could go to town on the Saturday afternoon and watch the football at Princess Royal park, the home of Deveronvale; then I could go to the pictures and have a fish supper. So the half crown went quite some way, especially if you consider that today it costs all of twenty pence to visit the loo in most towns! Yet my half crown was only worth twelve-and-a half new pence—happy days!

We had to walk about three miles to school, which involved taking a short cut through fields—so it was not too pleasant when it was wet. Boyndie School had three teachers and you could do your entire education there. It was quite a pleasant place. The headmaster was strict but fair; he used his tawse[1] frequently and had some of the pupils fairly frightened of him! It was a great school for football so I had no complaints. Our headmaster was a sly old codger—he had a huge garden round his house, so every Friday afternoon we had lessons in gardening! It was a cheap way of keeping his place tidy. Nevertheless I found it quite enjoyable—anything to get out of the classroom!

The house at Threipland was the most modern we had lived in with all mod cons. The school, too, was okay. I was enjoying myself and playing plenty football. Most of the lads around played so we had games at different venues each evening, usually in a farm field with the grass fairly long; you often had to dodge the cowpats as well, but it was great. I would soon be going for my higher-grade education in the qualifying class. I was no academic but I enjoyed the subjects that interested me and was fairly efficient at them, i.e. Geography, Natural History, Maths, Physical Education and Music. Algebra, Geometry, History, Science and English I hated and was bloody useless at them! But I had to struggle on. Another factor was that I had moved schools a couple of times and the education was slightly different each time. Sometimes we were behind, the next time we were ahead, so it made learning that little bit more difficult. My mother did her best to help with homework but she had a very busy life. I always felt my education should have been a lot better.

Everything was running along fine when out of the blue we were informed we were moving again! My stepfather and his boss had a difference of opinion and our man had to leave in a hurry; he was given orders to vacate the house at short notice. We managed to get a corner of my granny's house back in Cullen. It was just as we left it ten years previously. We were stepping backwards! She gave us the far sitting room, which still had earthen floors, so to avoid damp my parents agreed to get cement floors laid at their expense.

Cullen was a brilliant place to stay as far as I was concerned. We were back staying in a town. Every youth in Cullen was football crazy. There would be a game on every day, and on Saturday morning about twenty of us would congre-

---

1.   Belt.

gate down at the harbour. We would pick two teams, and using a garage door as the goals we would play a game called 'attack and defend'—one team was defenders, the other attackers. We would play for about an hour, then change round. It was like a cup final every Saturday! We were there for a few months and guess what happened—my Granny and my parents fell out and we were on the move again! It had not been easy for my stepfather in Cullen; he was unable to find full-time employment and all he had done was a few days casual work; the rest of the time he was on the dole. So we were going downmarket again. They managed to get a house in the village of Lintmill but the house should have been condemned—there was nothing but the basic four walls and a roof! We were back to carrying water from a tap in the street. The old thunderbox toilet was again part of our lives—things were not easy. Again my stepfather was unable to get employment, so they were beginning to struggle. I have no idea if work was scarce or what—no doubt the tractor was costing jobs as it became more widespread all the time.

Eventually my stepfather had success and got a full time job. The downside was that we had to pack up our goods and chattels and move again. For me the moving was a bit of a disaster. I would have been in three different schools during my qualifying year. We were moving east again, back to a farm near Gamrie. The name of the farm was Mains-of-Cullen. Why that name? I never found out, but it was a good few miles from the town of Cullen. We were back to the old bothy style of living, carrying water from a well, no electricity, and the cludgie was the usual six-by-four shed at the side of the house. One good point—the toilet wall was full of knotholes, so you could sit and look out of one of the holes and get a panoramic view of the Moray Firth! Another plus about this move was that the bus passed the house about one hundred yards away. The school was a couple of miles away. Longmanhill School was a two-teacher affair. After qualifying class you had to move to a Senior Secondary—mine was Macduff High School.

We were living within a mile of the beach, so I spent many happy hours exploring the rocks and doing some fishing. There was a wreck of a German aeroplane not far offshore, but we never saw it. Many years later I was talking to an amateur diver about the wreck and he told me he had found it. No doubt they would have removed the propeller for scrap.

Of all the places we lived I had a soft spot for Mains of Cullen and the Banff/MacDuff area. We had the choice of two picture houses for starters. MacDuff had an open-air swimming pool—it was there that I learned to swim. One had to be hardy as even in the middle of summer it was freezing cold, but it was in a wonderful setting. Sadly, like many of the older attractions, it closed down; no doubt it didn't come up to European standards. During the summer we spent many happy hours on the beach or the swimming pool. We also had a wonderful view of the Moray Firth. It is hard to estimate the distance, but the horizon was miles away, and then, if you swept your eyes from left to right or vice versa, it must have been sixty miles of uninterrupted view.

One outstanding memory I have is seeing the aircraft carrier *H.M.S. EAGLE* doing her sea trials off our coast. She was at least thirty miles out at sea. One needed powerful binoculars to see her, but it was quite a thrill—especially seeing her sheer size. Sadly she outlived her usefulness and was sent to the breakers yard a while ago.

Longmanhill, with its rural setting, was well in keeping with the modern trend, boasting a well-run youth club and also an amateur football team that played in a welfare league. The youth club taught Scottish Country Dancing which I enjoyed. It made you capable of being able to dance at local dances when we were old enough. Instead of being like a wallflower, you could enjoy yourself. Nevertheless, Longmanhill School was well behind the times; the only sanitation was the old dry toilet, a wooden building with a couple of buckets. I am afraid that system would not be tolerated today. That was the downside; the good side was that we had school meals! If I remember correctly, this was the first time that happened to us. During the potato harvest we were given an extra two weeks off to help with the tattie howkin; if you were fortunate enough to get twenty-four days work, you would earn £12 as the rate was 10/-(50p) per day. I was able to buy new clothes— my first pair of long trousers. It is a long time ago but I remember it as if it happened yesterday.

I had moved to MacDuff High School the Easter of 1950. We travelled by bus morning and night. We caught the bus home at a stop on the harbour front. We teenage boys used to get up to some devilment as we waited on the bus. On one occasion two or three of us were standing on a small landing platform below high tide level. It was covered in seaweed, and suddenly my feet went from below me. Next thing I knew I was under the water in my new outfit! First day and I was soaked to the skin! My mates thought it was hilarious, seeing me sitting on the bus with a trail of water from where I was sitting to the door. My mother had a very poor sense of humour and definitely didn't see the funny side. I was threatened with murder if I pulled the same stunt again.

I was able to attend the pictures on a regular basis and about that time made the first silly mistake of my life. At the age of twelve I started smoking—a habit I continued for the next twenty-eight years. In my later life I suffered blood problems and heart problems. Could this be the consequence of being hooked on the dreaded weed so early in my life?

My story began as a protest against war and from the end of the Second World War to the early fifties there had been skirmishes around the world, but nothing major. Palestine was a hotspot, as was Malaya with Gorilla gangs causing disruption. Suddenly through the magical powers of the wireless and the Daily Press a new name kept cropping up—Korea. Nobody had ever heard of it, so as soon as it was mentioned the locals would say, "Far the hell's that?" Before the year was over every body was well aware of it. "Far the hell" it was, because reports were soon coming through that there were hundreds of Chinese fighting against British and American troops. There was even talk of a Third World War! It was costing the lives of hundreds of young men on both sides. It was to last for three long years; I was too young to worry about being called up but, age wise, it was getting nearer.

Before I complete this rant about the evils of war I would like to mention a chap who worked alongside my stepfather at Mains-of-Cullen. I no longer remember his name but his face still remains familiar. He had been a prisoner of the Japanese for four years. The poor chap was a broken man. Like a skeleton, often unable to go to work, he was so ill and weak—it is sad that one human can inflict such misery on a fellow human being.

I really enjoyed attending MacDuff High School. My academic skills had not really improved—indeed, I would class myself as average. I now had to attend woodwork classes, which were okay, but what I did enjoy best was the organised football matches we played every Wednesday after school—so life for me was chugging along nicely. My social life was brilliant. I was now a member of the Air Training Corps. We attended meetings every week in the Drill Hall in Banff. This allowed me to attend a summer camp at Dyce Aerodrome, which in those days was still manned by RAF personnel. During my time at the camp I was lucky enough to get a couple of chances to fly for the first time in my life. My first flight was a twenty-minute stint in a Tiger Moth twin wings aircraft—no canopy, just the pilot and me. When we took off I had no idea what aerobatics were. Before we had landed I had looped the loop and carried out various death-defying manoeuvres that I never ever want to try again! A spare pair of drawers would have come in handy when we landed. My next flight was in an Anson twin-engined plane capable of holding about a dozen people. There were two seats in the cockpit and only one pilot. I was first aboard and when I reached the front of the plane the pilot told me to sit beside him. What a thrill that turned out to be!

I was given a set of earphones so I heard all the instructions given by the control tower. Then the magnificent view—it just great! We flew to Buchaness, Peterhead, Fraserburgh along the coast to Banff, and from there we followed the Deveron to Huntly, then turned back to Dyce. The flight lasted about forty minutes. The one incident I haven't mentioned yet was that we were each handed a parachute when we boarded the plane. I don't ever remember getting instructions about how to use it, but thankfully we didn't need it. I often think back and wonder if we had to bale out how we would have managed! We were all between twelve and sixteen. During the year we attended one or two athletics meeting sponsored by the Air Training Corp. It was quite a good day out and everything was free.

My football career had a bit of a setback that summer—we were at a picnic and as usual part of the afternoon was dedicated to a game of football. It was a fairly rough field. The ball landed in front of me and I drew back my foot and hit it! Unbeknown to me there was a boulder just behind the ball, which I hit full force. The pain was excruciating and I was sure I had broken bones! Luckily after x-rays it turned out to be just heavy bruising, though it took weeks to heal. I was picked to play for the local team in the Welfare League, but most of the other players were well into their teens and twenties so were much more streetwise than us younger lads and could pull one or two stunts. We took some heavy beatings and then a lot of stick from our schoolmates, so it was kind of embarrassing.

I was nearing my fourteenth birthday and entering my last year at school when, that winter, I hit the big time—I was picked to play trials for the Banffshire schoolboys. I got through the first trial and was picked for the second which was to be played at the Kynoch Park in Keith; but once again my hopes of football stardom were shattered when I woke up one morning covered in a rash and swollen glands. Yes, I had mumps and chickenpox at the same time! Sadly for me I missed the trial and, of course, I will have left school before the following year's trials. Some of my schoolmates went on to play for Scottish League teams. One I remember was Donnie Watt who played for Dundee United. I still have a great interest in football but I am afraid it's not nearly as exciting as it used to be—perhaps on account of the money. In my younger days Highland League footballers were paid a pound a week to play—very different from today.

My last term at school started in August, 1952. On returning to school after the holiday we were in for a shock. We were allocated our classes and given a timetable. Reading through the timetable, we thought they had made a mistake because, instead of woodwork we were getting cooking and the girls had to do the woodwork! We were quite embarrassed at first, worried about the ragging and leg pulling the rest of the lads would put us through. The explanation given was that many of the boys in my class were from fishing families and the first position the youngest member of the crew got was that of cook—so cooking it was and we had to get on with it! After we were used to it I began to enjoy it and would say it was possibly the best tuition I had during my life. When I left school I could cook as well as anybody and can still conjure up a mean dish when I feel like it.

One evening late that summer I had my first encounter with the opposite sex. Before we parted company I thought my end had come and put that experience down to losing my second life. It was not as painful as my encounter with the car but more frightening. One of my classmates and I were out on our bikes minding our own business when we caught up with a couple of girls from our school. We decided to tag along with them. They were walking while we stayed on our bikes, cranking slowly so we could keep abreast of them. After maybe an hour it started to get dark so the young ladies decided they had better get home before it got too late or they would be in trouble. Being chivalrous young men, we decided to escort them home so we paired off and parted company as they were from different parts of the town. I headed on up the road with my young lady, and when we reached her home there was a sort of lane about two hundred yard long with a high wall one side and a hedge on the other. I decided to park my bike at the end of the lane and walk to the house. I would say it was gloaming, not fully dark; we were getting on fine and were about halfway along the lane when suddenly my companion took off running. I was knocked off my stride and slightly confused until I realised there was someone running towards me from behind, using the foulest of language. I turned to face the person who was obviously going to attack me! Just as he made a lunge at me I dodged to the right. He had on tackity boots and was skidding as he tried to corner me. Being fairly fit I was able to out manoeuvre him and I feinted to the left. This insane bugger was at least six feet tall and seemed adamant that he was going to destroy me. I thought I was clear just as he swung his foot with a size twelve tackity boot on the end of it. I must have broken a world record for the high jump as I cleared his leg high hurdle style and took off running. I reached my bike about ten yards ahead of the lunatic, caught the bike and kept running. Thankfully it was downhill so when I had enough speed I jumped on the bike and kept cranking until I was well clear. The obscenities he was shouting after me are unprintable. The moral to this is never mess about with birds who live in dead-ends with their lunatic fathers—it's a health hazard!

Before I left school I fell foul of the headmaster, Lang Dod Goodall. He was a gentleman who was well respected. He was firm but fair, but unfortunately he and I had a difference of opinion over smoking before I left. We were sitting in the classroom when my classmate asked if I fancied a smoke. I said I did, so he asked to leave the room and a few minutes later I followed him. He had a twenty packet of Gold Flake cigarettes, so we lit up and proceeded to enjoy a puff. What we didn't know was that we were being watched from one of the classrooms. When we entered the school this teacher stepped out of his class and confronted us. We were made to go to the headmaster and tell him of our misdemeanours. We felt a right couple of tits as we knocked on Lang Dod's door to inform him that we had been caught smoking. He asked how many cigarettes we had left and we both produced douts; but he didn't believe us so Sandy had to hand over the other eighteen Gold Flake which the big fellow screwed up in a ball and threw in the bin. He then gave us twelve of the belt, six for smoking, six for saying we had no more fags. While Lang Dod was dishing out the corporal punishment, and even though it was quite painful, you always see something funny; there was a secretary in the room while we were getting punished and every time the strap crashed off our hand she would jump about a foot off her chair! It took me all my time not to burst out laughing.

During my final weeks in school the only class I really attended was the cookery class. One of my mates and I had the job of keeping the football pitch in order so we just did as we saw fit and pleased ourselves. One thing that amazed me was nobody ever gave me any advice on getting a job or emphasised the fact that from the Christmas holidays onwards I would need a job in order to survive. Somewhere along the line I had applied to join the Boys Service section of the army. I have no recollection of ever filling in forms or anything like that. One of my classmates joined the RAF Boys Service.

My schooldays drama was not over yet—my parents announced that they were on the move yet again! As I only had a couple of weeks of schooling left it was agreed I would carry on at MacDuff. Somewhere along the line we had acquired another sister Irene. The new job was outwith our normal circuit. This time they moved south to near Turriff, on the road between Turriff and Cuminestown. We were three miles from the main road and public transport. The new house was in the middle of getting renovated. We would have electricity and a bathroom as soon as the work was complete. My last evening at the school in MacDuff was attending the school Christmas party around the 18th of December, 1952—three days after my fifteenth birthday.

Before we moved to our new abode I had received instructions to report to Woolmanhill Barracks in Aberdeen to sit an Army entrance exam and have a medical—around the 20th December. I awoke the morning the medical was due to find myself covered in spots and feeling unwell. My mother diagnosed my condition as measles! There was no way I was fit to travel so mother phoned the barracks to say I was ill. About four hours later a Major from the Gordon Highlanders arrived at the door. He claimed he was passing the house so he called in to see how ill I was. The Major left and said to get in touch when I was fit. My mother was full of praise about the nice man coming all that distance to see me, but I think nearer the truth was the fact that he was more interested to see if I still intended joining the army.

After my final night at Macduff High School I never went back. I felt the Education Authority had done little to help me shape my life; neither did the government. Six weeks before my fifteenth birthday they informed my mother that the 50p a week allowance for my upbringing would cease to be paid. Nobody asked if I needed help to get started out in life. My father's sacrifice was insignificant. I may be winging on my own behalf, but I am sure there were thousands of war orphans like me in the same boat. I would have loved to have my father's guidance and advice on how to tackle this big bad world I was about to enter.

ALONE IN THE NASTY BIG WORLD

My new instructions arrived from the Recruiting Office. I had to report to Wool-manhill Barracks in Aberdeen on 6thJanuary 1953. I had to sit an entrance exam and undergo a medical. If successful I would then travel overnight to my depot in Nottinghamshire. The barracks were in a village called Tuxford. I had never heard of the place and I had never travelled so far from home on my own before. My mother and I had a tearful farewell that January morning. There was about a foot of snow on the ground. I had three miles to walk to get the bus, so there was nothing else for it but head down and head off.

My exam and medical went well and around 2 p.m. I took the oath of allegiance to serve Queen and country to the best of my ability. My only worry was having to travel on my own, as it was into the unknown. My luck changed dramatically when another lad about my age was shown into the room. He was Bob Barclay, from Aberdeen, and would be travelling with me. After the formalities of the introduction we were given travel warrants and expenses. It was roughly 3 p.m. and our train didn't leave till 8 p.m., so we were free till then. As we got to the waiting room a couple got up and came to the door. Bob introduced them as his parents. When they heard we were to travel at 8 p.m. they immediately invited me round to their house to pass the time till our departure. I was given a meal and the best of hospitality, after which they accompanied us to the station. I would never ever listen to anybody criticizing Aberdeen people ever again. We set off from a snowy Aberdeen and our fist major stop was Edinburgh. A young lad got on, entered our carriage and curled up in a corner and was soon asleep. We had to change trains at Doncaster around 3 a.m. I have done better things at that hour of the morning! It was freezing cold after the warm train. We had to wait awhile before our train arrived. The locals called it the milk train. We finally reached Retford at 6 a.m. and there was a guy in a fifteen-hundredweight truck waiting for us. We enjoyed a great conversation with the driver but it was one sided since he never answered. Eventually he asked if we were bloody Swedes as he couldn't understand a bloody word we were saying! I suppose unless you speak broad Doric, how are you expected to understand it? From Retford to the camp at Tuxford was about seven miles. We arrived just as breakfast was in full swing, which was handy as we were starving. It was lovely to get tucked in! As we ate we were surrounded by other lads asking what regiment we were going to and where we had come from. A few were going to the Gordon Highlanders but every regiment in the British Army was represented.

After breakfast we were shown our barrack room, which was empty except for the bases of thirty beds, fifteen each side. We were told to hang about until our full compliment arrived. They were arriving in dribs and drabs all morning. Two or three hours after we arrived the door of the billet opened and the guy who entered our train carriage in Edinburgh strode in—he had gone as far as Peterborough before he wakened! We had a good laugh about it. He was Tommy Davidson who made his name as an army boxer, winning the A.B.A title at his weight. By midday most of the lads had arrived from all over the British Isles. After dinner we were marched to the stores and kitted out with all our kit including blankets and sheets. We were then shown how to make a sandwich bed pack i.e. blanket sheet, blanket sheet, blanket; then the bed cover was wrapped round the lot to make it look like a sandwich. After the bed making demonstration we were marched to the Armoury. I didn't even know what the word meant and was quite shocked to find out it was where they kept the guns. At the age of fifteen and three weeks I had to sign for a deadly weapon with a lethal bayonet! Once they were screwed together it was taller than I was. We were then lectured about keeping the gun clean—our new best friend in the shape of a .303 rifle.

The following day I began my apprenticeship as a trained killer. Within weeks I could shoot people, throw hand grenades at them and kill with a bayonet—after being shown the most vulnerable parts of the body. For someone that detested the word *war*, what had I let myself in for? I would either be a killer or end up as cannon fodder if on the losing side. At six-o-clock in the morning the officers went through the barrack room like a dose of salts, as if they were demented, forcing us out of bed. Then it was a wash, dress and breakfast—sorry, you had to fuss over the bed pack first, making sure it was square. What a palaver! The barrack room had to be spotless, and only *then* it was breakfast. Back in the billet you had to get ready for muster parade, the first parade of the day conducted by a huge Grenadier Guardsman, our Regimental Sergeant Major, who was a big bully of a man who had all us young boys petrified. After twenty minutes listening to him shouting his head off you were dismissed and your working day began. The day was divided up into periods just like school used to be, except at school you were never shown how to kill people.

My second day at Tuxford started with much drama. We were lined up outside the billet ready to go on muster parade when my name was shouted by the C.S.M. He was screaming his head off and it might have been in a foreign language for I had no idea what was wrong! Finally he calmed down and explained that I had left my pyjamas under the bed pack! It was against the rules and I was on a charge. This was all double Dutch to me and my platoon corporal explained what would happen. I would appear in front of the Company commander at eleven-o-clock and would more than likely get confined to barracks for three days. If they only knew that was probably the first pair of pyjamas I ever owned, the one distinction I had over the rest of the squad. I was the first to be on a charge in our platoon. At ten to eleven I was in line with another half dozen defaulters. Dead on eleven the circus started. With much shouting and clattering of boots we were wheeled in to an office in front of our Company commander, a Major in the Seaforth Highlanders. When my turn came the charge against me was read out. I was asked if I had anything to say, which I didn't. I was then sentenced to three days confined to barracks. What a fiasco! We were already confined to barracks for the first six weeks as it was, so that was no hardship. The hardship was that you had to endure a lot more inspections. The first was at six fifteen in the morning—report to the guardroom; then again at lunchtime after tea at five-o-clock you had to report again. You were then given a duty like working in the kitchen or cleaning offices. They needed about twenty lads each evening to carry out these tasks so if you ended up on a charge you were automatically guilty so that they had enough skivvies to carry out these duties. My first evening I was sent to the cookhouse. I reported to Sgt Harris who asked if I had ever peeled spuds! I told him yes as I had done it many times at home. He showed me into a little room with a one hundredweight bag of spuds; there was a peeling machine so all I had to do was remove all the eyes and any rotten bits. Within an hour I had finished. I reported back to Sgt Harris who couldn't believe I had finished so quickly. He told me to sit down at a table and he disappeared. Five minutes later he was back with a huge sandwich, bacon and eggs and a mug of tea. We were good friends from then on and if he was ever stuck for a spud basher I would step in and help him out! When my hour and a half was up I had to report back to the guardroom. If it was one of the more sadistic regimental police on duty he could make life difficult—like making you report every half hour for the rest of the night wearing a different dress every time.

I kept my nose clean after that and our six weeks basic training soon passed. We were able to march in unison, clean our kit, and go on route marches which I didn't mind. We were also involved in sport. One of my favourites was hockey and cross-country running—a sport we never really heard of in Banff-shire so, before long, I was enjoying my army life.

Having survived our basic training we were now entitled to a bit of leave. Being privileged to be living in one of the most beautiful parts of the world has its disadvantages in our case, for it is far removed from England around which everything seems to revolve; consequently transport difficulties are a major factor, for to get home from the barracks meant travel. In my case it meant getting from Tuxford to Banff, a twenty-four hour journey; a half hour from Tuxford to Retford; then on to Doncaster, then York, which was the mainline station. Very often the train would be full to capacity. This meant there were no vacant seats: the corridors would be chock-full of mostly Service Personnel going on leave. If there was a ship docked in one of the South Coast Ports, look out—you would be knee-deep in sailors, many of them drunk and vomiting all over the place! The trains were dirty as they were pulled by steam engines belching soot over everything. There were no refreshments on board unless there was a buffet car; if not, they would have barrows at the station, so it was a mêlée trying to get a cup of tea before the train started off again. On my first leave the train arrived in Aberdeen in the middle of the night and I had no means of getting to Banff until morning. It was the mail train and someone suggested I should go to the mail depot and try and scrounge a lift in the mail van going east. Hoping he would be sympathetic (me serving my country and all that jazz), I found the postman who did that run and in my most pleading voice I explained my predicament. He was only too helpful but asked if I would walk clear of the depot in case anybody saw me getting in the van. So courtesy of the Royal Mail and a very considerate postman, I was delivered near home within an hour and a half. He dropped me at the end of the road, which was three miles from our house at a place called the Pole Smiddy. This was great! After thanking him I set off walking. The road had a thick beech wood on either side, with some lovely big trees. Looking up at the sky (it was still quite dark) I thought it was very open, not as I remembered the beech canopy we used to walk under—and I was beginning to wonder if I was on the right road. I kept walking and as it got lighter I could see all the lovely Beech trees lying in a tangled heap. That was the year of the severe gales that lashed the East coast from Orkney to Dover, causing untold damage and causing the deaths of quite a few people. We had no problems at Tuxford, just a few hours of severe gales, but the lovely Beech wood was gone.

I eventually reached home just as my parents were getting out of bed. Old age is catching up on me as I have no recollection of how I spent that leave. I wouldn't be hitting the high spots as the wages as a Boy Soldier amounted to 17/

6 (87.5p) per week. We were given 10/-(50p) a week to spend. The other 7/ 6(27.5p) was put in the bank so that you had money to cover your leave. We were certainly not in the millionaire bracket. When my leave was over I had to get the last bus from Turriff to Aberdeen, as we had to catch the first train south in the morning. This meant an overnight stay in the station. The bus arrived around midnight and by the time you got to the train station every nook and cranny had a body sleeping in it, all catching the first train in the morning. We couldn't afford B&B so you just had to rough it. We then travelled down during the day, getting back to camp around six in the evening. This gave one time to get organised for morning parade the next day.

The days were getting longer. This enabled us to get out in the evenings and indulge in more sports. I ended up playing hockey, basketball and touch rugby. We were really super fit. Later that year the Coronation was taking place in London. We had a bit of a rehearsal in case we were called upon to attend the parade. This never came off but six of the more senior lads were picked as part of the guard lining the route. I spent the Coronation with an Aunt and Uncle in Perthshire. They say in the services never volunteer for any event, but I used to try out most things on offer, just for the hell of it.

Once again they were looking for mugs like me so I signed up for another adventure. "Volunteers required," the notice board said in big bold letters, names to be handed in to Platoon Commanders. I went straight away and enquired what was going on. I was asked if I had ever worked on a farm. When I explained I had been brought up on a farm the Commander said, "You'll do!" and wrote my name down. I still had no idea what was going on. The only information I got was that we would be paid an extra 3/6 (17.5p) per a day for five days—that would double my wages for the week.

Twenty of us were picked the first week and we set off on Monday morning in the back of a three tonner. We had no idea what lay ahead of us till we got to the farm. I had never done this job before or ever seen the stuff, but we were there to pull flax. You just pulled handfuls of it and put it in a small stack! We were getting paid extra for it so got pulling! What the hell, you didn't need to be a brain surgeon to carry out this task. It was boring but where there's muck there's brass. Some of the wimps only stayed one day and the farmer told some not to come back; but I managed to stick it out for two weeks and earned £1.75. It was like winning the pools! Platoon No13 had some smashing fellows in it; at least half-a-dozen were Scots, some Welsh, some Irish, and the remainder were English. We all got on well and there were no problems among us. They were all honest guys who didn't touch any gear belonging to anybody else. I occasionally got homesick, but you just had to grin and bare it. You could buy yourself out but the cost then was £150. I did enjoy most of the things we did but the shooting and the war games didn't really interest me. I was stuck with it so had to make the best of it.

I am not sure if the government passed a Bill where it was stated that offenders should get the chance to join up as an alternative to going to prison, but all of a sudden we were inundated with thieves, burglars and violent aggressive characters who were in the Army against their will. There was no proper control over them, especially after five-o-clock in the evening, as most of the permanent staff had married quarters and were off the camp for the night. Shops were being broken into in the village and other crimes were being committed. For the first time in my life I heard the word *Poof*. I had absolutely no idea what the word meant, but with so many streetwise guys in the barracks it was soon explained in no uncertain terms. Another strange word new to me was the word *Arsonist*. On hearing the word I thought it was to do with Poof but I soon found out there was no similarity whatsoever! The word *arsonist* came to be used because of an incident that occurred that summer. Behind our barracks was a small farm; a lot of the ground in the district was given over to huge orchards, but this one smallholding was for arable farming. I often watched the old guy working away and wished I could spend my spare time helping him. He had a pair of horses and often had a woman with him whom I presume was his wife. That year he had six or eight haystacks, which he carefully built by hand himself, assisted by his wife and another couple of neighbours. When he had finished building all the stacks were like a line of Guardsmen. He went round morning and night, sticking his arm into the middle of the stacks, making sure they weren't overheating as they dried out. He would soon put a layer of thatch over them to keep them dry till they were needed. About a week later we were getting ready for bed when one of the guys shouted that there was a fire in the haystacks behind the camp. We all rushed to the windows for a closer look and lo and behold, the haystacks were well ablaze! There was no quick response Fire Brigade as we have now, so they were almost destroyed before the fire people arrived. When we awoke next morning the extent of the damage was there for all to see—smouldering heaps on the ground with a couple of firemen still damping them down. The rumour quickly spread that it was deliberate and the work of an arsonist. The police questioned a few guys in the camp but they had no luck.

I have often read in the press that there were no homosexuals in the forces. Nevertheless we had two different staff guys sentenced to civilian jails for affairs with young recruits.

Behind the camp they had constructed an assault course. We were booked to use it the next week. The usual water, ropes and walls were there—it would certainly toughen us up.

THE BEGINNING OF THE END

Do you ever get a gut feeling? Well, one morning I had one! I couldn't put my finger on it but I was not comfortable. This was the morning we were about to tackle the assault course! Remember, I was only fifteen and a half, still growing, and now about five feet four inches tall. We still had the same size packs as a guy six feet four, so we had to get over the same obstacles as the bigger guys.

Just before we left for the assault course I received word that I had successfully passed my third class education certificate. I was enjoying my education army style much better than school. We started on the course around 9 a.m. I successfully negotiated all the obstacles. It was hard going but the worst was to come—crossing a burn on a rope fifteen feet above the water! I was apprehensive about it, but luckily I was not first to go. The four or so guys in front of me managed with a struggle. Next was a big six-foot Irishman and he had no bother. Then it was my turn! The burn was about twenty feet wide, and I set off with some trepidation. By the time I reached the middle it was tough going, but I was confident. Suddenly the big brainless Irish guy started to pump the rope up and down, thinking it was great joke. I had no chance of surviving this and had to let go. There was a resounding cheer as I hit the boulder-strewn burn. I knew I had done damage to my leg for the pain was excruciating. Eventually the sergeant realised I was hurt and made moves to get me to the bank of the burn. The old meat wagon (ambulance) arrived and I was carted off to the M.I. Room. The orderly there had one look and sent me to Newark Royal Infirmary. After x-rays it was confirmed my ankle was fractured and so I was plastered and fitted with a calliper. I also had crutches for a couple of weeks till I was able to put my weight on my foot again. I was immobile for the next ten weeks. The big idiot that caused the problem got away Scot-free.

As you read this you will no doubt say to yourself, "This guy is a right bloody winger!" You are free to judge me—that's your prerogative and I don't give a shit. But from that day on the army as far as I am concerned abandoned me. I was left for weeks on end sitting in the billet and nobody came near me. You may ask, what did I expect? Well, remember I was still only a boy. They could at least have given me some sort of programme that would have kept me active. Apart from my education periods I did nothing but sit around and stare out the window. Also, bare in mind the accident wasn't my fault—I would put it down to bad supervision. So twice within sixteen years the government had abandoned me.

My appointment at Newark for the removal of my plaster was two days before I was due to go on leave. The doctor was quite happy with my progress but decided that I would need a light plaster for a couple of weeks, though I would be able to wear a shoe or boot. This was brilliant, as I didn't want to go home with only one piece of footwear. On the way back to camp I was studying the appointment card for my next hospital visit and was horrified to notice it was two days before my leave finished—so we promptly got a pen and altered the date for another week. I was holding my breath when I went back to hospital, but nobody noticed my little forgery. Returning from leave late afternoon on the Monday, we were confronted with a huge change to the camp entrance. We had been away for three weeks so were out of touch. The normal set-up was as you entered the camp, the Guardroom was on your right with a couple of Regimental Policemen hovering about; there was a clerk sitting just inside the door booking everybody in; then there was the Q.M office, the Pay office; and finally the C.O.s office. But the whole office block had been burned to the ground! All that was left was a heap of bricks. As usual there was speculation that there was an arsonist in the camp. There was major disruption as most of the records were destroyed, so it was utter chaos with the police involved once again.

There were always boys in the guardroom, normally the same half dozen trying to work their ticket. They were in trouble in Civvy Street, so the army didn't change them—they just couldn't behave themselves. A new secure place was required to house them while they carried out their sentences. The only place on the camp with barred windows was the sports store, so it was hastily converted to a temporary jail. After all the equipment had been removed, one permanent resident was a Scots bloke who kidded himself he was some sort of Glasgow gangster though he was just a plain evil bully. Another chap doing time then was a room-mate of mine, Phillip; he got caught up in some daft caper and ended up doing fourteen days in the nick. To add to the authorities' worries, there had been a massive robbery in the NAAFI. Hundreds of cigarettes and a lot of money had been stolen. It looked like a well-organised crime. The civil police were called in and every resident in the camp was fingerprinted, though to no avail—they hadn't a clue how or where the robbery was staged. My roommate Phil was released from the guardroom a few days later. He seemed to have loads of cigarettes and goodies we never had money to afford. When asked where he got them he insisted he had a windfall and that was as much as I was told anyhow. The only guys on the camp who had not been fingerprinted were the half dozen who were under lock and key. Nobody suspected that they would be guilty as they were in a secure place. The frustrated police decided to carry out another finger-print check of anybody who had missed the first run. Lo and behold, they had a fingerprint and they got a match with one of the guys who had been in the jail during the robbery! The six guys who had been locked up during the robbery were court marshalled, found guilty and sentenced to one-year detention in Colchester Correction Unit. So how did they manage to rob the NAAFI when under lock and key, I hear you ask? Quite easy—remember, they were in a tem-porary Guardroom, i.e. the sports store. Well, the windows in that store were barred on the *inside* so all they had to do was unscrew the bars, slip out, carry out their evil deed, slip back in—and they were never missed! The Guards would probably be half asleep during the night. The story that went the rounds was that they had socks on their hands, but one sock had a hole in it—and that's how the police got a fingerprint!

The drama of my fractured ankle was not over yet and I was dealt a sickening blow that virtually finished my army career; because of my three months in plas-ter I was behind with my education in the art of killing people, so I was down-graded to the squad behind mine! This was a nightmare as we had been together for nearly a year. We were like one big happy family; very seldom was there any hassle. Furthermore, they were all honest guys who you could trust. My new comrades gave me a hard time. As soon as I entered my new billet, there were comments like, "We don't want any rejects in our squad!" This was hurtful as it was not my fault that I had fallen behind; but as it turned out, most of them were rejects from society—they were thieves, liars and cheats from all the down and out parts of Britain. Some of them could barely speak proper Queen's English. They were the lads given the option of army or jail! It didn't matter which they might have chosen—they were essentially of a disruptive nature. One example of how callous they could be was apparent when one of the decent lads from the Peterhead area got word his mother had died suddenly; he had to leave in a hurry to get home. I doubt if he was an hour clear of the camp before his locker was burst open and a camera given to him by his mother stolen. I experienced a simi-lar incident myself. My mother used to send me some home-baked cakes and copies of the local newspapers, perhaps once a month. I used to share the cakes with the boys in my old platoon. They used to be waiting whenever I got parcel. The first parcel received while I was in my new platoon was destroyed before I got near it, and my precious newspaper torn into stamp size pieces. My enthusiasm for the Boys Army was diminishing rapidly. My new platoon Corporal was a Scot Cpl Chubb KOSB, but he lived off the camp so there was nobody to clamp down on the bullyboys.

ONE MORE FIRE

Lights out in the camp was ten-o-clock weekdays and eleven on a Saturday. This particular night lights went out as normal. We had been in bed for over an hour. I am sure most of the lads were asleep when, possibly around midnight, all hell was let loose with people shouting and banging. The noise was horrendous! All I could hear was the platoon Corporal from next door shouting to get out and head for the muster point as there was a fire. Corporal Bathgate of the Argyll and Sutherland Highlanders didn't need a loud hailer—he was kind of noisy at the best of times! We were a bit disorientated having been asleep, but we were soon wide-awake. When we hit the cold night air, the sight that greeted us was heart breaking: the whole recreational area was burning! It was an all-wooden building and was well alight; the heat was so intense that we had to move back. We were already the full width of the drill square away. Suddenly there was a series of explosions—it was like someone was firing shells into the air. Our corporal thought it was the Brasso tins—once they were heated up, the NAAFI was gone and the Leisure Centre was unstoppable, just a mass of flames; it housed a full-sized snooker table and a library with a grand selection of books. The rumours began to circulate the arsonist was at work again. People were seriously concerned—what if the stupid bastard set fire to one of the billets? We would have no chance. Possibly three hours later we were allowed back to bed, but the fire brigade stood by the rest of the night in case we had a flare up. The whole camp was tinder dry timber with a creosote coating; it didn't need much encouragement to burn.

To any younger people reading this, remember we didn't have the fire-fighting facilities available now. With the Brasso tins exploding it was very dangerous. There was also a big stock of boot polish, also highly inflammable. We spent the rest of that night without further incident. In the morning the recreation area was just a smoking pile of rubble. Our barracks were shrinking by the minute and there was no sign of any rebuilding of the area already burned. A couple of months previous, they just crammed us into other buildings that were still intact. Within a month the police had a breakthrough and an arrest was made. I can't remember how this was achieved but the lad responsible was a big Scouce fellow.

He was okay but in Banff-shire we would have said he wasn't the "full shilling"—he probably had trouble at home and been forced to join up instead of Borstal or prison. He was sent for trial in a civilian court and sentenced to be detained at Her Majesty's Pleasure, which meant his sentence was indefinite.

I had near completed my first year and was due a pay rise—another 10/-(50p) per week. Well, every little helped.

On the way back after my leave I had a narrow escape. You remember the routine—the overnight doss-down in the railway station in Aberdeen and catching the morning train south! As usual every vacant space had a body in it by the time I got there; but there were trains leaving and arriving at different times, so if you watched points you could squeeze into a vacant space eventually. I decided to have a wander around the platforms to pass the time—you could have a natter with the porters. It was around midnight and a train had just arrived; after the platform was cleared there was one weedy looking little guy still waiting and he asked me if I were waiting on somebody. Being a bit naïve, I told him my whole story—why I was there and how long I would be there. He said he was waiting for somebody to arrive but they must be coming on the next train. There was a strong smell of booze about him. He said the next train was not due till after 2 a.m. and did I fancy going for a walk to pass the time? Being bored and bloody stupid I agreed to go with him. We went around the back of the station and eventually came to a grassy bank. He sat down and motioned me to sit next to him. He produced a packet of fags and we lit up and started to chat. As soon as I sat down I started to feel uneasy. He was reeking of booze and was sitting so close I was getting the full blast of the fumes in my face. His chat soon turned to my leave and he asked what I had done with myself. He was very interested whether I had been with any girls and what had taken place between me and the girls. Then out of the blue his hand was on my leg! He more or less tried to push me onto the ground. I was fairly shocked and taken aback, especially him being a full-grown man. I was slightly afraid of him. Still on the ground, I drew my knee back and landed the best kick I could. He let out a squeal and let go. I didn't hang about but took to my heels back to the station. I never saw the little weed again but I was wild that a stranger had so easily taken me in—part of the learning curve, I guess! On telling the lads back at the barracks about this, the more streetwise ones said he would have been "an arse bandit"—another new bit of terminology for me!

Back from leave and things were on an even keel again. I was still not very contented with my new platoon but had no other alternative. I was quite enjoying the training although the guns and war games were never to become one of my points of interest. In February our hierarchy decided we needed a bit of toughening up so we were shipped to the battle training area of Sherwood Forest for a night of frontline training. When we arrived we had to dig trenches and were to be there for the night. I never felt so cold as I did then in my life. Some of the lads were quite ill after that little fiasco; in fact, I believe a couple developed pneumonia. Later that month we had a real calamity when one of the boys committed suicide; he shot himself at the back of the billets. I knew the fellow quite well—he was all right and had earned his sergeant's stripes, but all of a sudden things went wrong for him. When I think back, he was strange at times. We practiced a military funeral for a whole week marching up and down the square carrying a locker to simulate the coffin. Due to my size I was only a guard of honour. Eventually we were told he was being buried privately with no Military Presence. Maybe it was just a guise to add a new dimension to our normal drill routine. Suicides don't normally get military recognition, after all.

As I have stated, I am a football fanatic and that year I witnessed probably the best footballing spectacle every shown on the television. It was my first live match. We were given the afternoon off to watch it. The match I am referring to was Hungary versus England. It was pure brilliant! The Hungarians were a class act and England was beaten six-three. Can we gloat for a few seconds? But wait a minute, England couldn't have been all that bad—they got three against the best team in the world! Another statistic from that game—it was eleven English against eleven Hungarians. I often hear about the Eintracht versus Real Madrid European Cup Final, but Real Madrid was a multinational team who won seven-two.

The next highlight of my military career was being picked to be an usher at a huge Military Tattoo in the City of Nottingham. We had to show everybody where to sit. Once the arena was full we were free to watch the Tattoo. We decided to have a wander through the tented area where the performers were getting changed. Passing one of the Marquee tents, one of our lads lifted the bottom to see what was inside. Wow! About eighty young ladies, all at various stages of undress, were in full view. They were from the Women's Army Corps, comprising a physical training display team. We settled down to watch the view (well, you never know your luck!) when suddenly we were surrounded by an irate group of Military Police threatening us with all sorts of harm and calling us filthy names. Thus ended our live peep show!

We really had some great times. Earlier that year we had spent two weeks under canvas camping on the east coast near the Wash. We were close to an RAF camp at North Coates, a very important wartime airfield involved in the Battle of

Britain. It was now a training base for the RAF Regiment. We had about sixty tents, thirty each side of the grass area. At either end of the encampment were three rows of primed fire extinguishers. It made a lovely little football pitch, so right away we had a game of football in progress when somebody hit a block-buster of a shot amongst the extinguishers. As they crashed against each other like skittles, they started to go off, causing our masters great grief.

My body suffered further damage, again through no fault of my own. It probably happened to me because of my enthusiasm. We left our billet at eight-o-clock in the morning. Whatever task we were doing that particular day meant we were out till lunchtime. The normal routine was that you marched back to your billet about five-to-twelve once you were dismissed. There was usually a stampede to get to the billet first, pick up your eating irons and head for the canteen. If you were late there would be a queue of about a hundred guys waiting to be served. As well as having your lunch you would possibly have to change dress for the afternoon session, so the hour passed quickly. The day in question we were dismissed as usual. I was first in the stampede through the billet door—then utter chaos. Unbeknown to us there was a contractor repairing the floor just inside the door—no warning signs to say anything like that was happening. With the pushing and shoving from behind, the first three or four lads fell through the floor, landing on the geests. I was underneath the pile! I was sure my ribs were broken, for the pain was unbearable. We were a bit shocked at first. The medical team was sent for but luckily there was no lasting damage. I was told to skip duties for the rest of the day and rest on my bed. I was pretty sore for the next few days.

If you remember, a couple of chapters back I told you about the change in the quality of boys who were joining up. The problem was coming home to roost as there were nearly as many waiting for discharge as there were passing out. There was one barrack room allocated to guys waiting to be discharged. It was full all the time. Personally I would say there was a 40% failure rate. When I first joined there was hardly any guys who didn't make the grade.

Some of the smartest guys were Irish. There were quite a few of them, all from very poor backgrounds—you could tell that by the state of the clothes they wore when they arrived at the camp. One guy I remember arrived wearing an old greasy boiler suit that had numerous patches on the knees and the elbows. The patches were from an old jersey. I had never seen anything like it before. One thing about the Irish lads, though—once they were issued with uniforms they were really smart soldiers.

My feeling at that time was that the place was still in turmoil. After all the offices were burned down I had a feeling a lot of records had been destroyed and they were struggling to cope. I have always thought that I was possibly a victim of the chaos, for in the late spring of 1954 I was ordered to report to a medical office in Nottingham where I was interviewed by a Lt Col in the medical corps. I was under the impression I was there because of the pains and stitches I was getting in my side after falling through the floorboards. I told him about that incident and about being downgraded, but he didn't seem unduly interested. He asked me if I was happy in the army. I can't remember my answer, but he grunted and groaned before telling me that would be all. Back in the camp I went about my business as usual. I was about to sit my second-class education certificate when, out of the blue, one of the guys asked if I had seen the discharge board. I went across and had a look—and there, on the discharge order, was my name! I had to leave two weeks from Tuesday! I was gobsmacked to say the least. I immediately challenged the order and was more or less told that if it says you are going you are going—so there was nothing else for it but go! My only instruction was to make sure my kit was handed in before I left. I was totally confused—this was the only life I had known up till then! I was called in front of an officer and was told I would be unable to get any money till payday, which was the Thursday. Due to burglaries and fire they didn't keep any cash on site.

I didn't have much money on me but decided if the army no longer wanted me I was going at the first available date—so on the Tuesday morning, with about 2/-(10p) in my pocket, I entered the harsh world of Civvy Street.

WHAT NOW, MY LOVE?

Where I was at the time—in England—everyone called each other 'love', so I thought the title of this chapter would sound appropriate if I called it by the name of a popular chart song of the era! As I walked out the gate that morning in June 1954, it felt like I was being evicted from home. I suppose I was becoming a bit institutionalised but though I was gutted at the time, I never looked back after crossing the line at the gate. The other lad with me was going as far as Hull so he would be with me as far as York. Four hours at most would see him home whereas I had at least twenty hours more. Between us we had about 3/-(15p) but I was determined to get out as quickly as possible by not waiting until payday. I was cutting off my nose to spite my face. On that Tuesday morning I gave up my identity of 22839094 BOY SOLDIER A. SCORGIE and reverted to plain mister. The reason given for my discharge was ceasing to fulfil army medical requirements. I often wonder how I managed to work for forty-seven years with little lost time through illness. Some of my places of work were in the harshest environments found in Britain. I left early on the Tuesday morning in the company of my travelling companion (whose name I have since forgotten). He was quite a small guy, very heavily into music. I don't remember the reason for his being discharged. When we reached York he had a very short distance to go to his home, so he left the rest of the money with me. We were down to 1/6 (7.5p), and by the time the train got to Edinburgh I was broke. I had spent the last few coppers on tea and possibly a pie. I can't remember but the pangs of hunger were starting to set in. During our halt in Waverly Station two RAF guys joined the carriage I was sitting in; they were on their way home from Malta and were full of the great time they were having abroad. They also had stacks of Duty Free cigarettes. After listening to all the bragging they were doing about how well off they were, I told them my predicament and for the only time in my life I begged them for some money. I was desperate with hunger and only about halfway home. My final plea was to borrow a pound and I would leave my watch with them as security and would return the pound when I got home. These two guys were real saints—their generosity was overwhelming; they blankly refused my proposition. I had to pay a visit to the toilet and while I was away they must have had a summit meeting because when I returned they handed me 6d (2.5p) plus two Prize Crop ciga-rettes. It must have broken their hearts parting with large sums of money like that—the pair of miserable b....!! One lesson learned from that episode in my life was never ever to be landed without money. I often hear people say money isn't everything, but you canna' do much without it! By the way, my parents had moved again back near Banff in the Alvah district; they also had another addition to the family—our young sister Helen, who was to be the last. This move added another twenty miles to my journey so it was midday on the Wednesday when I reached our new abode. My mother started fussing and cooked a huge plate of bacon and egg. I was past being hungry and possibly due to fatigue I had diffi-culty eating the food. Just before my two RAF buddies left the train—I think it was Dundee—I was on the verge of asking for their home address so that I could return their Tanner. Before the weekend my final pay off from the Army arrived. If I remember correctly it was over thirty pounds. It was not a lot as I had digs to pay for; I also registered at the dole office but never received any money from them, nor advice.

I had a lot of problems ahead of me. I had no idea how to go about getting a job or the type of job to apply for. I was actually paid for a month's leave when I got home. It was undoubtedly time to try and sort my future out. Leaving the Army was like getting chucked out from your family. My only experience was how to kill people with a Rifle, Sten Gun, Bren Gun, Mortar Bomb, and Hand Grenade, but I had no practical experience—it was all theory. The only killer required in the local paper that week was a Gamekeeper, but you needed experi-ence so I had to content myself till the next edition of the paper.

Apart from my killing skills I had plenty experience of all sorts of sports, but outside the Army that was useless. I had just been medically discharged from the services—yet I doubt that there was any youth in Banff-shire with the level of fit-ness I had achieved. If I was no longer medically fit it was due to negligence on the part of the Army, or maybe they got it wrong. There was turmoil in the camp due to all the fires that happened. Did some clerk along the line get me mixed up with somebody else? After I got home and settled down I took my discharge papers along to my local G.P. and he was of the same opinion as me—they had surely discharged the wrong bloke. I will never know the truth, but it could just have been possible.

I was feeling pretty lost and had no idea where to go to get advice. The labour exchange did nothing to help. I felt the Army had dumped me at sixteen and a half. I deserved better than being thrown onto the scrap heap. Our location didn't help, either, as we were well off the beaten track. There was nothing but farms. I had very little knowledge of farm work apart from howkin tatties. My stepfather had worked at farming all his life, so he had no knowledge of anything else. Two weeks after I got home there was an advert in the paper—a sawmill labourer wanted. It was four miles from our house so I borrowed a bike and went to see the man. The man who required the labourer was a very difficult person to talk to—one could say he was dour. Nevertheless, he offered me a start on the Monday at half-a-crown an hour (12.5p), which equated to £5 per week. I had to start somewhere so I took it. Out of my fiver I had to give my mother dig money. By the time I cycled there and back every day I was away from home for over ten hours per day. I hated the job from the first hour I was there. Firstly, I had a boss that virtually ignored me. All he was interested in was cutting timber; he had a contract from the Coal Board to cut timber for the mines—lengths of 2"x 2"x 36". He could cut hundreds every day and my job was to barrow them away from the mill and stack them. You didn't need to be a brain surgeon to carry out this task. The monotony was soul destroying. I had definitely become institutionalised over the past eighteen months in the forces. Can you imagine leaving four hundred guys your own age, then be stuck in the middle of a forest at the back of beyond with a middle-aged, miserable bugger who found it difficult to say good morning? I had become accustomed to having thirty lads permanently around me with a lot of banter and hilarity day and night. This was bursting my head—the sound of the sawmill screeching eight hours a day was pure torture. Two memories stand out from this time. One was witnessing a Total Eclipse of the sun! I will never forget the eerie feeling as the day turned into near total darkness at midday; not a bird was chirping and everything went silent. The second memory was the reason I decided to quit. I had been a month there and on the particular day I am writing about there were severe gales. I had difficulty cycling against the wind and ended up a few minutes late. When I rounded the bend before the sawmill came into view, I couldn't believe my eyes! Every stack of wood was lying on its side blown over by the wind—a whole month's work! I uttered an unprintable adjective and decided I had had enough—I would be looking for another job. It was Friday and as soon as I got home I dived into the situations vacant columns in the local paper. There were very few vacancies—a couple of farm labourers required, and that was about your lot. I phoned one of them and spoke to the farmer. He asked if I could come and see him on Saturday morning. It was about eight miles away but I managed to scrounge the loan of a bike and set off for King Edward, arriving just before lunchtime. I was not desperately keen to become a farm labourer but it must be more interesting than what I was doing at present. This was my first proper interview and my nerves were taut as I neared the farm. It was right on the main Aberdeen to Banff road so it would be handy for the bus if I got the job.

The adrenalin was pumping like mad as I knocked on the Farm House door. The door opened and I was confronted by quite a smashing looking young woman. I explained why I was there and she introduced herself as Helen. The maid told me to wait there while she told the boss I had arrived. My nerves were playing havoc as I waited. She reappeared and told me to follow her. At the kitchen table sat a very overweight grumpy man looking at some paperwork. He didn't greet me with a lot of enthusiasm but started to ask me some questions about myself my experience. He then told me the terms and conditions. Because of my lack of experience he would only pay me £1.50 per week and every second weekend I would be required to look after the cattle at no extra payment. The going rate for a lad my age was £3 per week but this fellow was taking advantage of my lack of experience. I was desperate to get away from the monotony of the sawmill so agreed to start on the Monday, even though I was taking a drop in pay. It was live-in so I had no living expenses. I had a look at the bothy I was going to live in and confirmed I would be ready to start on Monday morning.

My first impression of my new boss was that he was a big fat bully. He was loud and rarely went to town to the Mart, but he returned well oiled, which seemed to give him an air of superiority. His main money earner was pigs, of which he had about two hundred and fifty. My job first thing in the morning and last thing in the afternoon was feeding the noisy squealing buggers. I didn't mind the job but, again, you didn't need to be a brain surgeon to perform the duties—feeding them and removing the dung, end of story. In the morning I had to perform the worst job I ever had the misfortune to carry out; at the back of the piggery there was a building with three hundred battery hens. The poor unfortunate creatures were kept in a cage all their lives. I would put it down to cruelty. The droppings landed on a platform; there was nothing mixed with it, just pure hen's poo. Along this platform was a scraper attached to a wire rope; by winding this rope you scraped the droppings along to the end where they dropped into a cart. If you were over zealous and went too fast the keech would plop off the end and splash all over the place. After a few splashes on the face and around the mouth you got into a routine of how fast to wind the rope. I hated that job and many times had to swallow hard to avoid throwing up.

My next task every day was to top and tail turnips—again, hardly a highly skilled occupation and the monotony was hard to bear. I would start at 10 a.m. until 3 p.m., turnip after turnip; there would only be me and ten thousand turnips in the field. It was soul destroying—the only cheerful bit was that you got two different colours that broke the monotony!

The social side in the evening was okay as there were quite a few lads my own age in that location, so we always had some fun after work. During my time there I came close to losing my life for the third time. When you read the next paragraph you may think it is a bit far-fetched, but I can assure you it is true. I was home for the weekend at my parents' house, due to return to my workplace on the Sunday evening. I managed to persuade my stepfather to give me his bike so that I could cycle the eight miles to King Edward. There was a bit of an argument with my mother as there were no lights on the bike and I had to go through the town, but I told her I would walk in the town so that the police would have nothing to say to me. At around eight-o-clock I set forth. It was really dark, but after a few minutes I got accustomed to it. There was a bit of a slope about half-a-mile from the house so I was out of the saddle head down and going pretty fast with zero visibility! Suddenly there was an almighty crash! Knocked off my bike and lying on the road somewhat dazed, it took me a couple of seconds to gather my wits about me. Then I realised that someone else was lying at the other side of the road, groaning and moaning. The only light I had was my cigarette lighter, which I lit the best I could. I recognised the man right away—he was from the next farm along the road. He was not a pretty sight—his forehead was split open with blood everywhere. He was still wrapped round what was left of his cycle.

Before dropping me at work, my stepfather had to get the car out and take Old Jock to hospital where he had six stitches inserted in his head wound. It was two weeks before I saw the extent of the damage to the two bicycles—they were both write-offs! Ours had the front forks wrapped round the handlebars, while Jock's bike had the forks bent right back touching the pedals—it looked like they had been steamrolled. How we both survived is a miracle. I got off Scot-free, not a scratch.

My latest job was probably not as monotonous as the sawmill as I had different tasks to carry out each day, but I still missed the company of my army mates. I was treated well by the farmer's wife and had my meals at the table along with them. The food was excellent. The farmer's wife must have thought I had the same capacity as her fat husband, as she used to heap plates of food as big as he had—enough to feed two normal men on each plate. He was a crabbit man in the morning and it was worse when he had been drinking the night before. He also had a sadistic streak in him. One evening he asked if I could milk the cow. He was going out with his wife and short of time. I had done this job many times for my mother so I could milk the cow although I was slow. I finished the job and handed the bucket of milk to the maid, who told me there was a packet of cigarettes from the boss on the kitchen table for me. I picked it up and when I got outside decided to light up. On opening the packet I found it contained only eight cigarettes—not very humorous, but no doubt he got a great laugh about it.

During this period of my life I made another blunder and got involved with alcohol. I was still under seventeen and got in with the wrong company. One of my old schoolmates with whom I had started to pal up with, who was about my age though six feet tall, had already started to go to the pub on Saturday evenings, enjoying a few drinks before attending the dance in MacDuff Town Hall. He persuaded me to go with him, saying I should just keep a low profile and nobody would even ask who I was, never mind ask my age. During the first visit I was nervous and uncomfortable—I didn't really like breaking the law, probably due to my army discipline. I had a couple of bottles of beer and bought a gill bottle of whisky before heading for the dance. Before entering the hall we had a "houp" out of the bottle—my first whisky! I was now well oiled and started to throw up. When I got home and went to bed, everything began to spin—it felt awful! In the morning I felt terrible and vowed never to touch booze ever again; but come the following Saturday evening we headed back to the pub. It was a wonderful way to spend an evening but played havoc with my thirty bob wages. We were having a good time and I spent the week looking forward to my Saturday evenings. I was beginning to know a few of the regulars so the crack was good. A couple of weeks later we were in our usual watering hole. I was on my way back from the toilet when I spied a couple of coppers at the table talking to my mate, big Jock. Having had a couple of drinks and maybe as a result of a bit of Dutch courage I kept going (I could have bolted for the door); as I approached the table I heard the copper tell Jock it was only six weeks since they had charged him the last time for under-age drinking, so he had no need to tell lies as they had all his particulars. I nearly died but was trapped! As I might have expected, the coppers turned on me. I was still under seventeen but told them I was over eighteen. They warned me if I was lying they would find out and it would be worse for me because of the lies, but I decided to brass it out. They charged the Big fellow and told him to leave the premises. They were still eying me and asked me again how old I was. Before I could answer Big Jock said, "You better tell them the truth as it will only be worse on yirsel when they check up." I had no other option then but to come clean—so we were both charged with under-aged drinking. Six weeks later we were summonsed to appear at the Sheriff Court. I was fined £1 and Jock £3. We were warned if caught again we would be given a custodial sentence. They were determined to stamp out under-age drinking, a problem that had become worse than ever.

I had been on the pig farm for nearly four months and it was Hogmanay. I had been invited to stay with a relative of mine for the festivities. He was working on a Hydro Scheme in the Highlands. When he heard the wages I was being paid he urged me to pack the job in and he would get me fixed up with him; but there was a snag—I would not be employed under the age of eighteen. So we left it at that and got on with the drinking—and I returned to my job at the piggery.

It was quite a severe winter in 1955. The boss travelled to some big sheep sale at Lairg and bought two hundred Blackface lambs. He got them for 50p each and when he had fattened them up he was going to make a fortune, so he bragged when he came home full of drink. We unloaded the lambs in a field near the house. There was about eighteen inches of snow in the field and these sheep were tiny. During the night there was a severe blizzard and another foot of snow fell. When I looked in the field there wasn't a sheep to be seen—they were all buried. We spent most of the day digging them out. One third had perished, so the profit was diminishing by the minute.

Shortly after the New Year, on a Sunday morning, it was my turn to look after the animals. I was in the byre mucking out when the boss came storming in the door. He was in a foul mood, most probably hung over. He asked why I was taking so long to get the job done. I can't remember my answer, but he lashed out at me and caught me on the side of the head. I was holding a four-pronged grape. He was a lucky man—I had just spent eighteen months learning how to stick a bayonet in a man's gut! The only thing that really stopped me was that they still hanged people for murder. If I had given way to impulse and launched an attack on him it's doubtful that I would be able to stop myself. I didn't particularly like this bully, and my dislike had now turned to hatred. I walked away, which was perhaps the best thing in the circumstances. I contacted my man in Garve that day and asked him to get me a job. I couldn't work on the bully's farm any longer, and fortunately I had a positive reply within a couple of days which necessitated travelling to Garve on Monday. That weekend I packed my few possessions and left. I wanted to cause this man as much hassle as possible, so I didn't tell him I was going.

The day I left the east coast for Garve was a milestone in my life, as I more or less settled in the Highlands with only a few brief sojourns back home. There was still quite a lot of snow on the roads, so the journey right up to Inverness was quite ropey. The worst part of the journey to Garve still lay ahead, for lots of areas on the road were single track. As I waited at the bus station a young Irish fellow tried to cadge some money from me—he needed his bus fare to get to Invergarry. There was a huge Hydro Scheme going on there. I had never heard of the place, but soon it would feature in my life in a big way. I refused to give the Irishman anything—I needed all the cash I had!

I was a bit apprehensive about going to Garve as I remember being told that you needed to be eighteen before you were allowed in the camp. On arriving at Altguish Inn, my friend was waiting for me. "Where will I be staying?" was my first question. "In the camp," he replied. I asked how he had managed that. "We told the clerk you were eighteen," he said, "so when he asks your date of birth, add a year on!" My nerves were shattered—telling lies was not my strong point. "What about your insurance card?" he asked. I didn't have it, I replied. "That's fine," he said, "it will take them a few weeks to get it. We'll think of something before then." I was not happy with the situation. Over the years I supposed everybody told a white lie now and again, but I hated doing so. I'm sure I always had a guilty look about me so I was all on edge as I lined up outside the clerk's office along with another dozen or so men who were also starting work the following day. My mate was next to me when I was asked for my date of birth. I said 1936—and he wrote that down and told me where my billet was. It put me in mind of Tuxford camp—thirty beds, fifteen each side, the only difference being the smell of sweaty feet: everybody wore Wellington boots and Donegal socks, i.e. corners off a blanket and wrapped round your feet instead of socks! They were all hung up to dry and the stench was sickening. Anyhow, I was there under false pretences—how long would it be before I would be found out?

This was my first time on a large construction site. I was quite awestruck with the size of the concrete dam and all the heavy machinery moving about. My job was on the batching plant along with my mate. Again, this job didn't require the brain of a surgeon—all I did was remove any concrete that spilled over the side of the skip, a pretty mundane job, but the money was way ahead of what I could get at home and there was plenty company, just like being back in the army without the discipline. I worked a twelve-hour day and the hourly rate was 3/3, approx 16.5p per hour—you were paid overtime rates as well—so that side of it was excellent; but I was there illegally and it worried me as I was sure I would get the tap on the shoulder and told to go and maybe charged for telling lies. I kept a low profile and had a couple of reminders that my insurance card and code number hadn't arrived as yet. The older guy who knew what I was up to gave me the most terrible advice, i.e. throw away the documentation when it arrived—as if I weren't in it deep enough already! We were into our fifth week and there was still plenty of snow about. Suddenly one night a blizzard got up and we had a blanket of snow three to four feet deep. As we sat at breakfast that morning the gaffers came and advised us to pack our belonging and go home, as the weather forecast was not good; they only had enough rations onsite for a few days. We were on the road before 10 a.m. Just at the Altguish Inn a Landover arrived—he was going to Garve with some parcels for the train: he invited us to jump in and he would take us there. It is just as well he had four-wheel drive as we slid off the road a few times. It was white-out conditions. Eventually we got to the station and boarded the train for Inverness. We arrived in Inverness late afternoon and there was doubt if there would be any transport going east for the roads were in such a bad state. We went to the train station and were in luck—there was a train leaving for Aberdeen just as we got there. We were in Elgin around six and managed to get on the last bus heading for Banff, though there was no guarantee the bus would get through on account of the snowdrifts. We had a little discussion and we decided to get to Cullen and stay with my Granny for the night. It was the safest thing to do.

For the next two days we had to sit tight as the storm raged. It is only in that part of the world that you can have roads blocked in minutes when the wind gets up and you experience white-out conditions. Eventually I made home to find a brown envelope waiting for me, the contents of which were my P45 and insurance card. So that was me sunk—there was no way I could go back to Garve. I was liable to end up in the clink! Nothing else for it but look for alternative employment until I was eighteen and then I would go back to the Hydro Work as it paid the best money. I had cleared £15 per week while I was at Garve.

I had a bit of luck when one of my parents' friends called for a visit. He was working on a Farm near Huntly. He told me there was a vacancy there, and that the wages were £3 per week with live-in accommodation. He said he would let me know if I was needed. That weekend we had a message saying this fellow would pick me up on Sunday evening and I would be starting work on Monday. This would be my fifth job in just over six months. So I started farm labouring again. There was £12 per week difference in the wages, but I had to take what I could get. It was still very wintry with lots of snow on the ground. My new boss was a bit old fashioned and was rather staid but he was okay to work for. My function was to assist the other fellow who was the tractor driver. I was the Go-For. I had had a taste of the better wages at Garve and I couldn't get to my eighteenth birthday quick enough to get back to where the pot of gold was. I was at the foot of the financial ladder once again—it was like a slippery slope where you keep sliding back to the bottom!

Bridge of Marnoch was something else! We were fed slightly better than the cattle. The farmer and his wife were behind the times but they did live in a rather outlandish place. If my workmate didn't have a car we would have problems getting in and out of the place. Back of beyond was the best way to describe it. Our main function was lifting turnips. There was still plenty snow about so the cattle had to be kept inside the steading and needed lots of feed. Again we had the choice of colours to break the monotony—purple or green! This place was okay but I was being used as a spare part. I would never learn anything just plugging the gap wherever it appeared, so head down and stick it out as long as I had a wage coming every week. But when you are a fairly intelligent person, monotony soon sets in if you don't have to use your brain occasionally. My workmate was quite a good crack—we had plenty banter going so it passed the time and, because he had transport, we could get into town and go to the cinema occasionally (no Telly in those days). About six weeks after I started I was home for the weekend and bumped into the farmer's son from the neighbouring farm to where my stepfather worked. He was looking for somebody about my age to train up in the art of general farm work. He asked if I would be interested. The money was the same—£3 per week and live-in accommodation; it would be like living at home and I could see my folks on a more regular basis. It was also a bit more civilised and I could cycle to town any evening I wished.

My new bosses were father and son. The son was about four years older than me and a proper gentleman. He also had three lovely sisters, but they were forbidden fruit and rarely spoke to us. I did a lot of tractor driving—nothing skilled, just the less experienced stuff. It was fine but I had a hard battle having to work on my own. I had been so used to company. The old father of the two bosses was very elderly and walked with the aid of a stick. The younger man was supposed to be the farmer but his father still had hold of the reins. He used to snoop around all day, never said much but never missed anything either.

We were given a rare day off one day to visit the Northern Agricultural Show in Aberdeen. We—the three hired hands—had a great day out. The thing that sticks out in my mind the most that day was that it was the day they hanged Ruth Ellis. The evening papers were full of it. We managed to get a lift home on a private coach. I was quite drunk, not being used to having a lot of alcohol. I must have overdone it because I slept in next day and didn't go to work. The older boss was none too pleased with me and let me know about it in no uncertain terms. We were into the harvest and I had the job of loading a cart, driving it to the stack yard, dropping the cart and hitching up to an empty cart. It was hard going keeping ahead of the guys building the stacks but the banter was good. The day we finished the harvest the old boss called me aside and said he was so impressed with my performance he was giving me a pay rise of 10/-(50p) per week. I thanked him but didn't let on I had itchy feet and was ready to move again.

Around this time I had been in the town on Saturday evening when I met up with some of my old mates from King Edward. They told me there was a football trial the following Monday evening and they were looking for bodies as they were short. They played in a Welfare League. I cycled the eight miles on the Monday evening to the football park I had no gear so didn't expect to get a game when one of the older guys handed me his boots and told me to get on and play. I was in the reserve team against the usual team. They had a star goalkeeper who was none too pleased when I put three past him. I was sure I would be signed but, alas, my football career came to a sudden halt once again. I was the fittest and fastest on show that night but never even got an offer of being a reserve. Shortly after that I met up with another old buddy. He was working in the Highlands in Glen Affric with a wood contractor. They supplied bothies for accommodation, the wages £7 + per week. There were vacancies so I asked my mate to get me a job, which he did. I gave my farmer colleague a week's notice and quit. We had no word of Gypsy blood in our genes but the wanderlust was in me.

Glen Affric was the most beautiful part of Scotland I had ever seen and I still think of it that way. To work there was just breathtaking. The job we were doing meant very little to me then as it was a means of making a living. It was new education as far as I was concerned, but now I am older and very keen on conservation it has come back to haunt me occasionally. We were clear felling the old Caledonian Forest at Benevein Dam, some wonderful old trees when I think back; it was destruction of wild life habitat, but then I was footloose and fancy free so it didn't mean too much. My boss Geordie Grant and his charming wife Margaret lived in a cottage deep in the forest near Tomich. The workmen's bothies were situated there as well; we were once again at the back of beyond. It was my first time in a bothy where we had to fend for ourselves. I had two mates so the three of us decided to split the chores. I was allocated the cooking thanks to my previous school training. The other two guys in the Bothy were ex-servicemen so we had already experienced comradeship in the forces. We spent most evenings gambling, playing Nap mostly for about sixpence a game; it passed the time as we had no wireless or anything like that (pre-transistor radio days). We were five miles from the pub and the only transport was shank's pony. We got our rations from the grocer's van that called twice a week. If you forgot anything you had to do without till he called again. Life was a laugh a minute! Where our accommodation was there was a river flowing close by, the River Glass, I think.

From our place to the nearest bridge where we had to cross to get to work was about three miles. It meant driving that distance morning and night and we actually passed our bothies but couldn't get across because of the river. Our boss Geordie came up with good idea—he would fell a fairly big tree across the river and we could cross that to get to the work's van which he would park at the other side, thereby saving himself quite a bit in petrol money.

Now, it's not everybody that can balance on a tree trunk and cross about eight feet above the water! One of our guys, Sammy, was just hopeless—he didn't have the balance to do it. The river was not very deep at that time so his mate Cecil said he would take Sammy on his back across the water wearing Wellington boots. Next morning, while we did the balancing act on the tree trunk, Cecil put the two pack lunches up the front of his jacket, then got Sammy on his back. He was about halfway across when the pack lunches began to slide from below his jacket! He bent forward quickly to grab them, forgetting about poor Sammy who took a header over his shoulders into the water. It was about half six in the morning, so the water would be none too warm! The air was blue with bad language as they tried to blame each other for being so bloody stupid. The rest of us thought it was hilarious! After a change of clothes we were able to get to work.

My time in Glen Affric was a bundle of laughs mostly. It had its other moments—there was a continual turnover of labour, so it wasn't long before Geordie had to recruit some new hands. He mostly got guys from our home area. He had been home to where his mother lived just outside Turriff on the family croft. Anyhow, he started a new lad, Joe, who had never been away from home before and when he arrived he was dressed in his best suit with a fancy suitcase! It turned out he had taken all his possession with him. We had been warned to get the bothy cleaned up so that it was sparkling for Joe's arrival. This we did. We were all at work on the Monday, Joe's first day. After we had eaten that night we asked if he fancied a walk to the pub, and he agreed. Before leaving we stoked the woodburner stove so that it would be warm when we got back. We were on our way back when we met the boss in his van. He asked if we had had a good night, then told us we better hurry home as the bothy was on fire. Now, Geordie was a practical joker so we didn't pay much heed of what he said! We had a wander around the old Stables near the ruined Mansion house before sauntering up the road. As we rounded the last bend to where the bothies had stood we were gob-smacked—there was nothing but heaps of cinders! Both bothies were burned to the ground and all poor Joe's clothes had gone up in smoke. We were in shock and if there was any trace of being slightly drunk we were soon sober as we realised that every possession we had was now reduced to ashes! Joe's two suitcases were clearly visible but turned to dust.

Our number one priority was where we were going to sleep that night, as we were miles from anywhere. The Grant family decided we could doss down on their sitting room floor until we figured out an alternative move. One thing we didn't need was a wardrobe, as we had nothing left to hang up. It was decided that we would have to rough it till the weekend. On the Saturday morning one of the company lorries would take us to Loch Broom to pick up a new bothy. On the Friday payday Geordie gave us £3 extra on our wages—that would buy a pair of working trousers or a pair of Wellington boots. We didn't alter our routine and headed for the pub after work. We were warned that we had to be ready to meet the lorry at Beauly Toll at 5 a.m. With that warning ringing in our ears we set off for refreshment. The next thing I remember is waking up sitting in a lorry at a lay-by beside the Corrieshalloch Gorge, not too far from Ullapool. In my jacket pocket I had a bottle of gin! I never touched the stuff, so unless I won it in a raffle or something like that, my mind was a blank. I had a horrendous hangover and began to wonder if I was off my head. The money I had spent on booze would have possibly bought me a new suit! Speak of being irresponsible.

Our new bothy was situated in the village of Tomich. It was a bit nearer civilisation if nothing else. We were quite upmarket there as we had a crystal clear burn running past the door—just perfect for getting fresh water and then having a bathe at the weekend (this was a summer time arrangement, of course).

Geordie Grant was probably the straightest timber contractor I worked for but he was the exception rather than the rule, for every good one there was at least ten crooks. To make a good living in the timber trade you needed to work jolly hard and not everyone was prepared to do that. A major downfall of timber contractors was heavy drinking, which ruined many good men.

Having spent the summer in Glen Affric I had itchy feet and was ready to move on. It was well into autumn. I had witnessed the Stags rutting—it was a sight to behold and quite frightening with all the roaring and clashing of antlers, but I could sit for ages just watching them. Most of the guys I met in the timber industry were always just one contract away from making a fortune, but alas, I never met one who ended up rich. The next man I went to work for filled my head with riches untold, but I am afraid it was only my head that he filled as my pockets were more empty when I left him than when I first started. I suppose you could put it down to a learning curve. The man I went to work for was one of the top sawmill operators in the country and he was capable of making a fortune. I was employed as his assistant (labourer) but unbeknown to me this fellow had a severe addiction to drink. He was undoubtedly a chronic alcoholic. He was a stranger to me but his promises of the money we could make had me hooked. The first contract we had turned out a disaster as the Timber Company supposedly went bankrupt two weeks after we started. We were assured we would be paid so we hung about for two days. Finally they said we would get a cheque on the Friday, which we could cash at the bank in Beauly. That evening, as we did every evening, we went to the local pub, talking to one of the locals. We told him about the cheque and he advised us not to move till we had cash in our hand, as this geezer would give you a cheque and by the time you got to the bank he would have cancelled it so you ended up with no money, as fly as a bag of weasels. But some were like that! I stuck it out till the Saturday and finally received a good part of what they owed me. We had been employed by a bunch of crooks, for soon after we left there the police raided the place and a lot of stolen goods were found—some of it from as far afield as Manchester. This was all part of life's education; the only problem was that I felt like a rolling stone and, instead of not gathering moss, it was money I wasn't gathering and I seemed to always be the loser.

There was no shortage of work in the Highlands at that time with timber jobs all over the place. Over the weekend we were offered a job with one of the established contractors in Lochaber, a whole new frontier for me. The boss agreed to pick us up on the Monday morning and drive us to where the contract was. If we were happy it was a case of agreeing terms and getting to work. Of course, my mate had a wife and family to think of, so he had more responsibility than me. Dead on 7 a.m. we were picked up in Drumnadrochit and in a very large car chauffeured to Lochaber—I thing it was a Jaguar, real luxury! It took just over an hour to be in Fort William where we stopped for a bite to eat, all paid for by our new chief who seemed a very pleasant fellow and chatted all the way. We then crossed the Corran Ferry to Ardgour and from there we headed for Strontain. I had my first close-up view of Ben Nevis that morning—very impressive. From Strontain we started to climb a very narrow single-track road. Near the summit we stopped and our prospective gaffer showed us some old disused lead mines and also the breathtaking view of the village of Polloch. We were told that the houses in the village were of the wooden Swedish style, all mod cons, and there was an empty one that my mate could house his family in. After viewing the lead mines and the magnificent scenery we started to descend into the village. It was like being in the Alps! I was totally taken with the place. My mind was working overtime thinking of how I could hide away here for a few months, save some money and indulge in my favourite past time—fishing! Mr Montgomery was explaining how the operation worked and we would be paid by every load of timber that left for the sawmill. It would be on a piecework basis, which suited me; we could then work to suit ourselves—perfect!

But my dreams of the future were suddenly shattered when my workmate whispered into my ear, "There's no bloody way I'm moving the wife and kids here! What if it doesn't work out? How the hell do we get back out of this hell hole?" So ended our sojourn to Polloch!

Shortly after that we had a real taste of west coast weather, when the heavens opened and it poured rain for the rest of our time there. Back in the car the boss said he would tell us what money he was paying. It was then that my mate blurted out that we wouldn't be taking the job. I could see Mr Montgomery's face changed colour with what I presumed was rage. Although he kept his calm, suddenly our Mr Nice Guy became Mr Nasty. As we approached Strontian we pulled up at the Post Office and he left the car to use the public phone (no mobiles then); as he re-entered the car he told us we would need to get the bus from Fort William as he had other business to attend to and would be staying in this location. It was getting on after 6 p.m. and we had no idea of buses and, worse still, I doubt if we had the fare between us; so there we were, stranded seventy miles from home in pouring rain, and destitute.

We were dropped off in the middle of town. I don't think there were any more buses that day so we started walking. About an hour later we were at the Road To The Isles junction. It had stopped raining but the traffic was sparse. Every set of lights that appeared we tried to get the car to stop. Suddenly our prayers were answered and a Forestry van pulled up. He was going to Struy so he said he would detour round by Glen Affric and drop us off at our digs. A lovely man!

It had been an adventurous day but we were no further ahead with employment. My mate had a plan: we would head for Inverness on Wednesday where we could visit some of the Timber merchants. They all had offices in town, but it meant another week without money. How my mate's wife managed to feed a family I will never know.

It was well after nine-o-clock when our Good Samaritan stopped. Thankfully it had stopped raining so we were relatively dry. Our journey took over an hour, which meant it was near midnight when we got back to our digs. We kept a low profile. Not having any money is a great way of being unable to enjoy yourself. Wednesday morning we were on the road early, hitchhiking to Inverness. We were waiting at the first premises to open—a Timber Contractor by the name of Armstrong. My mate was well known to him and within twenty minutes we had a job in Kildary Wester Ross—another new frontier for me and another new skill, for what it was worth. I was now employed as a talisman. My function was to help the saw miller to load the bench and clear away the slabs—real heady stuff but it was work. We went back to Glen Affric to pack my mate's goods and chattels. One of the company lorries was to pick us up on the Thursday afternoon. We would be starting work on Friday.

Kildary was a fairly civilised place. The pub was less than half a mile away. No doubt this was an added attraction for my mate. You could get the bus or train in either direction—Tain one side and Invergordon the other—both less than half-an-hour away. I didn't know anybody there but my mate was acquainted with a few of the people. There were possibly twenty guys employed in the sawmill. We were warned early on that there were a lot of families in the area with feuds going on all over the place. It was not a good idea to fall out with anybody as they were all related to one another. Soon after getting there I went along to the village hall to attend a dance. As the night wore on quite a few drunk guys began to appear just after the pub's closing time. Everyone was in fine fettle and the dance was going great guns when suddenly all hell erupted! Quite a few people, mostly women, made for the stage, me included. There then commenced a fight between two of the local families. They were lined up on either side of the hall and went at it for a good thirty minutes—until somebody said the police were on their way. Within minutes we were all on the floor, dancing! The feud was over for another night.

Invergordon was still very much a Naval Base in those days, with plenty ships in the Firth. There were also two or three RAF bases around the district, and then the Yanks had a base in Evanton, so it was still evident that there had been a war recently. A crowd of us from Armstrong's Mill decided to get the train to Invergordon for the Saturday evening. The Pubs were still State Controlled then, so they closed at 9 p.m. prompt, all very strict. We left the pub and headed for the dance hall which was heaving with servicemen. After being there for less than half-an-hour one of the guys in our party got involved in a fight, and within seconds there were all sorts of Service and Civil Police storming the place. We baled out and ran towards the station! With luck there was a train leaving; if not, we would have been murdered as there was an angry mob chasing us, throwing bottles and other missiles.

About a month after moving to Kildary I got word that my mate from Altguish was working in Ardross, again cutting wood. This was another job that would finish up with us making more money than we could handle (if you listened to my mate!); he convinced me that I should chuck Armstrong's and throw my lot in with him. Always gullible, it didn't take me long to realise that I had boobed once again this new contractor was a joke. The first joke—it was now near Christmas and we were asked if we would work overtime using the Tilley lamp for light while we cut down some trees! Second joke—when you come to the end of a log there is always six, maybe eight inches left over: this guy used to pay the kids a couple of shillings a week if they would drop these leftover bits through the stacks of wood; then, when they were counted he would be paid for a full pit prop when in fact all you had was two firewood logs in the stack! Another dodge he had was when measuring a fairly big tree he would put his fist between the wood and the tape so that it would measure a couple of inches more! He must have been desperate. I realised that I had jumped out of the frying pan into the fire once again.

We were barley making enough money to feed ourselves. It was also winter with snow on the ground, so we decided to stick it out till the last week in December, then head for home and see if we could pick up another job; if not, we would soon be in debt. We managed to get fixed up with a Polish Contractor, Mr Zigman Glass, whose headquarters were in Inverness; but the contract was in Glen Gloy, near the Commando Memorial at Spean Bridge. We could have digs in the Forestry Hostel there, so we had no problems with food. It was dead of winter when we got there and the job was only to last three weeks. We were to stack peeled pit props. This was a joke, for the pit props were like eels! We had difficulty handling them. Within days it started to rain, making this even more difficult. We were unable to work and it was like that for the next twenty days. Our Jewish gaffer was going mental but we were helpless. Thankfully we were paid by the hour, otherwise we would have been sunk. Eventually it dried up and we finally cleared the place up but well outwith the date they were required to be finished.

We were now into February 1957. Steve the foreman who was also Polish offered us more work in a place called Invergarry. We finished in Glen Gloy on the Saturday around dinnertime and headed for Fort William where we would get a bus to this Invergarry place. It had started to rain again and our bus didn't leave until around 8 p.m. It was dark as we left Fort William. Our instructions were to get to the shop at Invergarry, then walk for about two hundred yards west and we would come to an old bus that had been converted to living quarters. We got off the bus in pitch darkness and pouring rain and headed west as instructed. Finally we came to where this old bus was parked. The door was wide open so that was a good start with the wind and rain howling around the place! I have no recollection of what we did for heat or light that night but I do remember wakening in the morning and my underwear was soaking with the damp off the dirty filthy bedding that had never been washed since the day it was bought. The crockery was the same—old chipped plates and cups! The whole place was bogging—I had never experienced anything like it in my life. The place was a pigsty and no shops open to get rations! My life was at its lowest ebb. Again I have no recollection how we survived until the shop opened on Monday morning, but I told my mate as soon as a bus appeared I was off, as I had no intentions of living in those prehistoric conditions. But fate must have persuaded me to stay and after we cleaned the old bus up it was a bit more presentable. One of the reasons I stayed was because I had no money to get me anywhere else!

We were to be working with a guy from our home area known as the Kit Glove Woodcutter, as he always wore Kit Gloves when he was dressed up to go out. He also fancied himself as a bit of a lady-killer. I didn't particularly take to the guy and my mate who knew him said he was bloody useless and hadn't a clue what he was doing; but we were penniless so beggars can't be choosers. The job we were given was clearing blown timber, one guy snedding the branches, the other two cross-cutting into lengths with the old Herring Bone saw. There were power saws on the market but ours was powered by brute force and ignorance. After working for an hour our leader, who was working the saw with me on one end and him on the other, did nothing but moan. He was more or less insinuating that I had no idea how to pull a saw. We stopped for a tea break and our man sharpened the saw. Back to work and within an hour and it was hard going—the saw seemed to be as blunt as ever. This went on for a week, sharpening the saw every break and it always seemed to be blunt. At the weekend our leader took the saw to the Saw Doctor in Inverness; he had one look at it and said it had been roasted in a fire and there was no way it would stay sharp as all the temper was gone. Our man came back tongue in cheek and told us what was wrong. He also had to buy a new saw. We had nearly come to blows over the saw but my mate had stepped in and cooled the situation. The Kit Glove Woodcutter never even apologised for the slagging he gave me, but that's life.

THE NIGHT THAT CHANGED MY LIFE

The new saw made a huge difference and we started to make progress—and our leader and I managed to see eye to eye again. We had the bus as comfortable as possible and we were handy for the shop. Our place of work was behind the shop. The young assistant was a smashing redhead, bubbly and full of fun. We used to have a blether with her. She was right into making the community spirit worth getting involved in. There were still quite a few men about Invergarry clearing up the remains of the Hydro Camp just past where we had our bus. The second weekend we were there the redhead informed us that there was a local dance in the village hall! She would be looking for us to attend, as it was a fund-raising dance to help build a new Village Hall. As the entertainment was pretty sparse we decided to attend. After work on Friday evening we got dressed up had a few beers and went to the dance. It was quite amazing the amount of people who attended! There were quite a few drunks but it was going well. I had a dance with Joan (the girl from the shop); she was in the company of another female so I enquired about her. I was told she was Joan's mate. She looked a bit of all right so I asked her up the next dance she said her name was Jess.

I ended up having a few dances with this Jess and eventually asked to walk her home, hoping she didn't say she lived in Tomdoun or some other far-flung place. She reluctantly agreed and it turned out that she lived less than half-a-mile from the Village Hall. She told me she worked in Inverness and was only home till Sunday evening. I asked if I could see her on Saturday evening and she agreed. I have no idea what spell she cast on me but I couldn't get her out of my mind and the time couldn't pass quick enough till I met her again. Now there weren't many warm places you could do any courting in about Invergarry during the first four months of the year—the back of the Church was the favourite if you could handle the draught! I spent as much of that weekend with my new found girlfriend as was possible before we parted on the Sunday afternoon and she returned to work. Whatever there was about this young lady, I was hooked! I felt terrible when she left me. We were writing each other daily and I realised I was madly in love. We saw each other as often as was humanly possible, and within weeks we were meeting each other's parents. This was getting dead serious. By the time we met up with my parents they had moved again, back south to Fyvie.

My girlfriend was an instant hit with my family, although she had slight problems with the Doric (we were all broad speakers!). My mate and I also moved jobs. Still employed by Mr Glass, we were offered the Sawmill job. It was okay—we worked the Sawmill all day, then had a side line where we cut pit props in the evening, still with the same company. This allowed us to earn roughly £10 per week. My mate moved his wife up to Invergarry and she took over my job in the mill. I was given a job on the transport side. The attraction there was that I had been promised to sit my driving test when I was capable. In the meantime my parents had moved *again*—this time back to our home area of Cullen. It was handier for me to go home for a weekend. During a visit home one of the local farmers offered me job at the harvest; it would last about six weeks and they paid good money. This was pre-combine harvester days. I went back to Invergarry and worked a week's notice. My Polish boss told me to come back as soon as the harvest was over and I would get my job back.

I left Invergarry on the Sunday. One of my workmates decided to travel into town with me. We had a snack in one of the cafes in town before heading for the east coast bus. As we passed the old La Scala we were approached by a guy who asked if we were interested in buying duty-free cigarettes; he told us he was a seaman and they were docked in Invergordon and he was selling his duty-free ration 10/-(50p) for two hundred. I bought £1 worth and then carried on to the bus station. I bade my mate goodbye and left for home ready to start work the next day.

It was great to get a few weeks home. I hardly knew my brothers and sisters and they were growing up fast. The harvest was great fun—it was fairly hard work but there was always plenty banter with the guys working there. The Tuesday week after I started it was a very wet morning, so we were unable to harvest. We were usually employed clearing up the steading or some other mundane task; that day we were winding up the old rope from the previous year's harvest, locally called Glesga Jock; we were having a bit of a yarn when someone spotted a couple of well-dressed guys crossing the farm yard—they were sticking out like a sore thumb. Coppers. I realised! What would they want? The foreman went to meet them and after a couple of minutes speaking to them my name was called. I could feel the adrenalin rush—what the hell did they want! I had done nothing wrong. As soon as they spoke to me they had my name and address in their notebook. I had to confirm that I was the guy they were looking for. After identifying myself, the next question was, "Have you smoked all the Woodbine you bought from the guy outside the La Scala picture house in Inverness on Sunday?" I was flabbergasted, wondering how they knew all this information so quickly. I told them all the fags were gone, as I had given them round the family; in fact, the truth was that I had sold half to my stepfather, possibly making a small profit. I then explained to the cops what the guy had told us, even telling them about the mate who was with me. They said they knew all this. They started getting a bit heavy-handed and pointed out that what I had done was illegal, as the duty-free goods were not for resale and I could end up being brought to court. That would be up to the Procurator Fiscal. Immediately they changed course and really stuck the boot in, telling me I was in bigger trouble as what I had done was reset the cigarettes since they were stolen, the result of multiple break-ins to shops. Now they turned Mr Nice Guys again and told me the guy was in custody and if I would co-operate and identify him, they would do their best to persuade the P.F. to look kindly on my case. They then produced a couple of photo albums with mug shots of some evil looking characters and I had no problem identifying my guy. He was sentenced to five years for his dishonesty.

I often wondered how the cops got on to me so quickly and I soon found out—the fag seller had been heading for Fort William and the police were on to him; they happened to call at the sawmill in Invergarry, showing his photo and asking if anyone had seen him. My mate George told the police yes, he had been with Bert Scorgie when he bought cigarette from that guy a week ago; so I was passed on to the cops as easy as you like. Thanks George, you were always a pal!

The six weeks of harvesting soon passed and I headed back to the Highlands and my old job. Jess and I decided to get engaged and set a date for our marriage in December. Her boss was being moved to Edinburgh and she was offered a job with them; this meant we would hardly see each other due to the distance, so we decided to make it permanent and we could see each other every day. I only had one major drawback—I had no money! It was hard to keep yourself and save £7 per week. Of course we all smoked then. She was worse off than me as she earned £8 per month, but lived in so we would need to tighten the belts. Work was very scarce at the time so we were stuck with what we had.

A few weeks after returning north I met a guy from the east coast. He was in the same boat as me and needed money rather quickly, as he was also committed to getting married soon. He told me there was loads of work in England and they were paying good money on the Preston Bypass. We both jacked in our jobs and headed for where the streets were supposed to be paved with gold. We arrived in Preston early morning and tramped around construction sites and factories. Every place told the same story—sorry, no vacancies. It was soul destroying. We managed to get fixed up in a bed and breakfast joint costing 10/-(50p) per night. We decided to start heading north next day. Our first stop would be Leyland. There were plenty factories there where the buses used to be manufactured.

Our landlady for the night was a big fat loudmouthed Lancastrian. I never felt less welcome in a house in all my life. As soon as we spoke she replied, "You're Irish, aint yer?" We quickly replied that we were not Irish but Scottish. She more or less implied that we were little better. The bedroom was just about habitable with wallpaper peeling from the ceiling, but it was a one-night stay so it would suffice. We needed to eat so we dumped our cases and were about to leave when we were accosted at the front door by our ignorant landlady. The ground rules were laid down—in by ten-o-clock "and if you are drunk your cases will be placed on the pavement and you will be out on yer necks"—charming fat bitch! We headed for the dining room at seven-thirty next morning and were quite shocked to see about eight black men sitting having breakfast. We were the only whites there as they were all West Indians, except for the landlady, of course. Were we Scots below the level of coloured people? We were at the station early and bought tickets for Leyland where we tramped the streets for hours with not one offer of work. About midday we decided to head for Carlisle, arriving there mid-afternoon. We were in luck! At the Labour Exchange we were offered work digging trenches to bury cattle, the victims of a foot and mouth outbreak. It was a start, but again luck was not on our side—there was plenty work around Carlisle with a big power station being built nearby, but the snag was accommodation. It was impossible to get digs. We spent ages going from door to door, but it was the same everywhere we went—"Sorry, full up!" We were in despair. Of course, a major factor was that we didn't have transport, so we were very restricted as to how far we could travel.

We headed back to the Railway Station and over a bite to eat we decided to have one last go at getting a job. There was a huge Hydro Scheme in progress in a place called Glen Lyon. We had to get to Stirling, then to Killin; after that we would be into the unknown. Money was getting short so to save on bed and breakfast we would travel overnight to Stirling. We arrived in Stirling early morning, had a breakfast and cleaned up in the station. The train for Killin left about 10 a.m., arriving there about an hour later. This was our last throw of the dice—if we didn't get a job there it would be back home. It was now Thursday, so fingers crossed.

Glen Lyon is like all the rest of the Highland Glens—it goes on for miles with very little traffic. There were at least half-a-dozen construction sites, but miles apart. We tried one or two with the same response—no vacancies for labourers.

Finally, and near at the end of our tether, we were offered work with Mitchell Construction as machine men in the Tunnel. Neither of us had ever done anything like it before and were apprehensive about it. If I had known how easy it was I would have taken the job, but our inexperience was showing through—so we had no option but turn down the only offer we had that day. The day was starting to catch up on us. Another couple of hours and it would be dark, so we started heading back to Killin—but it was miles away. If we didn't get a lift shortly we would be stuck there for the night and probably have to sleep in the open.

On the way into the Glen I had noticed a huge Dutch barn. I said to my mate that if we hadn't got a lift before we reached there we should perhaps think of dossing down there for the night; at least it would be dry and fairly warm. We reached the barn and jumped the fence across the field. It was about fifty yards. We walked in the entrance and near collapsed—there must have been about fifty guys already there with the same idea as us! Some of them were fairly rough looking characters. As soon as we appeared they were asking if we had any fags on us. I gave my mate a nudge and pointed back to the main road. Our first bit of luck happened soon after that—a Mobile Cinema van drew up alongside us and offered us a lift back to the railway station. The driver assured us we would be in time to get the train back to Stirling from where we boarded the Inverness train and set off back to where we had left a week ago. I intended going back to Mr Glass, my old gaffer, to see if I could get my old job back. It had been a fruitless week and my resources were badly dented. Life was a struggle!

We arrived back in Inverness at night and I had to find bed and breakfast. The house in which we stayed is no longer there—it is now a car park in Castle Street. I was shattered, so fell into bed with the minimal of washing myself. I slept like a log and was up early. I needed to get to Mr Glass's house as soon as possible, so after a good wash and shave and a decent breakfast I decided to make the bed—an old Army habit. I near died when I saw the pillowcase! It was filthy with me travelling about all week in dirty steam trains! My hair must have been covered in soot. I turned the pillow case outsides in and skidaddled as quickly as I could. A lot of landladies used to nip through to the bedroom while you were at breakfast—they were interested to know if you were into water sports (i.e. piddled the bed)! Needless to say I never stayed there again. To save the bus fare I hitchhiked back to Invergarry.

I was given my old job back starting Monday morning and my old bothy was as I had left it. Apart from being rather broke it felt as though I had never left the place. It was head down and save as much money as I could. We had twelve weeks until our wedding day. We had secured accommodation in the form of a caravan parked in a most romantic setting down by the shores of Loch Oich.

Over the years and with the many different jobs I have worked at, you meet and get to know people and everyone is different. Most people I got know were decent friendly people who would do a good turn before a bad one. There are a few exceptions, but thankfully they are in the minority. One guy who sticks out in my mind was Big Donnie. He was a smashing big fellow but had the vilest temper I ever came across in any human being. Donnie was wonderfully placid one minute, but the next was like a raving lunatic. We were attending a dance in the Old Village Hall in Invergarry when I bumped into Donnie. As was the norm, we both had a half bottle in the hip pocket, so we would go for a dram outside the hall. There was a veranda with seats round the front so we would relax while having the normal tipple. Donnie was the first to sit down. Remember, it was pitch dark. He immediately jumped to his feet as if he had sat on a sharp instrument! The curses he was letting forth are unprintable. When he finally calmed down I found out that somebody had vomited on the seat. In the dark the big fellow had plonked his arse on top of the mixture of whatever the guy had had for his last meal—disgusting! I was near bursting with the need to have a good laugh at his expense but, seeing the mood he was in, I thought better of it.

We had our wedding arranged for the 14th December 1957—the date of my 20th birthday. It was to be a quiet affair with only the four of us, including Joan the redhead from the shop and my cousin Edwin (sadly both passed away a few years ago, two relatively young people).

We were married in the Church manse. The old minister of the Queen Street Church agreed to marry us. I must have done everything right as it is now nearly fifty years later and she still can't get enough of me. Every penny we had was precious and guarded like the crown jewels as we struggled to meet all our commitments. We got quite a few presents from family and friends, but none of the presents was money—unlike the custom these days. But we had each other and even if times were hard, we gloried on and made the best of life and started married life without even a wireless. We appreciated the little we had.

I'M GETTING MARRIED IN THE MORNING

The coach that carried me to my wedding was the 11 a.m. MacBraynes Fort William to Inverness single decker bus complete with utility seats. I met my cousin in Farraline Park bus station. We headed to the Clachar Bar (now extinct) for a dram—a bit of Dutch courage maybe. We arrived at the Manse ahead of time and were waiting for the minister to tie the knot. Our small ceremony went okay and we must have had the correct ingredients as we are still together nearly forty-eight years later! Life has not been without its difficulties and has not all been plain sailing, but I don't think we would have done it differently. We stayed in Inverness in the Old Cummings Hotel, then caught the bus back to Invergarry on Sunday morning. I needed to get back to work on Monday; if not, we would have been broke by the end of the week as we only had about a fiver between us after squaring up with the hotel.

It was ten days before Christmas as we settled in our love nest by the Loch. The caravan was a new experience for us. Within days the weather was very frosty with quite a fall of snow. The first morning of severe frost Jess near had a disaster; our caravan was very small so we had to fold the bed away every morning to give us more room. I was at work before she got up, but as she caught the blankets to pull them off the bed she nearly did her back in. With the condensation running down the wall of the caravan, the blankets had frozen to the wall—that was with us sleeping in the bed. She also had to thaw the hot water bottle every morning, as it was also a block of ice. It was a hard winter weather wise and also for us. Most mornings we had to thaw the Calor Gas Bottle before we could even have a cup of tea. How we survived I'll never know. Things have changed so much today with central heating and all that jazz. Later on in the spring Jess went to do some spring-cleaning only to discover her clothes were ruined in the wardrobe—the damp had stuck everything together. I suppose it was another learning curve. The caravan was great during the good weather but very Spartan during the winter.

Most of the guys in Invergarry who were about my age worked on the Civil Engineering sites. There were various contracts around the area. The money was better than the timber trade, if only because you worked longer hours and they paid overtime rates.

There was a fairly big contract due to start in the spring of that year with the construction of the Invergarry/Glenmoriston road. It was about fifteen miles long through virgin land. I contacted the Site Agent and was given a start date. Once again I had to tell Steve my Polish boss that I was leaving him for about the fourth time. He was a lovely person and wished me luck in my new venture. All the guys employed on the construction site were old hands at the Construction Game; they had nothing to learn and many of them worked together for years. They were well educated in the do's and don'ts of site working. There were about sixty of us working on the Glengarry end—for the road was being worked from both ends. The road was built by a company called Farrans and has been known as Farrans road since the day it was completed. If you are not acquainted with the area, you will be sucked in by the magnificent scenery when you reach the summit and look down towards Poullery. At the height of summer it is a dream come true. But I can assure you that when the weather changed it was the most hostile place I ever worked in. Firstly, in the summer, it was wonderful working in the blazing sunshine—that is, until early morning or late afternoon when the midges performed! As soon as the diggers moved peat the midges would swarm all over you, nearly driving you demented. Then there was the rain! When it mixed with the soil in that area it went into a quagmire, bogging down machinery and near impossible to walk through. It was tough going but the wages compensated for the hardships.

The summit of Farrans road would be the highest point of the road to Skye. Standing there looking west you would be in line with Loch Hourn. As soon as late autumn appeared the sleet, snow and rain would come driving down the glen, possibly straight off the Atlantic Ocean which would be in the region of fifty miles away. At times it was near impossible to work, but no work meant no pay, so we had to make the best of it.

We found out that spring that we were to become parents—we didn't hang about! We also had a stroke of luck when a couple of rooms became vacant. They were on a croft belonging to an elderly lady who was wheelchair bound. She needed some help with her daily activities so the deal was we would get the rooms in return for helping this unfortunate lady. It was just perfect, as our daughter would never have survived a winter like the one that had just passed. We moved into the rooms well before the birth of Doreen in September and were heading into another winter. This again was quite severe and possibly worse than the previous one. Just after the New Year conditions were so bad that the site was closed down indefinitely. For the first time in my life I had to sign on the dole along with all the rest of the guys. Work was at a low ebb that winter. Having filled in all the forms to claim my dole I sat back and waited. Within days I received a letter telling me I was short of insurance stamps on my card so my dole money was cut by a pound from £4.50 to £3.50; that, believe it or not, was quite a drop, but we had to carry on regardless. One thing in our favour—we didn't pay any rent. It was going to be a struggle. We had to plan how we were going to make the money last the whole week so we acquired an old W.R.I. Cookery book wartime edition and started to cook meals. From that we came across one meal that looked appetizing so we bought the ingredients—1lb of mince, 1lb of rice and 1lb of oatmeal. We never thought about the fact that the rice and oatmeal would swell when cooked! We had to change the pot twice as it kept coming over the top as it cooked. We ended up with a delicious smelling concoction that filled two cooking pots. It tasted lovely! The first three days as we ate it hot, cold, fried and any other way we could think of. We were broke and could not waste any of the food so we just had to grin and bear it. After a week we were a bit scunnered of it.

The weather finally cleared up enough for us to return to work. We were off for about eight weeks. We were still getting sleet and snowstorms but with the weather getting warmer it was melting pretty quickly; but melted snow means water and our next problem was flooding—but we worked on. Another big contract was due to start in Glenmoriston later that year so we would get continuity of work. This job would start running down later in the summer so if everything went to plan there was no fear of being unemployed for the foreseeable future.

The income tax year ended on the 5th of April and rumour had it that every worker in Britain was due to get a tax rebate due to a clerical error of sorts. Every week we were waiting to hear if it had been paid out. I can't remember how much it was to be but it would come in handy when we got it. Finally word went round that the rebate was in the pay-packets that week (we were paid in cash then), so everybody was excited about it. We were to receive between £8 and £12 extra depending on your code number. Normally we received the pay about 2 p.m. which gave us time to check it and if any queries needed answering we were allowed time to get that done. Our normal pay out time passed and no sign of the pay! Another hour passed and still no pay. The bears were beginning to growl: "Where the hell's our money?" Eventually word filtered through that there had been a burglary and the office had been broken into and the wages were gone. We near had a riot! We had to hang about till the C.I.D. arrived from Fort William. The guy in charge of the site was called out of the line of men being sized up by the police while the rest of us were told to get on the bus and go home! There was mutiny as we were given no money! The guy in charge who had been standing near me kept saying it's a disgrace, this happening the week of the rebate.

Later that evening we heard that the Site Agent had been arrested for the theft of the company payroll. We were quite happy as we thought we would get paid out next day, but alas, we were in for another shock! The police were holding the money as evidence! The place was in an uproar next morning as we tried to find out what was to happen. A lot of guys lived from week to week so a missed pay was a severe hardship for them. The company let us down very badly and it was two weeks before we received any of that week's pay. Even then it was only part payment and it was over eight weeks before we were finally squared up with the full amount. I often wondered if the guy who stole the wages realised the hardship he caused many families with his selfish behaviour. It was all down to his alcohol addiction, so probably he was desperate and in need of help.

The drama of Farrans road was not over yet. Shortly after the wages fiasco we had finished our shift and were heading for the company bus, about twenty of us walking in a group having a bit of banter as usual, when suddenly one of our foremen stumbled and fell to the ground. He made a gurgling sound and then fell silent. The moment he hit the ground he showed no sign of life. A lovely big friendly man had passed away on one of the most barren landscapes imaginable. As it was a sudden death we had to get the police involved. One of the guys set off running for the office (no mobiles then); the police and doctor were at least twenty miles away. It is an incident I will never forget. As we sat with the big man's remains the wind was whistling through the heather. The sound was so eerie, just like the sounds from a haunted house! It was late that evening before we were able to get home. Word had gone before us that there was a death, causing worry till the wives found out who it was.

Midsummer we eventually heard that the new construction site had opened a labour office and would soon begin to employ men. The company, A.M. Carmicheal of Edinburgh, had been awarded a five-year job from the Hydro Board. On the Friday I left work early and headed for the labour office at Dundreggan. I was keeping my head down in case I didn't get a job. If the Farrans boss found out he was liable to give us the sack. I was in for a shock as I rounded the side of the office for I bumped into half of Farrans workforce! They had beaten me to get there first. I was given a start date a week on Monday. This would work out great as I could give Farrans a week's notice. Our gaffer at Farrans had been trying to find out who had been to the new site office. It looked as though we had just beaten him to the punch. I would have been well up his hit list as I had had a run in with him over the way they were paying overtime, so no doubt I would have been a marked man. It's great how the sadistic get their kicks.

We decided to join the trend of that time and buy a residential caravan, which we managed to site in Fort Augustus. That meant the travel distance to my new job would be less. There was also talk that Carmichaels' would have a site up and running as soon as they were established. The caravan was handy as I could move the family with me much better than staying in camps with the smell of sweaty toe rags in every billet.

I had been at Farrans for over a year, a kind of work record for me, but it is easier to stick a job that is of interest than doing the same mundane tasks every day; another plus was that on the construction sites there was always plenty company.

TIGERS UNDER THE TURF

A whole crowd of new starts were lined up at A.M. Carmicheal's office just below Logan's Dam at Dundreggan that Monday morning. We were being allocated to different gaffers all over the site. My new gaffer was an Irish fellow, James O' Donnell, from Dunlough in County Donegal, Ireland. He was a smashing, easy-going man who never bothered you as long as you did what he asked of you. He took a shine to me right away and said if I stuck with him he would make sure I would get a job in the tunnel when it got underway. At the moment we were working on the approach access way, mostly drilling and blasting rock, but they were looking for six dumper drivers for when the tunnel got underway. Four or five weeks after I started a few of us were told we were being moved to another job on the Monday morning. I immediately got in touch with my Irish gaffer and asked what the score was. He assured me my job in the tunnel was safe but in the meantime I was required to help out somewhere else for about six weeks. Eight of us had to report to a gaffer at Blairaidh road end, from where we would be given instructions on what we were going to be working on. I knew most of the guys so it was no problem fitting in. We were to be employed with the Engineering department building stations on top of sixteen hills (mountains, even) along the Southern Heights of Glenmoriston. This sounded exciting as I loved the open spaces and the wild life and nature was right up my street.

The company had hired a helicopter to fly the material out to the top of the hills. Our first job was to load the chopper and two guys were flown out to do the unloading. It was quite a small machine so it could only carry a few hundred-weight at a time. I never managed to get a flight but it was great fun! After three days all the material had been successfully landed where it was required. Then the donkeywork came. We needed to drill holes in some places to get an anchor, so we had a petrol-driven drilling machine (a Cobra) that weighed about one and a half hundredweights. Two of the guys volunteered to carry it. All the time they would wait at the foot of the hill while we climbed to the top. If it was needed we gave them a shout and they would humph it up to the top. Sometimes we could dig a hole deep enough to anchor the station, using concrete. To make concrete was sometimes a problem as well, as there is never a lot of water on the top of a hill! This required a bit of donkeywork as well, so we had a water carrier if required. One thing in our favour was that the weather was brilliant! We were our own bosses and nobody really checked up on us. If we had a rather hard time erecting a station we would only do one per day, so we plodded on. Those five weeks were some of the best days of my working life—working in glorious surroundings, and we had a good little squad, plenty crack, good long lunch breaks—just perfect. But all good things come to an end and we were soon back in the humdrum work on the access road into the tunnel. There was a huge difference from when we had been there last time. It was estimated that we would start working underground around the first week in November.

Once I had got established with Carmichaels' and was settled down, we decided to move the Caravan down to the company site at Levishie Lodge. It was pretty basic and all the fresh water had to be carried from the Lodge. My good lady Jess often had to fetch the water herself as I was working twelve-hour shifts, but to give her credit I don't recall ever hearing her complain about it regardless of weather conditions. This was a much better option as I could be in the caravan twenty minutes after my shift finished compared with having to travel at least half-an-hour each way daily. Another problem was the state of the roads in the winter, so we had quite an acceptable set up.

Traditionally Saturday evening used to be the workingman's night out. Women were not yet welcome in the pubs and nobody could afford to eat out, but the men would make their way to the nearest or favourite pub and pour as much drink into themselves as possible before closing time, which was 9 p.m. in the winter and 9.30 p.m. in the summer. They would then stagger home with a carry-out, and maybe a screw-top for a reviver in the morning. Many a poor wife had to suffer slagging for no other reason than the man was drunk; she would be pleased when he fell asleep and the house was quiet once again.

In Invermoriston things were slightly different. When we got home from the pub we would gather in somebody's caravan and have a celeidh! There were Gaelic singers, Bothy Ballad singers and musicians. The carry-outs would be nearing empty but around midnight the licensed grocer would arrive and we would get a top-up, which would keep us going till the middle of the night. Some of us would still have to get up and go to work come morning. It is also traditional that men who work in dirty, dangerous jobs are often referred to as Tigers! The Tunnelers work in a terrible environment, so they were given the exotic nom-de-plume of Tunnel Tigers. Let me put the record straight: *exotic* was definitely *not* the word to describe the type of work that happened underground and the surroundings were anything but exotic! It was dangerous, dirty, unhealthy strength-sapping work, not a place for the faint hearted. I became a Tunnel Tiger in the autumn of 1958.

The guys that risked their lives working in Tunnels were second to none. They were quite an international workforce, but were the most loyal workmates I ever encountered in my working life. They stuck together, helped each other and, if anyone was down on their luck, they would pull together to help them out. My first Tunnel job was easy for me—I was driving a dirty Smokey dumper, moving the waste from the tunnel to a tip-end. We would be called upon four times a shift. The quicker we did our function the quicker we could swing the lead till needed again. The dumper would spew out thick black fumes night and day. Every now and again the oil pressure gauge would burst. You only realised that had happened when you felt the hot oil running down your leg! Within a month you were coughing up phlegm similar to black boot polish, but it was easy work and the money was okay.

A lot of the terminology used was of American origin. I suppose this was due to the amount of Irish immigrants that went to America to start a new life, e.g. the guy in charge of the explosives was always referred to as the powder monkey; the guys who looked after the narrow gauge rail line were referred to as the Gandy dancers—all American slang. The Powder Monkey was in control of issuing and stock control of the Gelignite and detonators required to blow up the rock in the tunnel and any other area that required explosives. Most of the Monkeys were Irish so it would have been easy for them to stockpile some sticks of gelignite to send home to their terrorist friends (though, of course, the real terror threat in Ireland was not yet at the forefront). Nevertheless, the control of explosives in those days was pretty lackadaisical. We used about a ton every twenty-four hours, so a few sticks here and there could easily have not been accounted for.

My first tunnel job was the roadway into a huge underground Power Station. It was about seven hundred and fifty yards long and twenty by twenty in diameter. When we reached the entrance where the power station would be hewn out of the rock, our team were to be shifted to another part of the job further into the hills. We were working round the clock. The only shift not worked was Saturday night—that was used for the changeover of shifts and I suppose to give the men a short rest. The site was a hive of activity with about five hundred men employed full time at its peak. On a Friday afternoon Scottish Brewers would deliver a lorry-load of beer to the canteen. Spirits were prohibited, but the people that ran the bar used to sell the beer by the crate. I think it was 30/-(£1 50p) for a twenty-four mixed case. By Monday morning not one bottle would be found—just empties lying around.

Early spring 1959 we completed our part of the Tunnel at Dundreggan. We moved to a much further away site to a small tunnel eight by eight feet in diameter. It was known as the Outfall and collected water from outlying lochs to feed the Dam. We were working from one end and the tunnel would eventually end up approximately one mile long. I was still working for the same Irish squad, and Big James asked me if I was interested in taking on the job of Handyman. This meant a better rate of pay and a full share of the bonus, so I grabbed it with both hands! It was also a more interesting job. My job was to service and repair any broken machines, which happened frequently. I also had to keep advancing the service lines, i.e. air, water and ventilation, so it could be fairly busy. We also had to install a length of railway line at least every twenty-four hours, depending how far we travelled each shift. It was not always the same as the rock formation could change two or three times a shift. We used eight-foot long drills. If the rock were red and very soft or 'rotten', as it was called, we would manage to blast nearly ten feet each blast; but if the rock was the other extreme, a type of very hard rock called Grey Fern, we might only blast two or three feet. This was a dangerous situation because you would have six feet of the old holes, or sockets, left in the rock face; a socket could hold an unexploded detonator and if your drill slipped into one of these holes you could end up with an explosion. It was a reality, as it happened in another tunnel on that site but at a different location from where we were just now. The lad who was on the receiving end was partially blinded. Of course we had the usual headcase who would deliberately go into the old hole as it meant he had less to drill next time round!

Tunnelling in Invermoriston must have been a Geologist's dream as the rock formation constantly changed and we had at least four or five variations. I have already mentioned two types of rock; another was like marble and when we drilled it crumbled like granules, very soft but difficult to work, as the inch drill hole would end up about three inches in diameter, making it difficult to charge with gelignite. Another was Mica, like Perspex in layers, possibly four to six feet thick—again soft and very difficult to work but to me very interesting.

A few months later they were struggling to get machine men for the drilling at the rock face. The gaffer asked if I would be interested as I had done the job often enough. There was no more money but at least it was learning another skill; it was always handy to be able to do as many different skills as possible. A couple of weeks into this job and I was wondering if I had made the correct move. We were obviously working under a burn or a loch and the water began to seep through the tunnel roof just above where I was working. Every time we blasted it got worse and continued like that for six weeks. My opposite number and I were the only ones soaked every shift. Two suits of oilskins made no difference. It was now wintertime and as soon as we reached the surface our boiler suits were stiff with frost; they could near stand up by themselves! The water underground was always freezing cold, even in the middle of summer.

The management structure on these jobs always amazed me. Everything was governed by a Senior Engineer. Under him were two or three junior engineers plus their chainmen; then there was a Tunnel Boss, a Shift Boss, and possibly a Leading miner. In my eyes half of these guys were only hangers-on, as they never did a lot except sit around and drink tea! The Tunnel Boss would venture into the tunnel once a day, if at all. He ordered all the spares and equipment (a store man or site clerk would have done this function). The shift boss would appear when we were about to set off a blast. The leading miner could have done the same function as he often did on night shift when the shift boss was asleep. What I am getting at is that we were on a Bonus system; we would never make a fortune but it was an incentive. All these guys I have mentioned were included in the bonus, i.e. the Tunnel Boss got three shares, while the rest were on a sliding scale depending on status with no input whatsoever.

The outfall job was completed without a hitch. I can clearly remember the night we finished the job—it was around 2 a.m. We blasted a hole in the hillside and in the pitch dark we could see the stars! This is one of the bits that I remember and still find very funny: one of the Irish guys, Soldier Doherty, said to me after we had secured a ladder up through the freshly blasted hole, "Come on young fellow, we will climb out the hole and scale down any loose rock so we can leave it safe." As we stepped outside in the darkness we could see nothing but the light shining out of the hole, which was about six feet in diameter. Doherty stripped off his jacket and threw it down behind him so that he could get stuck into the work. What he didn't know was that about six feet behind and below us was a fairly fast flowing burn! His jacket landed in it and was never seen again—just another comical incident that occurred occasionally during my working life. (Perhaps it was just my quirky sense of humour that caused me to perceive these incidents!)

My next port of call was less than a hundred yards from the Outfall. The Site was known as No 9. This was another tunnel, about three miles long, being worked from both ends. It was well established before I was transferred over and would possibly be about half-a-mile underground. The new squad were mostly Scots who travelled from Inverness every day; they were smashing guys to work with and we had some good laughs. One very funny incident from that job that springs to mind was the day they finished the slope shaft; this was the tunnel running from the Power Station to the Dam. I think it was about a mile long and the gradient was something like 1 in 6, which was fairly steep and quite an achievement to complete on time. As it was a major milestone, there was a big party for the guys working on that particular part of the job. The company supplied two cases of whisky, which worked out at six bottles per shift. Of course, six bottles didn't go far, so they were soon collecting money for a carry-out so that the party could go on. When we arrived at the offices to go on nightshift there were a few of the engineering department, as we would say, 'well gubbed'. One of my workmates, Big Jimmy from Inverness (now deceased), looked in one of the office windows and saw this guy lying prostrate on the floor. He handed me his lunch bag and left me standing. What happened next was astonishing! Jimmy pulled the brand new Wellington boots off the drunk guy's feet, tried them on and walked out, leaving his old stinking boots alongside the man lying drunk. I would have loved to have been there when he sobered up! We jumped in the transport and headed for work. As we had nothing to do with the site where the party was taking place, we got on with our work, but the news was filtering through that as the guys got more drunk old wounds were opening up and soon there was fighting between the Scots and the Irish. Eventually they were moved and sent home to wherever they were staying. No doubt there were a few sore heads and black eyes next morning.

As soon as we were far enough underground we had to stay there the full shift. It was about three-quarters-of a mile; the tea maker would send in hot tea when we required it but the conditions were well below Hilton Hotel standards! We had to do all our toilet functions about a hundred yards past the area where we dined, so it was pretty dog rough. During my time there we had a severe outbreak of dysentery, which affected three or four hundred men—not a very pleasant experience, especially with the toilet facilities the way they were.

Another experience I would like to relate from that era occurred on Easter weekend. The site was closing down for four days and one of the gaffers approached me and asked if I was doing anything over the holiday. We weren't, so he asked if I would be interested in working. I jumped at the chance when I heard it was doing security on the site near the dam. He then asked if I had a mate who would share the job with me, as we were required for seventy-two hours. Big Frank, my neighbour, was also keen to do it as they were staying on the caravan site with nothing to do—just as well get paid for it. Frank and I had a little confab about how we would cover the hours. He decided we should do thirty-six straight hours each; then we would still have some time with the kids.

If you have ever done solitary confinement you will know what that thirty-six hours felt like! You can amuse yourself for maybe eight hours. After eighteen hours the time starts to drag. Even on solitary confinement the Warders would look in periodically. At night it was like being in a haunted house—no phone and no company, plus we were about four miles from the main road and the only transport was shank's pony. Never volunteer into the unknown—thoughts of topping oneself did occur!

Later that year I had a bit of a disaster when I was injured at work. On the night shift our boss, who was a decent Arcadian man, used to allow us out of the tunnel for a hot meal. We had to be discreet and not abuse the privilege, so to speed things up we all used to pile onto the Locomotive that pulled the muck skips to the tip. It was rather overcrowded but we could be on the surface in minutes as opposed to walking. On the way back to the tunnel face, the strap of my lunch bag caught on a steel pin and I was thrown off the Loco onto the steel track. I was slightly stunned and had done damage to my hand. I was sure something was broken. I was carted off to the medical room where they could do very little except tell me there was an ambulance going to Raigmore Hospital in the morning. "At nine-o-clock be ready," I was told, "and they will pick you up. Your hand needs to be ex-rayed; here's a couple of codeine to ease the pain—off you go!" What they would have done in a serious situation I have no idea! It makes me shudder to think about it. At the hospital they confirmed I had broken a bone in my hand so it was plastered and I was signed off for six weeks, not too handy with Christmas on the horizon. A couple of weeks before the Christmas break I managed to go back to work but had difficulty trying to handle vibrating machinery for ages after that mishap. The day I went to get my plaster off, one of my neighbours, a big rough Irish fellow, needed someone to accompany him to Inverness as he was sitting his driving test. He asked if I would go with him as his experienced driver. This was no problem except that the man had a glass eye. I asked him on the way to town whether he had any special restrictions because of his eye, and he said he had no idea as he hadn't told them about it! I was a bit shocked as I was responsible for the daft bugger; so if the test inspector found out I could be in a lot of bother. Anyhow, I accompanied him to where his test started and off he went. About an hour later he arrived back and was over the moon, having been given the pink slip saying he was successful.

Big Willie was just another of the characters I worked with. I met guys from all walks of life and from all over the world during my working life, so there were characters! One other I must tell about was a big rough customer called Charlie. He was originally from Sutherland. Charlie was the most dishonest, thieving, lying human being I ever came across; nothing was safe if it was moveable. Each Monday morning the junior engineer would measure our last week's work so that they could calculate the bonus. He needed a hand to hold the tape. Charlie always grabbed one end while the engineer checked the other end. What he didn't know was that Charlie would have six or eight feet of tape wrapped round his arm. Of course, the engineer was about two hundred feet away and the lighting was none too good; there must have been a lot of head scratching when they did an overall measurement and always found they were short. Charlie's claim to fame was that his uncle was the Governor of a famous Scottish Prison. How Charlie wasn't his best customer I will never know. Another stunt he pulled going home off nightshift; he had to pass the site of where a big new hotel was being built and he stopped to have a nose around. He was telling us about it on the Monday when we got back to work. He finished up by saying there were eight brand-new barrows on the site, so he threw two into his van and took them home. He argued, what would a man with two hands need two barrows for? The company who owned them was lucky Charlie didn't have room for all eight or the lot would have gone. He was a thief of the highest degree.

There were a couple of incidents worth mentioning, both caused by excessive drinking. The first concerns an elderly timekeeper. He had got himself hopelessly drunk and made it back to his room in the camp. Possibly he was on the verge of oblivion. The camp had individual rooms heated with 2-inch pipes running along the wall. This old geezer must have fallen asleep with his neck against the pipes and he was very severely burned before he wakened or was found. He died a few months later, probably due to the shock of his dreadful injuries. Another gory incident involved another middle-aged guy and most likely plenty booze. It was Cup Final weekend and Rangers were to play Kilmarnock. One of our workmates was a staunch Kilmarnock supporter, although he belonged to the North Caithness/Sutherland area. He was a rather loud brash sort of person but he was okay and a decent workmate. He left work on the Thursday night and travelled to Glasgow on the Friday, where he was going to have a weekend in the big city, taking in the match at Hampden Park. He never appeared for work on the Tuesday but word got around that he was back in the camp though feeling a bit poorly. He lay there for two or three days before a doctor was sent for, but it was too late—the story was that he had got into an argument in Glasgow and was hit over the head with a bottle. Whatever damage was done it caused his lungs to fill with fluid and eventually caused his death.

Those are just a couple of incidents caused by excessive drinking. With four hundred hard drinking men in the one place, there was always plenty drama.

It was over two years since I started working underground and it was time for a break, as it was really unhealthy work. The atmosphere in the tunnel was contaminated all the time with oil, diesel reek or gelignite reek, and of course all the bodily functions that were dumped along the side of the tunnel. We lived in total darkness from October until May, only seeing daylight for a few hours on a Sunday. If we were lucky our skins were a paltry grey colour from lack of sunshine! So I was on the lookout for a job out in the open air for a while, but I had got used to the tunnel wages that gave me a take-home pay of £27 per week for an eighty-four hour week.

Three of us were on the lookout for another job. Big Frank, my security mate, my brother Geordie and me, got a whisper that there was work in Ullapool—a new hotel. They were working six twelve-hour shifts trying to get the hotel completed for the tourist season. And so we took the day off and headed for Ullapool. We chose the cheapest option of getting there, i.e. hitchhiking. On arrival in Ullapool we managed to get hold of the Site Agent. He was over the moon to get three guys who were willing to start a week Monday; he also promised us the moon—sixteen hours a day and ten on a Saturday. Sunday was rest day as the locals protested against working on the Sabbath, but we would be happy with that and a more or less guarantee of six months work. On our way home we stopped off in Inverness so that we could arrange to have our caravans towed to Ullapool. The only available day was Sunday, so we agreed a price and told the guys to collect us early Sunday morning. That gave us a couple of days to finish up with Carmichael. Giving them four days notice was better than walking off the job and leaving them in the lurch. You are never sure when you would have to come back.

It had been a hectic week but much as I enjoyed the tunnel work I needed a break and some clean air. Ullapool would just be the place—plenty seaside, pure clean air. Monday morning we were ready to report for work. The three of us headed for the site and we lined up with other new starts and were allocated work. Unfortunately we were split up, however. I was sent to one job and my two mates somewhere else, so from the word go I felt very uneasy. There seemed to be an awful lot of men standing about and not a lot of work taking place. By the Wednesday rumour was rife that the owner was bankrupt and there was going to be changes like the hours cut to eight hours a day! What a disaster for us! Just before the morning tea break on the Friday a crowd of guys were waiting for the hooter to sound; they were early—the foreman walked up to them and took their names and told them they were all dismissed. My mates were in the crowd.

I was told that I still had a job but would be working an eight-hour day as of the Monday. I told them just to make up my cards and I would leave along with my two mates. We were bloody well annoyed—it had cost us a bit to get to this godforsaken place and they must have known what was about to happen when we were given the job! We went to the pub to drown our sorrows and ended up steaming drunk, got a carry-out and went home and had a party with the wives.

On the Monday morning we were on the road at the crack of dawn heading back to civilisation, to see if we could find work. We would try Strathfarrar. Our first lift that morning was on the back of a coal lorry that took us as far as Garve. We eventually got to Strathfarrar at midday. The first site we managed to find was a small dam being built by Duncan Logan, Muir-of-Ord. We got started right away. We contacted the caravan towers and they agreed to bring us back to Beauly on the Saturday. We had managed to find a site at Beauly Toll—handy for the girls to get to town.

Monday morning we were waiting for our transport, which was an open-backed lorry belonging to Logan Construction, one of the many Logan lorries heading for Strathfarrar first thing in the morning. We travelled in silence although there were at least ten other guys sitting beside us (ever get the feeling you're not welcome?); these fellows had travelled from Cromarty, which was nearly an hour's drive from Beauly. Remember, the roads were pretty basic, single track with passing places, so the speed was restricted. It was about an hour from Beauly to the dam at Strathfarrar and we started at 7.30 a.m. We were definitely treated like aliens. Even the jobs we were given were the lowest of the low and the boredom would have eventually driven a man with half a brain insane; but we three needed to get a wage coming in as our little adventure to Ullapool had been costly.

Some of the Highland residents were none too keen to have us from the east coast working alongside them, and referred to us as Seagulls. I got a whisper that Logan had a small tunnel a bit further up the glen and there were vacancies, so I knocked off early and headed for the tunnel on my own. I got started, no bother, but one downside was that it was another half hour travelling every morning and night—but at least I was interested in what I was doing. During my first shift I had an uneasy feeling about the place—there seemed to be a lot of bad blood. It was like the United Nations—there were only eight of us, made up of Poles, a German, a Russian, two Irish brothers and me. They never spoke as a team. The only one who really gave me any acknowledgement was the German. I had worked with him before. It was a difficult situation so I gave it six weeks and chucked it. I was finding it difficult to settle in to Strathfarrar—they were very different people compared to Carmichaels' folk.

My next port of call was the labour office at the Mitchell Construction Site. I got a job, no bother, and never missed a day—but I am afraid it was another soul destroying job, standing with a shovel twelve hours a day and occasionally pushing some lose rock in front of a scoop. I was young, fit, and had a fairly good brain, but this work was vegetating me!

So I gave this job a week and went back to the labour office. I told the guy unless he could give me something better I was jacking it in. He told me not to be too hasty and he would have a look. He had a job in the tunnel if I was interested, so I took it. This was a huge tunnel, twenty by twenty. Seven miles of it were completed and they were now lining it with concrete, using a creeping shutter. It was a new venture for me so I would give it a try. My job was painting the concrete behind the shutter with black bitumen paint. You needed to wear gloves and oilskins to keep clean. The snag was that the temperature was about twenty-five degrees centigrade so it was a most uncomfortable environment to work in. The plastic cloves were soon soaked and started to chap my hands. Our boss was an ex-Nazi Hungarian and, boy, did he throw his weight about! I asked for a second pair of gloves so that I could dry them and change them and save my hands from the mess they were getting in after a couple of days. I got an outburst of rage from this Hungarian thug and was told in no uncertain terms I had a pair of gloves. When I asked for the second pair of gloves I was polite and respectful. I have no idea what triggered this Hungarian lunatic into a rage—he was ranting and raving and shouting at me like a man demented! His English was not the easiest to understand and all the time I was answering him back in Doric like saying, "I dinna think yir aw there, min, in fact I think yir a bloody feel!" He was high all over a pair of gloves that possibly cost 25p! I didn't get the gloves so my hands would be badly chapped by the end of the shift. This guy always had two or three Big Eastern Europeans near him; some guys said they were bodyguards as he was such a horrible little man! His life was in jeopardy if he went about on his own. He was hated for his bully-boy tactics and sacking innocent men. Because of his attitude he was a top dog with Mitchell Construction—they would be quite happy with him as he got the work done regardless of the cost in human sacrifice. It was also rumoured that he had his Nazi identification number tattooed on his arm. One guy came over to me and said, "I see you had words with Andy!" I said yes, I had, so this chap told me I would be well advised to pack the job in because the next rage our Hungarian friend went into I would more or likely be 'run off—that was how he operated. My card would be marked. I didn't wait to be told anymore—I just walked out back to the Labour Office and told the labour manager I had a run-in with a nasty little foreign pig and could not work with him anymore. He replied, "Oh Andy can be a little bit difficult now and again …" I proceeded to tell him what I thought of Mitchell Construction employing displaced persons and allowing them to treat good honest Scots like shit on their own doorstep. (My father gave his life for low life like this guy!?) The labour manager shook his head and in the next breath asked if I was interested in going to work in another area, under an old Irish guy. I turned it down and headed home to the caravan. I am sure my dear wife Jess must have despaired, as once again I was unemployed, but I never took to Strathfarrar. There had also been a few fatalities so there were breaches of safety. Another thing I found out—it helped if you were well known.

Next morning I was heading back to Glenmoriston to try and get back with my friends there. The past few weeks were a learning curve, maybe a costly one, but nevertheless it increased my experience. I was in no hurry to get to the Carmichael offices as I had a better chance of getting a job from one of my old gaffers. It would be evening before they were available so I hung about. The first guy I bumped into was my old boss from No 9. Before I could ask for a job he asked me when I could start! I said in the morning if he could get me a bed in the camp, which was quickly arranged. I contacted my wife and told her to get the caravan back to the site at Leveshie whenever she could, and I went to work on the shift I had left eight weeks ago.

On the Saturday I was heading for Beauly early in the morning. When I got as far as Levishie I could hardly believe my eyes—there was our caravan! Good old Jess had managed to get it shifted fairly quickly. I was delighted, as living in the camp was a poor substitute for getting home every night. We had at least a year's work left at the No 9 Tunnel, so I decided to dig in and make the best of it.

We soon had a few pounds saved and decided to buy a vehicle so that we could visit my family more frequently. We ended up buying a Blue Ford Van. It had a six-volt battery system and turned out to be the most controversial brute that was ever made. If you failed to get the engine going after the second rev the battery would be flat; then you either had to push it or try the cranking handle. I used to park on a slope and if it failed to start mechanically I would let it run down the slope, hoping it would kick into life (this was usually around 6.30 a.m.); if that failed, Jess would have to push! One morning it was about to give up the ghost when it burst into life. I was so bloody angry I rammed it into reverse and headed backwards to the road junction. Unbeknown to me there was a fellow walking along the verge. He had to jump for his life, landing down the embankment. He was none too pleased with me and called me a list of unprintable names. He was possibly the only fellow on that road at that time for the whole year.

JACK OF ALL TRADES—EVEN MOUNTAIN RESCUE!

I had settled back in Invermoriston and it was heading up to Christmas again. It had started to snow early that year and before long the roads were getting a bit difficult. We also had severe frost, so bad that the vehicles were freezing as they were running! We had no anti-freeze so we had to drain the vehicle after every usage. We got over the New Year celebrations and had returned to work when the weather took a turn for the worse. We had a severe snowstorm one night and every road in the area was blocked; worse than that, there was a shift of men trapped in the furthest out site at No 4 tunnel. It was a single-track road, about seven miles from the camp. It was impossible to get a vehicle out to No 4. Nowadays they would have had chopper there in minutes. One engineer, a ski enthusiast, managed to get to the site. He carried a few bars of chocolate with him as the guys would have had very little food, if any. One of our neighbours, an elderly man, was among the party of trapped men; his wife was going frantic, as he didn't keep too well. At times there seemed to be very little effort on behalf of the company to get these men home.

On the second day my neighbour's wife was getting ready to climb the hill and find out what was going on. The storms had abated and it was a clear frosty morning when another neighbour of mine, a Norwegian fellow well used to snow, asked if I would accompany him and we would go looking for the trapped guys. The site was more or less in a straight line above Levishie caravan site, possibly three mile distant, but a steep climb for at least half the distance. The wife of the trapped neighbour got a haversack and loaded some easy carried biscuits, fags and a half bottle of whisky. My Norwegian neighbour Karl and I set off about half past nine in the morning. It was a bright clear day, very frosty, and we had our fingers crossed hoping the weather stayed that way. It took us till nearly 2 p.m. to reach the site. It had been a hard struggle as the snow was very deep and all we had on our feet were Wellington boots. The guys were over the moon to see us! It was quite funny—two of the younger men had left the site that morning to walk to the camp; when the guys in the cabin heard us shouting they thought it was the two who had set off earlier and that they had got lost and returned; but no, they made it safely back to camp.

It would be dark in little over an hour so we told the guys we were not stopping and were ready to return the way we had arrived. They all wanted to come with us. Two of them were quite elderly, but were determined to get home that night, so a motley crew set off and we were well down the hill when darkness started to catch up with us. We got two of the young guys to run ahead and warn them that we were on our way with the result that some body had the sense to point a few cars up the hill with the lights switched on. It made our last half-mile of the journey that bit easier. It had taken Karl and I nearly ten hours to do that journey, one of the hardest day's work in my life. We did it a few times. After that the boss of Carmichaels' got hold of us and thanked us for what we had done; he then asked if we would go back up every second day and check the water pumps in the tunnel, because if they were left unattended the tunnel would flood. We would get paid a twelve-hour shift every day we did the journey. I was delighted doing something I enjoyed and getting paid—it couldn't be all bad. It was over two weeks before the snow cleared sufficiently to allow the men back to work. Again, none of the guys were any worse for their ordeal of being trapped for forty-eight hours, and it was the talking point for a few days—something very different.

We were well tested out that winter. Life in the caravan was hard going and the birch trees around Glenmoriston took a hammering that year, as they were one of the main sources of fuel to keep the place warm.

The heroics of the mountain rescue were soon history. We received a small mention in the press before it was forgotten and life carried on. The time changed and the days got longer. The tunnel work was starting to run down, so it was getting time to move on again. I met a timber contractor in the pub one evening—he was desperate for men who could work a horse dragging trees. My brother and I both knew about horses, so this guy pleaded with us to come and work for him. A horse needs at least an hour to eat in the morning before it starts work; this was the contractor's biggest worry—that his horses were not being properly cared for, so to give the job to young inexperienced kids was taking a gamble. He would pay us by the tree so it was up to us how much money we made. Once again my pocket ruled my head and I agreed to go back to the Timber Industry.

I wondered if I needed my head seeing too, but in for a penny in for a pound! It didn't take us many days to find out that the wages we could make were half the money earned in the tunnels—we had boobed again! It was always my ambition to learn a skill, something that needed me to use my brain. I was fed up doing work that was really depressing and boring; when you felt that way you never worked to your full potential.

I had been applying for jobs through the National Press but had never had any luck—as often as not, I would never get a reply. Either that or they would say they were full up but would keep your name on file—most likely the file that was put out to the scaffies every week in a black bag! But perseverance is a great virtue and eventually I got a reply form a company based in Warwickshire. They did Inland Dredging, something new to me. I had never heard of it but they promised to train people up and on receipt of an application they would send me details of the terms of employment if they thought I was suitable for the job. Within a few days I had a reply telling me they had a vacancy for me in North Wales and if I made my way there they would reimburse my train fare. They were looking for me to start on the following Monday. I needed to get a move on as we had the caravan in Glenmoriston; this would leave Jess rather isolated if she stayed there, so it was agreed she would get the van moved back near her folks in Invergarry and if the job in Wales was any good we would move the van south so that we would be together again.

My train left for Wales on the Sunday evening. Wales was a new frontier for me (I now know how Livingston felt!). I had one change at Crewe, which took place at an ungodly hour of the morning. Crewe was not the liveliest place I have visited, especially around 5 a.m. I caught the train for North Wales via Chester, then travelled along the North coast Line following the river Dee directly opposite Birkenhead. I was fascinated with the amount of factories—all very new looking and bearing the name Courtland's along the top of the highest buildings. They were a world leader in the manufacture of nylon. Eventually I reached my destination, a little village called Mostyn. Its claim to fame was that it sported a huge Iron Ore Smelter. It was fairly easy to find the site I was looking for and found the foreman. They were just about to have breakfast so I was invited to join them. The foreman had three other lads with him and he asked me if I was ready to go to work or whether I needed time to rest after my overnight journey. I felt quite fresh and was ready to start as soon as I changed my clothes. It seemed a reasonable set up; the company supplied a workmen's caravan with bedding and a woman to keep it clean and do the cooking. We paid for the food with five of us sharing—it cost about £1 each per week.

There was a small harbour that held about three ore carriers that came from Africa, periodically fully laden with Iron Ore. The harbour used to silt up and had to be kept clear to allow the ships to berth. Behind the harbour there was a huge lake. When the tide came in it filled the lake with water and then the sluice gates were closed. When the tide was fully out they would then open the sluice gates and the rush of water would wash the silt out—quite an ingenious way of operating. Our job was dredging the lake, as it got silted up as well. All day long the chimneys at Mostyn belched out yellow smoke; it was some kind of sulphur but it made the atmosphere nearly as bad as the tunnels at home.

North Wales was a very busy place in the early sixties, packed all summer with holidaymakers. This was pre-Spain and other exotic foreign holidays. One Friday evening that sticks in my mind we were heading for the railway station, which was situated on the opposite side of the main road. This would probably have been changeover weekend for the holidaymakers, but the cars were nose-to-tail, all shapes and sizes, laden down with everything bar the kitchen sink. We were standing for forty minutes before there was a sufficient break in the traffic to allow us to cross.

Just across the road from the harbour where our workmen's caravan was parked stood an old fashioned Welsh Hotel/Inn where we were able to get Sunday lunch, a roast beef dinner with trimmings, that cost 25p. The Landlord was a friendly little man from the Newcastle area, a Geordie. One Sunday after lunch he asked if I would go with him in his Dormobile van. He was learning to drive and needed an experienced driver with him. I was delighted with the request, as it would give me something to do to pass the time. It didn't take long for me to realise why none of the locals would accompany him on his driving lessons! His driving was atrocious—the poor guy had no idea! To give you one example—we were driving through a small village that had a double carriageway that suddenly changed to a single carriageway. My man never noticed this and ran into the gable of the house that jutted out into the street! Thankfully he was creeping along at twenty miles an hour so the only damage was a dent in the van. My only thoughts at that moment was how fast I could get back to the hotel before this guy killed one of us or some other poor unfortunate soul.

Rhyl was the main town nearest to Mostyn, so we would head for there. Most Saturday afternoons they had a football team and there were loads of cinemas, but it was always heaving with people. I only had one dress shirt in those days so I would wash it on Saturday morning and get it dried and ironed before heading for town. One Saturday I hung my good shirt on the chain barrier round the harbour. There was a good breeze so it wouldn't take long. An hour later I went to check my shirt and, horror of horrors, it was floating face down in the green slimy oily water of Mostyn harbour, never ever fit to be used again! I just left it to float.

The company I was employed with were Bomford & Wilkins, a small Warwickshire concern that specialised in Inland Dredging. Most of their work was on Estates and with the Coal Board they also did work for local councils. Their contracts were fairly short, lasting from a couple of weeks to maybe twenty weeks, depending on the amount of work. They moved their equipment by road, having to hire low loaders for the really heavy stuff.

We were soon ready to move from Mostyn. Our next job was at a teachers training college in the hills behind Conwy, a back of beyond place. Everything needed for comfort was at least three miles from where our accommodation was parked, but it was only for five weeks so it was a grin and bear it situation. The nearest village boasted a post office, shop and pub. On our first visit to the pub we were eyed with suspicion. To make matters worse, the locals spoke their own brand of Welsh Gaelic; apart from nodding of heads in acknowledgement, we were virtually ignored. Then we got involved in a few games of darts. After soundly thrashing them a few times we were gradually accepted. Back at work nobody wanted to work the steam engine as it meant getting up at 5 a.m. She had to be fired up early so that there was a full head of steam ready for our 7 a.m. start in the morning, I decided to take it on—it was more money and another skill. Few people could work a steam engine then as they were becoming obsolete. It was a dirty mucky job, but where there's muck there's brass. Being the steam engine driver held a bit of celebrity status; there were few working steamers in the country, so it was a bit of a novelty. Everybody wanted pictures taken standing on the running board, while some would slip you a couple of quid just for the privilege of standing like a dummy with their hands on the controls.

FILM STAR STATUS

It is amazing the amount of people who are Steam enthusiasts! We were inundated with people of all ages wanting photos and Cine Camera footage. They would stand for hours just awestruck when the engines were at work. These engines were built for ploughing the huge Lincolnshire fields. There used to be one at each end of the field; they would pull possibly a ten-furrow plough, then turn the plough over and pull it the other way. No time was wasted pulling an empty plough. Our engine was a Sentinel built by a company called Fowler. One enthusiast, an elderly gentleman, appeared every day around two-o-clock; he would nod to acknowledge me, then point to the footplate, asking permission to get on board. Once established, he would produce a hand-rolled cigarette. Most people used fag papers made by a company called Rizzla. My old friend had his rolled in an old newspaper and they were about eight inches long. Seeing the scruffy old fellow, I would feel sorry for him and offer him a real cigarette, which he refused, carrying on puffing at the newspaper one! Thinking he was a bit senile, I asked one of the locals if he were the full shilling. I was told that if I could spare a moment next time my friend paid us a visit, to have a look behind the tall Hawthorn hedge and then form an opinion of the old guy. This I did and near collapsed when I saw that he ran around in the latest Jaguar car! I am sure even that far back they would have cost around fifteen thousand—but I was assured it was small change to this old guy since he was a Millionaire hill farmer and had all his marbles. He was just a bit of a loner!

We had an old couple that used to travel round with us. She did the cooking while he did odd jobs. Joe was of the old school, up at the crack of dawn every morning. He would wander round the fields gathering the most delicious wild mushrooms, some of them the size of soup plates. Ivy, his wife, would fry them in bacon fat ready for our breakfast at nine-o-clock every morning—lovely, makes my mouth water thinking about them! Our postal address was Betws-y-Coed. The only outstanding feature in that place was it had a Post Office and a public phone box; otherwise it was another remote village.

We were getting near to completing our contract and a few of the local lads wanted us to have a night out in Rhyl before we left. After a bit of a pub-crawl we were heading for the chip shop when we saw a guy playing the Bagpipes. We waited till he finished playing and approached him for the crack. He asked me where I belonged and I said Inverness. He corrected me by telling me, by my accent, that I was from somewhere along the Banff-shire coast! I said I belonged to Cullen, and he told me he was from the next town, Portsoy, and he was descended from travelling people. His name was Kelbie, and, as it turned out, many times his mother had tea from my mother as the old lady used to sell goods around the houses from a pack! I also knew one of his brothers very well.

Our small contract soon finished and we were on the move once again. The next destination was in Yorkshire, a small village called Wentworth near Sheffield and a five-day journey. Our gear was stowed on the various means of transport with the steam engine on the hired Low Loader, and we were ready to move early the next morning. We were making for a place called St Asaph where we parked in a pub car park—where else? It was ideal and we all ended up severely hung over the next morning, but again it was on the road at the crack of dawn! Our next stop was in Northwitch. I was driving an old Fordson Major tractor pulling our living accommodation; the rest of the transport was very slow—we were lucky if we were travelling at fifteen miles per hour! Nevertheless it was a great adventure—something new and we got paid for it!

Our next port of call was Buxton, an overnight stop before we tackled the Snake Pass, a horrible twisting narrow road in Derbyshire; but we successfully managed it and reached Wentworth late afternoon. This was paradise! We were in the estate compound complete with electricity and a flushing toilet—could we handle such luxuries! We were there to tidy up after the Coal Board. It was a fairly long contract by B&W standards—three months.

Of all the places I have worked in over the years, Yorkshire could have been my adopted home. It was a marvellous place with lively friendly people. Within days of our arrival we were being treated like locals. The village of Wentworth was situated in a triangle made up of Sheffield, Rotherham and Barnsley, each being about five miles away—a paradise for me as there was a major football team in each one, Sheffield Wednesday being in the top league. So we could have a decent match every week. The village was the accommodation of the original estate workers but as was usual after the war these Estates were sadly depleted. The owners of Wentworth were a family called Fitzwilliam, very wealthy people. Their main residence was an estate in Peterborough. Although Wentworth House was huge, it had been split in two; one half was a ladies Physical Training College while the other half was still residential, occasionally used by the Fitzwilliams for pheasant shoots, etc. As I mentioned, we were spoiled for choice on a

Saturday, wondering which match we should go and watch. Tottenham Hotspur was the top English side at the time. Sheffield Wednesday was very good but lost most of their top players due to a bribery scandal. I was also able to go and watch my favourite team, Man. United; they had just signed Denis Law from Torino—he was in a class of his own and he was Scots so he was a joy to watch. Stanley Mathews was still playing occasionally, having signed for Stoke City. They were in the English Second Division at the time. We went to a couple of places to watch him but both times they decided the ground was not suitable for a man of his age, so we never saw him in action live.

Yorkshire was a hub of industry in the early sixties—Coal Mining, Steel Works and various spin-off industries. I considered staying there and settling down, but as with lots of ideas, it never materialised.

About that time of the century a new phenomenon hit Britain—Chinese Restaurants! We sampled our first one in Sheffield. It was brilliant and you could have a full meal for 40p—but remember that was nearly two hours' wages; but the food was out of this world. Later that year Jess managed to get the caravan down to Yorkshire. Bless her—she was hardy but we were back together again. She was asked if she wanted the job of doing the cooking and keeping the workers' caravan tidy. She accepted, was paid by the company, and was more or less her own boss. Doreen, our eldest daughter, was still a bit away from starting school; we were doing all right and managing to save some money at last—we now had two wages coming in and I just had my grub along with the rest of the guys, costing around a pound per week; so things were looking up for us at last.

It was coming up to the end of the year and we decided to stay where we were for the festivities. Sorry to say, it was the worst Hogmanay I ever had in my lifetime! We were used to a good couple of days celebrations at home but in England it was just another day.

Just after the start of the New Year the weather broke. We had heavy snow and frost; coupled with that, we experienced smog for the first time in our lives—not a pleasant experience, I can assure you! It was so thick we were unable to see across the street. It lasted for seven weeks! We were unable to work, as the two winches we needed for our operation were about a quarter mile apart. We needed to be able to see each other as it would otherwise be dangerous; so we sat in the caravan playing cards night and day until we were able to resume working again. The first thing we had to do was get an order of coal for the engine, as some nice souls had stolen the ten tons we left when the storm began. I had to dig out the football boots again as they had a Sunday league in the village; so I got involved most Sundays. It gave my fitness a boost.

We had to make a major decision before Easter. My daughter was due to start school so we decided to take her home to stay with my mother until we had made a decision on our future, like settling down somewhere. I was enjoying my job but it was so short-term between contracts it would be no good for a child of school age. In May of that year I saw my second televised Football game; it was exactly ten years since I saw the Hungary English game—this time it was the English Cup Final. We were invited by a local family to watch the game on their black and white telly (there was no colour in 1963). The game was Man United versus Leicester City. We were both die-hard Man United fans while the rest of the company were rooting for Leicester, so it was quite a lively afternoon! Our team won 3-1; our hero, Dennis Law, got one of the goals.

Sadly our contract in Yorkshire came to an end and it was time to move on again. It was now well into summer and our next move was to Northampton-shire. Our destination was a small English village complete with thatched houses, village green and a couple of pubs. It was situated not far from the town of Northampton, but the nearest sizable place was Corby (little Scotland), so called because of the amount of Scots who moved there during the Fifties. There was a lot of work at the Stewart & Lloyds steel works. Many of the people came from my own area of Banff-shire. Walking down Corby Main Street on a Saturday afternoon, you could easily have mistaken the place for Buckie or Banff. The broad Doric accent was quite distinctive. The steelworks are no longer in opera-tion so it would be interesting to know what all the Scottish immigrants do for a living now as Stewart & Lloyds employed thousands in their heyday. We trav-elled to Rockingham by tractor pulling our own caravan. Jess was hanging on for grim death! Every time we hit a town she would go inside the van till we had passed through, as what we were doing was not strictly legal. It was quite a messy journey. The weather was very hot and the melted tar was flying everywhere off the tractor tyres. The heavy lorries were breaking through the Tarmacadam sur-face and bogging down on the main roads. It is the only time I ever witnessed this in my lifetime! We were there during a bank holiday weekend; all the guys were going home but Jess and I decided to stay put. The Gaffer asked if I wanted to work—quite an easy job keeping the pumps going while the site was closed. We were there to dredge a pond just below Rockingham Castle. The Castle was built in medieval times and was preserved more or less as it had been built.

I started pumping on the Friday morning. It was glorious weather so as soon as everything was fired up I lay down on the bank to enjoy the morning sunshine. Suddenly I had a feeling I was not alone; then I heard this female voice shouting, "Yoo-hoo!" I turned in the direction the voice came from and at the edge of the wood was standing the most gruesome female I ever had the misfortune to look at! The hairs on the back of my neck began to rise! She was quite scary—she had shoulder-length white hair and a very weather-beaten wrinkly face. She made her way towards me and introduced herself as the wife of the Lt Commander who owned the Castle! He was a war hero from the Spanish Civil War. She then asked all about me and what I was doing. Then she turned to leave but before going told me the Castle was open to the public that afternoon, and that if we wished to have a look inside.... What she didn't say at that point was that they charged twenty-five pence per person to get in but it was money well spent—a very interesting place.

Another place in Northamptonshire we were able to visit was the Motor Racing Circuit at Silverstone. We decided to go and watch a day's racing. It was not Formula One but it was for a trophy called the Martini Trophy. We caught a bus in the town. We had just experienced the most glorious weather anyone could wish for, but on the day we visited the racetrack we had wall-to-wall rain! It never halted the whole day. The guys who were driving the cars must have been complete lunatics, for the conditions were atrocious. There were numerous accidents resulting in one poor sod losing his life. It cost us 50p to get in that day; now I am told it's nearer £100 to get in to watch the practice session for the Formula One!

Our contract at Rockingham was coming to an end and we were soon on the move again. We had another two small contracts in that location, so we continued our adventure with Bomford & Wilkins.

Old age must be creeping up on me because I can't remember the name of the next two estates we worked on; but our contract was to dredge small ornamental lakes that had become silted up over the years. We were about thirty miles from London so you would imagine this area would be lively with plenty of life about us. Our nearest town was Buckingham. Well, I have worked in some of the remotest parts of the British Isles and was never as isolated as we were on that contract. There was nothing around us and the bus only travelled to town about once a day. The first estate we worked on was owned by two eighty-year-old sisters. They were part of the original family that owned Dulux Paint. They drove around the estate in an old Model-T Ford car. Anyone else would have had this ancient vintage model in a showcase in a highly polished state, but not these two—they would come careering down the field to where we were working daily, the old car bouncing feet in the air as it hit the various bumps. Most of the older estate owners seem to be very eccentric types. I noticed this a few times—filthy rich but something strange about them. All the hired hands on that estate came from Sicily and were very poorly paid, their only perk being free housing.

Our foreman got hurt and was off work for about a month. I got my first big break in Supervision when I was asked if I would run the job till he was fit again. I was over the moon—at last I had been recognised for my ability! I revelled in my new post till the gaffer returned.

We soon completed that task and moved to our next small assignment. Again, this was a small Estate—in fact, it was a weekend residence of an Arab Oil Tycoon. He was Sir Nubar Gulbunkein. It was said that he earned one thousand pounds every minute of the day. The estate house was a fifteen-room affair. There was a Spanish couple, permanent residents, who looked after the place; there were four Welsh ponies with a permanent groom, and three gardeners. Most weekends the family drove out from London. They arrived in three separate Rolls Royce cars. The man spent most of Saturday fishing in his pond. It was full of coarse fish—there were so many you could almost put you hand in the water and pull one out! He must have caught about a hundred every day—same routine every time: hook the fish, lift it out of the pond, unhook it and return it to the water—his idea of relaxation. On the Sunday the groom would dolly up the four ponies in their brasses and harness; he would then dress himself in top hat and tails, yoke the horses into a four-wheeled carriage, then drive the family round the country lanes. They were easily pleased! Sir Nubar was a mate of the Duke of Edinburgh; they were both into carriage racing and would often be seen on television at the various events.

Apart from our wireless, we had very little entertainment. The nearest pub was three miles away and the only mode of transport was to walk. Life in Buckinghamshire was fairly Spartan, but our stay there was quite short and before long we were on our way back to the depot at Bideford-on-Avon, referred to as the Garden of England. Our nearest sizable town was Stratford-on-Avon. It was about twenty minutes away by bus so we were back in civilisation again.

Shortly after getting back to the depot I was asked if I had a current driving license that covered agricultural tractors, as they needed someone to go to Birmingham to pick up a unit from there. I jumped at the chance! It would be a change from the repair work we were doing in the workshop. Next morning the young lad from the office picked me up. We set off and it was over an hour before we reached our destination. All our equipment was in a field but no sign of a tractor. I turned to my driver and asked about the vehicle I was supposed to be taking back to the depot. He nodded his head towards a huge American Army truck, left-hand drive and two vertical winches on the back! I near collapsed! I had never handled anything like it in my life. Worse was to come as they hooked a flat trailer, then an accommodation caravan behind that—the total length being about forty feet. I near had heart failure! I needed a second man with me, as there were no indicators—and we set off. One good thing, it only travelled at twenty-five miles per hour. I was a bag of nerves!

After the initial shock we settled into a nice easy pace. Nobody would argue with us due to the sheer size. My gaffer drove in front on his motorbike so we just ambled along. The truck was a Studebaker. The nose was about eight feet long and it had thirty-two gears. It would have weighed about twenty tons. My second man was a mouthy little man from Coventry, Jack King. He was a bit of a fly man who was up to all the dodges; he had been well briefed on what his function was, i.e. hand signals whenever I prompted him. Our first big challenge was a huge busy roundabout at Blackheath. This was well before Spaghetti Junction was ever thought about, but there were at least five busy roads converging on the roundabout. I think it was the busiest in Europe at that time. This was the first time I had to depend on Mr King to use his skill at hand signals. When I glanced over at him to make sure he was ready I couldn't believe my eyes—the old pig was sound asleep! Normally I am quite a placid easygoing person and three things that can change that are laziness, inefficiency and punctuality. I had an example of all three sitting next to me! I was uptight with the task I was performing but to be let down by this lazy old bugger sitting beside me ignited the Blue Touch Paper. I totally exploded and a full-blown riot took place in the confines of that lorry cab! I grabbed a spanner and started to flail about with it, making sure I never actually hit old Jack but close enough to frighten the daylights out of him! I did leave a few dents in the cab, otherwise no blood was spilled. He got the message and near drove me batty the rest of the journey as he grovelled and tried to get in favour with me. He told some of the other guys never to upset me as I was a bit of a nutter when I lost the plot.

The drama of that journey was not over and worse was to come. In those days the M1 motorway from London finished at Bromsgrove. We had to cross over it on a flyover. We were about halfway across when the cab filled with steam or vapour! We stopped and bailed out. One of the injector pipes had burst so it was vaporised Diesel that had filled the cab. Within seconds we were surrounded with police motorcyclists! They put a cordon of cones round us while the Gaffer headed back to the Depot to get a spare part. Within two hours we were repaired and ready to roll again. The rest of the journey was incident free.

The vale of Evesham was beautiful countryside and the old town of Stratford-on-Avon was a lovely place to spend our Saturday afternoons. From the depot we managed to get home for a couple of weeks holiday. When we left my daughter was not keen to stay without us but we had no option but leave her; but we would need to make a decision soon about getting a permanent residence. When we returned to Bideford we were informed that the company had been awarded quite a sizable contract for Birmingham City Council. We would be working in the city. Great! With all those top football teams playing every week I was going to enjoy this move. Our first port of call was a place called Cradley Heath. This was all new territory for me since I had never been in Brum before. I can assure the reader it was an education on how the other half live. I thoroughly enjoyed my stay there!

RUDE AWAKENING

Cradley Heath was something else! It was like a bombsite. We had our living quarters on a piece of waste ground near to where we were working. The next eye-opener was the contract we were about to carry out. The year was 1963 when most houses in Scotland had flush toilets connected to a sewer system that was underground. Here less than half-a-mile from the centre of one of Britain's largest cities the sewage ran through an open trench! It was about eight feet deep and twelve to fifteen feet wide. All the household waste flowed through this trench—that was before the mindless morons who lived there started to dump their discarded household goods in the trench, i.e. three-piece suites, bed ends, mattresses, old bikes and any other items they had no more use for.

Our contract was to remove all the obstructions and dispose of them on the corporation dump! Sounds disgusting? Well, it was, and all caused by thoughtless lazy people.

The district of Cradley Heath was okay. We were parked across the road from the Speedway stadium. I spent some smashing Saturday evenings there watching the motorbikes, or else the Greyhound Racing. The dog racing didn't really appeal to me but it passed an evening. Mind you, there were some real fanatics! You would think their lives depended on their favourite dog winning every race. Next door to the stadium was a family pub where we would end the evening having a couple of pints before returning to the caravan.

Earlier on the Saturday afternoon we would take in a Football Match. We were spoiled for choice! You could take your pick every week—Aston Villa, West Bromwich, Birmingham City, Wolves, Leeds United, Coventry, Walsall, and Stoke City with Stanley Matthews and Jimmy McIllroy making the occasional appearance. They were all within easy travelling distance. The entertainment was fabulous! We were doing okay, but all the time I was on the lookout for a permanent job so we could settle down and get together as a family again.

My time in Birmingham was educational at every turn. We would talk to the youngsters and the Brummie accent was the most awful imaginable! When I spoke to them they would say, "Dount youw talk funnie mate!" They were not used to the Doric. We spent the first week getting the rubbish in one big heap ready for the hired trucks to shift it to the Corporation Dump. The first truck was loaded and I went with him in case he needed help. When we arrived at the site I could hardly believe my eyes! There were at least three hundred kids digging amongst the rubbish pulling out bits of scrap iron and any other article that would sell! Our load was a bit of a disappointment for them as it was wet, useless waste. The only other time I witnessed anything like it was in Documentaries on the Telly from India or South Africa. It was disgusting! This was way before companies issued rubber gloves and any cuts or injuries needed a typhoid injection—just in case.

Another fascinating feature of the children that scavenged the dump was that they all carried a nine-inch length of a willow branch with them. They also had a pocket full of gravel about the size you mix in concrete. When they would fall out, which was frequent, they would form into gangs and have a fight! The twig was used like a catapult or a sling! They were deadly accurate and the attacker thought nothing of splitting a foe's head wide open with this rather lethal weapon. How none ended up dead I will never know, but it was miracle it never happened.

Another form of daredevil entertainment in that area emerged from the fact that all the boys were Speedway enthusiasts. They would get cinders from somewhere and construct a track similar to the Speedway ones; then, on ordinary pushbikes, they would race round the improvised track, cornering as the motorbikes would do. They were really expert at it and it was quite fascinating to watch. There would possibly be about thirty of them, all going flat out, when suddenly one guy would skid, causing most of them to end up in a tangled heap of bodies and bikes. Again, I never heard of any serious injuries.

ONLY SECONDS BETWEEN LIFE AND DEATH

We moved from Cradley Heath to Old Hill, another district of Brum. Our new site was on the edge of a Municipal play park. We had a grandstand view of the Welfare Football games most evenings. It was sheer luck we never had a broken window in the caravan as a few blockbusters ricocheted off the wall of our van. This was probably the worst and most disgusting stretch of our contract! On this site there was a council housing scheme on one side, a private housing estate on the other side, and then the play park somewhere in-between. The nearest private houses to the sewer were less than ten feet away! There was a major blockage just below where the council houses were. Just about every household item had been chucked in the sewer, completely blocking the flow of waste. This was before the Pill became the popular form of contraception, but going by what was floating in the sewer the condom must have been the in-thing! There were *thousands*, all floating about in the water! Each had a knot tied in it and they were all suspended in rows, just like a battalion of soldiers. We had to use a huge scoop to dredge this sewer. It was rather prehistoric and had to be pre-set by hand. If the ground were hard a couple of the guys would stand on the back until the scoop had dug in. On the particular day I am speaking about I was operating the winch, and just as I started to pull the chain snapped with the result my brother Geordie took a header over the scoop and was completely submerged in the horrible liquid that flowed along that awful trench! He was none too pleased with me, blaming me for jerking the winch, causing the chain to snap. The names he called me were disgusting and unprintable! He had to go to hospital and be given a typhoid injection.

The 21st October 1963 held very little significance to me. It was the day after my wife's birthday; otherwise it was like every other day—I don't recall any outstanding features for the first four hours of our working day. Just before midday there was a truck loaded up, ready for the dump; the driver decided to get it done before lunch break, and we were on our way back and should arrive at the site as the lads stopped to eat. We had to drive down a slight slope from where we could see the caravans. As we neared our base I could see smoke billowing from the workman's caravan. As we got nearer I could feel a strange knot in my stomach! I realised the van was well alight and Jess would be very near it, as she did the cooking in there.

I was not fully prepared for the sight that greeted me. My lovely wife had taken a severe burning and there was hardly any skin or hair left on her face and head. I felt totally devastated. The Ambulance and Fire Brigade had been sent for and we could hear the siren in the distance. We were like headless chickens as none of us had any form of First Aid training. We had no idea how to try and relieve the pain—just utter panic as we awaited professional help. It was only a few minutes before the Ambulance arrived but it felt like hours! When it did arrive the medics they took over and soon had the situation under control. Jess was rushed to The Dudley Guest Hospital. I had often witnessed Ambulances rushing past, Blue Lights flashing, but it is a different feeling altogether when you are sitting in the back of the vehicle as it races towards the hospital.

More shocks awaited me when we got to Dudley. We entered a huge Auditorium and Jess was whipped straight through to a repair bay. I had to wait in the seated area. Obviously this was the waiting room—its sheer size was breathtaking: there must have been three hundred waiting to be seen by various consultants. I would say every nation on earth was represented that day—there were West Indians, Pakistanis, Indians, Africans and various Orientals. It was like a meeting of the United Nations. Of course I was there representing Scotland, but it was a colourful gathering of people. And wasn't it lovely to see everyone agreeing, regardless of his or her colour or creed! That was a day never to be forgotten.

Jess's injuries amounted to third degree burns to her face, neck and back. Her back injuries were made worse as a result of her nylon petticoat that melted with the heat and penetrated the skin. She was still receiving treatment in March of the following year. She had another surprise for me when she told me she would be having our second baby in May. Life is full of good along with the disasters. The reason for the fire which caused the disaster was that we were due to move to another site further along the sewer; it was just off the Wolverhampton road at a place called Oldbury, alongside the canal which was still working then as a means of shifting produce. Oldbury was a bit out of the city and not so handy for shops etc so the boss had instructed one of the lads to get some provisions in before we moved. One of the items was metholated spirits for our lamps and primus stove. When Ronnie put it in the caravan, he laid it on a shelf near the coal burning stove chimney. Nobody is sure what happened except that it was quite cold outside and one theory was that the heat expanded the bottle, causing it to blow the cork, thus releasing the vapour. This in turn exploded when it reached the stove, and in seconds the place was ablaze. Jess had been below the bottle and she was covered in the spirit. There was a stable-type door on the van and she had been leaning out, talking to Ronnie as he left to go back to work. Luckily he had the presence of mind to grab a bucket, run to the filthy stinking sewer and fill it with the disgusting water which he then threw over Jess, probably saving her life and from further burn damage. There was nobody else around to help and there was not an abundance of clean water; the good news was that there was no complications from the sewer water.

There were no beds available at the Hospital so they had to send her home with me to the caravan. The hospital sent an ambulance every day to take her in to have her wounds re-dressed. I had to do the Florence Nightingale bit and nurse her for the first few days. Her mouth was so badly swollen it was difficult to get a drinking straw between her lips. The Doctors decided she would be fit to travel home ten days after the accident. It was pretty hopeless where we were with very inadequate facilities in the caravan; also, because we were due to move again, we decided she would be better off at home where she could stay with my mother and be reunited with our daughter. We travelled home and I stayed for a couple of days, and then had to travel back south as I still had a job to do. Our contract around Birmingham finished and we returned to the depot in early November 1963. The thing that sticks out in my memory was the evening I walked into the local pub and was told president J. F. Kennedy had been assassinated. It was a Friday.

We were in the depot for two or three weeks before the manager announced that we had a contract in Ascot alongside the racecourse. It was on a big estate between Ascot and Windsor. The owner was a top man with I.B.M.—the communications people. His working week was split between America and Britain. He was a very rich man, Sir Leon Baggilt. His estate was more or less a hobby. I saw him once and I would say he was of the old stiff upper lip brigade; he wore a bowler hat and spats all the time. The gardens of his estate were overgrown and our contract was to dredge his ornamental pond that was loaded with the biggest Pike I have ever seen. At one end of the lake was an ornamental arch similar to the kind you see in Japanese paintings; someone had deemed it unsafe and it had to come down. There was no cement in the structure—dry stone held together with a keystone in the top dead centre. The Royal Engineers were called in to blow it up. This was a disgrace as it was a lovely piece of Architecture and was a work of art! The engineers needed three goes before the structure landed in a heap, so in my opinion it would have been safe for another hundred years.

To get the estate looking a bit more shipshape there were one or two young managers employed in various departments; one was in charge of a herd of cattle, another of a flock of sheep. The man in charge of the sheep offered me a job complete with a house if I would train as his shepherd. We were only twenty miles from London, so it was certainly tempting. Nevertheless, I had to decline the offer of the job as a shepherd—the timing was wrong: I had a pregnant wife six hundred miles away who was recovering from severe injuries, so to commit myself to anything like that would have been foolish.

Bomford and Wilkins were one of the best companies I had ever worked for. They treated their workers well; you were allowed to get on with your job with the minimum of hassle. But I was getting disillusioned with my lot. I had to get a settled job and a home base soon. As long as I followed this line of work I would constantly be on the move. The manager, Len Hunt, had sounded me out to see if I would be willing to take over a squad of men. I would be allocated my own contracts and be responsible for running the show. I was flattered to be given the opportunity, but it would mean getting an odd weekend at home now and again. With us due another bairn in the late spring this was out of the question. I know other people lived their married lives like this, but it was not for me. One Thursday after lunch, walking back to the worksite, I made an instant decision—I wanted to go home, so I told the foreman I was quitting. He asked me when and I said two minutes ago! I explained my reasons, one being not knowing the score at home, how my wife was coping. Unfortunately in those dark days you couldn't go about with a mobile phone stuck to your lug all day. The foreman called the depot to let the manager know and the manager told him to get me to stay and he would drive down and talk to me—he was sure we could sort something out. I told the foreman I would be on the Inverness train at eight-o-clock that evening and I wouldn't be coming back. I asked him to thank the manager and I would write a letter when I got home. I packed my few belongings and set off for London, the first leg of my journey home.

My family had moved back to Invergarry and were in temporary accommodation, thanks to kind friends of ours who put us up in our time of need (thanks Betty & Jimmy!). Our caravan was still down in Bideford-on-Avon awaiting transport to tow it back home. My luck was in work-wise as work on the new phase of the road from the A82 to Farrans new road had just begun. I got in touch with the man in charge and was told to start the following Monday. Most of the men working there were the same crew that worked on Farrans Road, so I was acquainted with most of them. I had another stroke of luck—the plant foreman was a friend of mine! He told me there were two new ten-ton Dump Trucks arriving the next week and he had earmarked me to drive one of them. It eased the heartbreak of having to leave Bomford and Wilkins—things hadn't turned out too badly.

We soon had the caravan back and our lives became more settled once again. Our second lovely daughter was born in May. I bought a second-hand van so that we had transport to get to town and we could have trips down the East coast to visit my parents.

Not long after starting work with Tawse I was waiting for my dump truck to be loaded. The Digger driver swung the bucket round, loaded with muck, and hit a branch of a big beech tree. The branch was about six inches thick; it snapped and came crashing down on my head, catching me just above the hairline. There were no safety helmets worn in those days, so I got the full impact, apart from a big bump!

I felt fine, maybe a bit groggy, but I carried on and finished my shift. Next morning I woke at my usual time and I started to get out of bed, but was overcome by a dizzy spell. It was so bad I couldn't get out of bed! Jess was debating whether to get the doctor or not when suddenly my nose started to pour blood—clotted blood. Her mind was made up and she called the doctor. When the doctor arrived he signed me off work for a few days and told me I had been extremely lucky—if the bruised blood had not been released by the nosebleed I could have ended up having a brain haemorrhage.

I was a bit shaky for a few days but was soon back at work. Our caravan was a modern residential van but it could be quite cold in the winter. We were living a fairly Spartan existence with no power, water or proper sanitation. We were depending on Jess's relatives to let us share their facilities, not the best of circumstances, especially with a young baby to care for.

We were in Inverness shopping one Saturday when we bumped into Frank and Hilda, the ones who accompanied us on the ill-fated trip to Ullapool a couple of years back. They were living at a place called Bunchrew, a residential caravan site with all mod cons. They invited us out for tea. As soon as we saw the place we were hooked! I went straight away and enquired about a site. Where could we be better off three miles from Inverness and plenty work around! Frank was working with Wimpy at the Raigmore housing scheme and said he would get me a job, no bother, as they were desperate for men. So, without giving it much thought, we moved to Bunchrew. Everybody on the site had television, electricity, running water and there were shower and toilet facilities close at hand—just brilliant. Civilisation at last! We hired our first television from Radio Rentals (50p per week, I think). Jess had and still has an ongoing love affair with flowers and plants, and she decided that the top of the new television was the ideal place for a vase of flowers—that is, until someone knocked the vase over and the water ran into the body of the television, which was on at the time! The picture started to whirl just like a gramophone record! It was going quite fast when suddenly it blacked out. We switched the set off and looked at each other, wondering what to do next—would we have to pay for a new set? We left it switched off for a period of time before switching it back on, holding our breath. But our fears were unfounded as the picture came on as bright as a button and the set functioned for as long as we had it!

Wimpy was the top job in the North that winter. We worked a twelve-hour day right up until the contract finished. Some of us were transferred to a private housing development at Culcabock—which was the worst job I ever encountered in my colourful career! It was slave labour! I soon had a difference of opinion with the Irish gaffer. I was well aware my stay in that awful job would be short.

There was not a lot of work in the town of Inverness. Things were quiet so I had to hit the road again. I applied to the Forestry Road Squad for a job back at the Rock Drilling. I got the job and was sent to Glen Gloy Hostel. I had been there with the Jews in 1957, with the Forestry; you were paid a very substantial subsistence for the first six weeks of your employment—it was something to do with the disruption of your lifestyle, so for the first six weeks you were well catered for. I had never worked for a government concern before, but expected everything to be up to scratch. I was in for a shock! The equipment we were given to work with was dreadful, in some cases downright dangerous and badly neglected. Being employed as a driller, I had to use a compressor. The one given to us was not producing enough air to do the job with the result that the operator had a lot of stress on his back as he tried to hold the machine in place—something the air should have done. At the end of the shift your back would be in agony! We also had stilson wrenches that we needed frequently; the teeth were so badly worn they were downright dangerous! They were so bad that the least bit of pressure on them and they would slip, causing unnecessary injuries to the operators. I tried talking to the guy in charge—he thought my complaint was funny and had a good laugh about it (of course he wasn't the Organ Grinder); after a couple of weeks I decided to look elsewhere—if this was how the Government operated I was totally shocked. How they measured progress I never found out, but rock drilling was hard enough work without working with inferior tools. The Forestry Commission no longer exists as such, but then this does not surprise me. I got the feeling that it was like a little club! Perhaps you had to be a member to progress. Entering my sixth week and the end of my big subsistence, I got word of a job in Glen Sheil with R. J. MacLead. The forestry guy was not at all pleased and referred to me as another six-week wonder, having a dig about getting the big subsistence then jacking it in. His sarcastic remarks were like water off a duck's back. I got my work through ability, while some got theirs through more devious underhand means. To me it was another day, another dollar, Glen Sheil is one of the most beautiful places I ever worked in (except when it rains!).

There were a lot of characters employed in the Construction Industry. R. J. Macleod had more than their fair share of them. The Site Manager was a character in his own right—a tall Irish fellow named Jimmy Black. We had words the first day I was there. I had been promised a job as a driller but was given a labouring job. There was a huge difference in the wages, i.e. the drillers were paid a substantial sum compared to the earnings of the labourers, and he asked why I thought I should get a job as a driller. When I said because I was the best in the North of Scotland he gave a grin and drove off! It was about three weeks before he would give me a try; within half-an-hour he had agreed to give me top rate and my dig money. Where I was drilling I needed a labourer with me, and this takes me on to my next R. J. MacLeod character. The guy allocated to me was called Bob Lindsay who sounded more like an Oxford Don than a construction worker. Bob talked with a cultured accent so it wasn't long before one of the wags gave him a nickname—and so Bob was immediately christened Lord Peel! I have no idea of the origin of this title. To begin with, Bob was a very old man, I am sure well over seventy, though I never did find out. He was from the Sandeman's Wine and Spirit people of whom, according to himself, he was the Black Sheep. He had a birthday during our time together. The reason I remember this was because he got drunk and fell asleep at the door of the caravan, and spent the night under the stars! How he never perished I will never know. If I had been asked to put an age to him I would have said somewhere between seventy and eighty. He certainly looked it, for he was a tough old codger and never shied away from any of the work, and it could be hard at times.

We used a great amount of explosives on that job. The company was restricted to how much they could hold in the magazine. I think it was something like three hundred boxes. The magazine had to be three hundred yards from the road, so the company used to bulldoze a track from the road to the magazine, which meant all the new boxes had to be hand-carried for the three hundred yards, quite often uphill. Normally six of us would be sent to unload the carrier van. We normally had twenty boxes each to carry—tough going even for us young guys! We would tell old Bob to go and have a seat but never once did I hear him complain—he was marvellous! Bob always maintained he went through Sandhurst along with Montgomery. According to Bob, when they passed out, Monty was told he would never get anywhere in the Army though he was told he would get to the top as he had what it took. (Funny, I never ever saw Monty carrying boxes of Gelignite up the hill in Glen Sheil!) Another of Bob's tales was that he transferred from the Army to the old Flying Corps (pre-RAF) and took part in the Iran/Iraqi war around 1916. That was about the first time planes were used in war; they were the old double-winged with pram wheels on them! They could only carry one bomb, so according to Bob, they would load up a couple of dozen fist-sized rocks in the cockpit and after dropping the single bomb they would dive down and pelt the poor Arabs with the rocks! Another one of Bob's dubious stories was that his wife was supposedly part of a sister-singing duo that performed in the old music halls.

All I can say of Lord Peel is that he was a tough old nut, no longer with us, and that he had no family—so I will never know if his stories were true or not. I'm afraid we don't have characters like that now and I believe the world is worse off without them. They were inoffensive people telling the truth or living in their own little fantasy world—I am not sure which—but they certainly gave us a laugh with their tales and folklore.

I was happy in Glen Sheil. Although I was away from home all week, I managed to have the weekend at home every week—not ideal, but it could have been worse.

Another amusing incident from my time in Glen Sheil and yet another character—we were into winter (January, I think) and there was about a foot of snow on the ground. I need to fill in some background detail to let you understand where I am coming from. In the sixties the sea between Inverness and the Black Isle was teeming with sprats and a delightful little herring called the Kessock Herring. Half a dozen Kessocks and a few new Tatties and you had a meal—lovely! There were often between forty and sixty pairs of boats fishing the Moray Firth in search of these precious little fish; they would be there for three to four months, so you can imagine how plentiful they were in those days (sadly they wiped the lot out—no boats to be seen now). One of the guys who shared the caravan with me in Glen Sheil was big Jimmy, the one who stole the Wellington Boots off the drunk Chainman in Glenmoriston, another construction character. Jimmy was one of the most devious guys I ever came across, but he also had a heart of gold and would give you his last. Every Tuesday morning a couple of Jimmy's cronies from Inverness would arrive at our caravan with boxes of Kessock Herring. They were heading for Skye where they would sell the fish. Then they would fill the van with scrap metal to sell in Inverness, always making sure they were home in time to sign on the Dole on the Friday (a nice little earner). Jimmy's forefathers had been travelling folk so he was part of the Clan, even though he was a hard, honest worker.

The fish sellers would always drop about three dozen fish in our caravan, and in return they were sure of a cup of tea. Before departing for Skye where they sold the fish at 12.5p per dozen, the night I am writing about just after we had eaten our evening meal there was a knock on the door. Standing outside in the freezing cold was one of the fish sellers! He was in a pickle since the van had a puncture and he and his mates had so much scrap metal in the van that the jack wouldn't lift it. We told him not to panic and drove out to where there van was stuck, right opposite Kintail Lodge Hotel. We got my jack under their van and within minutes had their wheel changed. They were very relieved, as otherwise they would be stuck for the night. They handed us 50p to get a pint at the hotel before we headed into the night for Inverness. It was about eight-o-clock. Jimmy was waving like mad and shouting cheerio as they disappeared into the distance. Once they were out of sight he asked if I had an empty sack in the back of my van, as he had something he needed taking to Inverness at the weekend. With that he started digging in the snow at the side of the road, finally producing lumps of lead and other metals. While we had been changing the wheel on his friend's van, Jimmy (nice guy that he was) was stealing their spoils from Skye! We took it to a scrap yard in Inverness on Saturday on the way home and he was paid £15 for it. There is no honour among thieves! Jimmy's theory was that they were screwing the DHSS so why not have a free-for-all! He could not see the error of his ways.

My boss approached me (I was now his star man) and asked what my intentions were about staying in Glen Sheil. He was about to get a brand new Drilling Machine, one that would do the work of half-a-dozen men. He needed to train someone on it but he needed a bit of commitment to stay long term. I didn't really commit myself because if somebody offered me a better deal or a good job at home there was no way I would turn that down. Anyhow, he put his faith in me and I was sent with a salesman guy who showed me the ropes on how this new machine operated. The instruction lasted about an hour—that was my training session over, but you didn't need Brain Surgery skills to operate the thing since it was fairly straightforward. There was to be a Causeway built across the Loch and R. J. Macleod wanted to establish a Quarry at Invereniate, as close as possible to the site—hence the reason for the new machine. Unfortunately the rock in that area was very rotten soft material, so it was unsuitable for the task in hand. It was difficult to drill and we encountered many problems, especially with water seeping into the hole while we were drilling. This caused the machine to jam—very frustrating! I had been struggling for about six weeks making very little progress. Picture this scene: it is raining as it only can rain in Glen Sheil. It has been like this for three weeks. Suddenly I hear a car horn blowing. Looking down the hill I can see the Gaffer waving me to come down. I shut the machine off and head to where he is parked. As I get near the car the Big Fellow holds out a yellow envelope—a telegram. He hastily adds that the Post Mistress said it wasn't bad news (what do they say when it is bad news?). We have just endured almost three weeks of continuous rain and the last thing at night before falling asleep was rain drumming on the roof of the van. The next morning it's the same music, so it's a battle to get the work done. I open the envelope and there's one line from Jess: "Received cheque for one thousand pounds."

I handed the telegram to Jimmy Black to read, and then had a look at the rain pouring out of the Glen Sheil sky and jacked. The cheque was compensation for the injuries Jess got through the fire in Birmingham! Big Jimmy Black was an excellent gaffer but there was no way I was putting up with that rain another hour! I told the Big Fellow I had just quit. His parting words were that a thousand pounds wouldn't last for ever! I couldn't give a damn at that moment—it was my passport out of that horrible incessant rain!

I got home and headed straight for Hilton where Wimpy were just starting a new phase of Council Houses. I called at the office and was told there were no vacancies—disappointing, but that's how it was. I was about to start the van and leave when somebody banged on the side. I wound down the window and, standing grinning as he usually did, was my old boss from Raigmore. He asked if I was working when I told him I had been knocked back in the office. He told me to hold on while he spoke to someone. About ten minutes later he returned and asked when I could start. I told him right away, if he was desperate, but he said first Monday would be time enough—so everything worked out just fine.

I was there until they paid me off some four months later. My big mate Frank (of Ullapool fame) had changed jobs and was working for Unilever in the food distribution section of the S.P.D. He asked if I was interested in working for them as there were vacancies. The money was about the same as the Construction and it would be a change, so I decided to give it a try. I was granted an Interview and the job was explained to me. I would be making up orders in the Cold Store. This was fine by me and it meant I would be home every night. We didn't work Saturday afternoons, so I would be able to follow the Football! Again, yes, I would start the following Monday.

The job in the Cold Store was a whole new concept for me. Again, you didn't need a university degree to follow the routine! The pay was reasonable and we worked shifts—nights one week, days the following week. The job was fine, *but*—the class of people I had to work with! They were the pits! Firstly, the management were very weak they listened to people carrying tales about one another. I had never been used to this type of behaviour. One morning I was finishing off the work left over by the nightshift on my own when the Supervisor called me over to tell me one of my workmates had complained about the length of time I was taking to complete the job. I near burst a blood vessel! I put the grovelling Supervisor on the spot by asking what he thought of my performance, and he was so embarrassed he was near sick! He couldn't answer me, and at that point I told him where to stick his job. I was just plain devastated. My work performance had never ever been questioned before, but that was the class of people employed by that company.

Our supervisor was off sick and we had an old guy sent up from Leith as a replacement. He was near retiring age so he didn't want any hassle. He was very red-faced and not too healthy looking. He hated being away from home but he had to spend a month in Inverness before getting a weekend leave. The morning he was due to go home I passed him on the way to work. He was about two hundred yards from the gate of our works so I just left him to walk. His name was Adam Souness. I found out later that he was an Uncle of Graeme Souness, the present Football manager of Newcastle Utd. Graeme was still a schoolboy then. Adam had his wee suitcase with him, ready for off!

I parked the car and headed back to meet the old guy and have a banter with him. I looked along the street to where Halfods now stands and there was no sign of Adam. I leaned a bit further out of the gate and was shocked to see the old fellow lying on the pavement! He had collapsed! I ran to where he was lying but there was no sign of life, no pulse, and he was a deathly colour. The ambulance was called but everything was too late—Adam Souness was gone. It was another sad day in my life. Years later I contacted Graeme Souness just to tell the family that we had done our best for their uncle and we tried to preserve his dignity as he lay on our Inverness pavement, his final resting place before burial. Graeme phoned me at home which I really appreciated and we had a great blether about our heart problems. Funny—here was a great Scottish footballer talking to me on the phone and we never once mentioned football!

With the S.P.D. I had the opportunity to sit my heavy goods driving test. I jumped at the chance! The day of my test was an ordeal—it was a Saturday morning in Aberdeen, and we had just left the test centre when a kid was hit by a car and killed outright! Not the best preparation for a driving test, but I pulled myself together and passed. On the football front, Celtic had reached the final of the European Cup. I am not a Celtic fan but was keen to see the game on television. The kick-off was about four-o-clock and I had permission to leave work at three. Just before I was due to clock off the manager sent for me. As I entered his office he looked at me and said, "I have bad news for you, my friend—you are going to miss the match." Before I could protest he told me the driver on the Skye run had been rushed to hospital with appendicitis! He had a fully loaded van of frozen food and it would need to be delivered first thing in the morning. We left Inverness about kick-off time and arrived in Broadford just as the final whistle went. As we entered the hotel you would have thought we were in Parkhead—it was a sea of green and white scarves with many of the wearers well drunk! We had a quick look around before leaving, as I had to pick up the van and get it plugged in for the night; otherwise we would lose the whole load. Then I had to find digs. Having done all this I rejoined the Celtic supporters for a few beers. I had an early morning and was driving, so I left early. The party was in full swing and was possibly like that for a few days.

Although the men I was working with were a different breed to the Tunnel Tigers, I quite enjoyed the job. Now that I had a heavy goods ticket I would get out of the depot. If someone was sick or on holiday it gave you an insight as to how the way the vans were loaded, which made life easy or difficult for the person delivering. One day the manager sent for me and asked if I would go on the road permanently as one of the older drivers was having difficulty meeting his targets. I asked what the alternative was, only to be told the older guy would have to be made redundant if I did not come aboard to share the load. No way could I stand back and allow someone to lose their livelihood, so I agreed to give up my job in the store and drive full time. Within a couple of weeks I realised I had made a big mistake—the pressure on you was tremendous to meet the times allocated. Every day the van would be loaded to capacity. There were cash sales so you had to collect cash. A lot of the shopkeepers were awkward, as they wanted to check their deliveries before they would pay. The girls in the sales office were on commission so they would disregard any item that was sold out and keep taking orders with the result that when we went to the shop the order would be short, all adding to your delivery time.

I soon realised the driving was not for me! I had done another man a favour but ended up worse off. I would have to get another job. An old acquaintance of mine called one day and asked if I was working—it was just at the time when I started working my notice. He was starting work on a big hotel in Aviemore at Coylumn Bridge and required a labourer to work with him and his mate; they were plasterers—another new field—but they assured me they would keep me right. Plastering was a skill achieved with years of practice! I would say the labourer had the best job—probably less boring.

STILL PROTESTING ABOUT WAR

1967 and another war—this time in the Middle East involving Israel, Egypt and Jordan. The ordinary people in the street were worried as the Middle East was always a flashpoint ready to flare up at a moment's notice. Luckily this was only a small war that lasted six days, but the cost in human lives between the three countries were fourteen thousand dead, over twenty thousand injured, and then of course the dependants—no known figure was ever put on these unfortunate souls.

My job at Colyumn Bridge was coming to an end. We were in the last few weeks and the company, Grey of Dundee, were laying people off. I got a whisper that Logan Muir-of-Ord were looking for people at the new Ice Rink being built at the Bucht Park. I gave them a call and got started right away. It was general labouring but it was home every night to my own bed and to see the kids on a regular basis.

A few weeks after starting they were ready to lay the floor of the rink. Three of us were allocated the job. There were three layers of concrete. The first was dead easy as we managed to use a machine to carry the concrete. When the first layer set they laid out miles of alkathene piping—which meant the only way we could transport the concrete was by barrow. We had a great little squad—Ian (now deceased), Ronnie and I. It was hard work pushing a barrow full of concrete ten hours per day and I can tell you there are hundreds of barrow loads in each mixer truck! Well, it felt like hundreds, but somebody told me there were forty; but when the crack is good the day passes marvellously.

Unfortunately those jobs have a short lifespan and it was soon time to move on again. In the meantime we decided that ten years in the caravan was long enough and we spent Jess's compensation on a two-bedroom flat. Out of her thousand pounds we got £1 change. The same flat today is selling for sixty thousand pounds plus—the mind boggles.

My next job was back at the rock drilling with a new sophisticated drilling machine for John Mackay Plant, Muir-of-Ord. I was sub contracted to R. J.

Macleod at Balmacara on the road to Skye once again, on the section between Balmacara and Kyle-of-Lochalsh. It turned out to be the best paid job I ever worked on. Mr Mackay asked if I was interested in taking the job on peace work, i.e. paid by the yard. I had never done this before but decided to take a chance and boy, did it pay off! Nevertheless, it was hard work. My old boss Jimmy Black was still the main man with McLeod's and showed he was a true gentleman and never mentioned the fact I had let him down rather badly in Glen Sheil. In fact, he gave me a bed in the camp and never charged me one penny all the time I was there. There's not many Jimmy Blacks in a pound.

McKay's had the most up-to-date equipment on the market. Shortly after I started with them a new machine arrived, still in the packing cases. We had to assemble it before we could start work. When I say "we", I had a workmate with me—Donnie Macdonald (The Moon Man)—who was employed to do the shot blasting. After assembling this very expensive American Drilling machine we started to travel to the worksite. It was a slow process as the ground was virgin hillside, very difficult terrain even to walk on. We had travelled about half-a-mile and the ground got really difficult. We hit a bump and the new machine toppled onto its side, then continued to cartwheel to the bottom of the gully! I was totally gutted and fully expected the sack, even though I was helpless to prevent the accident. The foreman phoned the boss and explained what happened, and his only concern was whether the machine was still in working order! We up-righted it, made a couple of adjustments, and it was none the worse for its tumble.

We always tried to let off a blast on Friday afternoons just before we left site—it was easier when everybody had gone home. This particular Friday we were all wired up and minutes after the last guy had passed us my mate Donnie lit the fuse. It should have exploded in about a minute but nothing happened! We were supposed to wait half-an-hour before checking what went wrong. When Donnie got back to the fuse he got the shock of his life. Just below where the debris from the blast would have landed were two men in a boat casting their fishing lines with not a care in the world! Little did they know how near they had come to being blown to kingdom come! We didn't enlighten them as to what had happened (or didn't happen!), but asked them to get well back as we were about to detonate a charge. It would be a waste of time fishing there that day, as the vibration would possibly scare the fish for miles around. The Moon Man was a bundle of nerves for a while after that incident.

Donnie, my workmate, got a job nearer his home area so I had a new mate to get to know. We had a marvellous summer that year and everything went like clockwork. The contract was supposed to last till Christmas, but we were a month ahead of schedule. We had one piece of rock to finish before we were moved. This was the huge rocky outcrop just west of the village of Balmacara. We started there on a Monday morning and sixty hours later were ready to move. Every rock driller in the country wanted to drill and blast that particular lump of rock, it was so inviting! (Sorry guys, I beat you to it!) We had the equipment on a low loader and were bound for Bower Quarry in Caithness. It was dirty, dusty, windy and remote. The rock in the quarry was like coal—we ended up each night looking like the black and white minstrels.

This contract only lasted a month and we were on the move again. I was not sorry to leave Caithness. Our next move was the other side of the country—to Strontian near Fort William. I arrived on the Monday morning. The main contractor was P. L. J. Heron from Fort William and the first man I met was Donnie (The Moon Man); he was running the show for the main contractor. Strontian was very exposed to the West Coast which often means wet weather and that is just what we experienced—incessant rain every day. We had problems with the drilling due to the structure of the rock formation, so life was anything but a bed of roses.

I was home for the weekend and got the offer of a job at Daviot Quarry—very convenient and home every night. I had been travelling for near a year, so it was good to get home for a spell. I worked at Daviot all summer. It was a good easy job. The wages were average but the days were getting shorter and the hours would be cut shortly.

I got wind of a job in a fish factory in the Ferry area of the town. They would work long hours right through the winter. I made enquiries and was offered a job starting in a couple of weeks' time; that suited me down to the ground, as I was able to give a week's notice of leaving. The fish factory was another kettle of fish (pardon the pun); the smell, for a start, was overpowering until your nose got used to it. Again, you didn't need to be an academic to work there! The first few weeks were spent cutting the heads off the herring. They were then packed in barrels in a mixture of salt sugar and cinnamon (a marinade). When we had a full shipload they were sent to Denmark or Norway. We were paid an hourly rate plus bonus for every basket of herring we filled. I could make £5 extra per night.

Back to my favourite gripe—war! There was a full-scale war going on between America and Vietnam. There was wholesale slaughter going on and it is difficult to say which side was the more aggressive. The Americans as usual were going to clean up and go home victors once again, but I am afraid it didn't work out that way—the Americans were soundly whipped and sent home with their tails between their legs.

One of the latest weapons used by the U.S.A was Napalm. This was magnificent stuff—it was dropped from a plane and on impact it burst into flames and sprayed wide areas with burning liquid. Everything and everybody was incinerated—men, women and children, animals and vegetation wiped out in one fell swoop. Ever wondered what kind of sad human being invented that W.M.D. or the sad human beings that sanctioned its use against innocent defenceless women and children? I often wonder if the terrorists of today are retaliating for what has gone before us. Some of the stories from Vietnam are as harrowing as any war stories ever recorded, but no doubt it will happen again and again. It seems we are not meant to live in harmony.

IT WAS AN EDUCATION

Working at the Fish factory was an education. Most of the guys working there were casual workers, often on the Dole. They were frequently up to all the dodges—if you needed to find out how to beat the system, there was someone there who could keep you right. The spicing of the herring lasted about six weeks before the freezing started. Work went round the clock as long as there were fish available. The frozen slabs were stacked on pallets and shipped to the Continent when we had a shipload ready. The company was Norwegian-owned and controlled. It also owned the ship that carried the cargo, mostly to Germany. The round trip usually lasted ten days. The first twenty-four hours in port the Norwegian crew would be drunk as they reckoned it was a nightmare to cross the North Sea in the boat they were using. After one trip the whole of the bridge had been staved in by a huge wave—maybe they had reason to get drunk!

The first winter I was there the manager asked if I would be interested in promotion. They were looking for shift foremen and I decided to give it a go, the salary being quite attractive. I suppose it was a baptism of fire for me as my supervisory experience was practically nil. I had never dealt with a squad of men this big before and there were a few tough nuts working in the fish factory; but to be fair I never had a lot of hassle—most guys, when they are working, behave fairly well. Of course there are always a few disruptive people that want the wages but don't intend doing a lot in return. On many of the shifts we would have thirty or forty casual labourers unloading lorries. They were undependable people! You would put two guys to work on each lorry stacking boxes on pallets. Some nights there would be up to sixty lorries queued up waiting to be unloaded. We would have between ten and fifteen lorries being worked at the same time by the time I had done a circuit of the worksite. Half of the labour force would have downed tools and gone home. This was the quality of people available so it could be hard going at times. How these people survived I never really found out, but we would only give them one go; if they didn't perform the first time we didn't take then on again. We usually ended up with the old faithfuls pulling us out of a hole. Mind you, they didn't do it for nothing—we usually ended up with a job and knock situation where you offered them so many hours to do the task and when they finished they could go home. They would get maybe a couple of hours pay for nothing. There were very few shifts without drama of one sort or another.

A lot of times it was funny and you got a good laugh, but the police were regular visitors. A couple of funnies I recall: the boat would bring back illegal duty-free brandy and cigarettes. We paid a pound for a carton of fags and a bottle of three-star brandy; we had collected £100 and paid the crew to bring back the goods. The first mate on the ship had wrapped the cigarettes in a waterproof cover and was about to throw it on to the quay; it was dark in the evening, and just as he heaved a postman in uniform walked round the side of the factory. The mate thought he was Customs so panicked and the package landed in the harbour which is the River Ness, fairly fast flowing; soon about a dozen guys were running along the bank as the package neared the Beauly Firth! Luckily there was a bit of a wash and the package landed on the beach feet from the firth, but it was a funny incident.

The second incident could have had serious consequences. Our factory was full to capacity but we had a facility at Dalcross to take overspill. One rather irate driver was really upset when told he had to go to our other facility. He jumped in his wagon and reversed at speed out our gate. What he must have forgotten was that there were a couple of phone boxes just outside the gate. It was dark but inside the nearest box was a woman phoning. The lorry struck the box, pushing it on its side. One minute the woman was standing up; next she was horizontal, badly shaken but unhurt. Luckily she didn't complain about it. The driver was gone and probably didn't even know what had happened.

At the end of the season ending April 1972 I decided to finish at the fish factory. I had worked there for three hard seasons, very long hours during the winter; there were six of us kept on permanently, mainly doing maintenance getting ready for the next season. There was always a pay-off at the end of March when the Herring season finished, so I asked to be added to the list. We had bought another house and it required some renovation. My plans were to have a few weeks off and get the work done before the summer started and I got another job. But as Robbie Burns once said, "the best laid plans of mice and men aft time gang agile"—and on the Monday after I quit the fish factory I was busy getting measurements and a list required for my renovations when, mid-afternoon, there was a knock at the front door. I answered it and found a man whom I had never set eyes on before. He introduced himself as Charlie Mackenzie, a manager with the Highland Haulage. He told me he had heard I wasn't working and asked if I was looking for a job. He went on to explain that their forklift driver had broken his ankle that morning and they were stuck—so would I be willing to pull them out of hole till the guy was ready to start work again? I agreed to help them out and downed tools and made my way to the H.H. depot. I did not really need a job that soon but better to keep as many options open as possible (you scratch my back and I'll scratch yours!). The next morning I was at the depot bright and early when this guy came limping up to the forklift and said he was back—he had only sprained the ankle. I handed over his machine and went looking for Mr Mackenzie, who was full of apologies for mucking me about; but I told him no hard feelings and I would get on with my renovations.

As I walked away he called me back and said he could make me an offer of a job. They had a vacancy on the back shift unloading the trunkers—start at 9 p.m. and work till all the platforms were empty; the harder we worked the quicker we could finish. He told me the pay and conditions and emphasised that most nights the squad would be finished around 4 a.m., which in fact suited me down to the ground: home around four, in bed till midday, then a few hours at the renovations—bingo! I felt like I had hit the jackpot!

The shift at the H.H. depot started at 9 p.m. We had eight trunkers to empty before morning. Most nights at least a couple would have full loads. We didn't touch them as they were delivered direct to whom they were addressed to. The job was a doddle! It was so convenient for me it was unreal! Again, it was a fairly unskilled job but you were usually so busy the time flew by. Most days I was able to get few hours DIY done before going to work and I was earning a fairly decent wage.

Near the end of the summer there were two adverts in the local press—one was men wanted to train in new skills for an oil construction yard opening at Arderseir in the near future, while the other job was with British Telecom, also looking for trainees to work in their establishment. I applied to both—maybe at last I would have an opportunity to train for a job that required me to use my brain instead of my brawn! I heard nothing for a few weeks. It was then seven months since I started with the H.H.; then one morning the postman dropped not one but two brown envelopes through my door—one from McDermott, the Oil Rig builders, the other from B.T.—what a dilemma! Both offered me an interview practically on the same day, same time. Which do I choose? What a decision! My big mistake was choosing one, whereas I should have made arrangements to attend both—but I chose McDermott's. Perhaps I made the wrong decision. Financially I definitely did, but as far as learning a skill is concerned, I was probably best off with the Americans. At my interview they said I would have at least thirty years work with them! I was over the moon with that prediction as I would be an O.A.P. within that thirty-year period. My time with the H.H. had been very enjoyable but I had done ten months steady night shift and covered a lot of work on our house, so I was looking forward to a change. Believe me, it was a huge change!

The McDermott interview lasted four hours this included an aptitude test, a medical and an interview with about half-a-dozen people round the table. I faced a rather embarrassing moment when the guy asked me to fill in all the jobs I had been in since leaving school. He only handed me one sheet of paper. If I remember properly I needed two and a half pages—that was using both sides! I was amazed that in twenty years I had worked for forty bosses. I did a quick recount and scrubbed six of them—thirty-four sounded better than forty.

Not all the jobs were as promised at the interview or over the phone; in a lot of cases you would be promised the world, then end up with nothing. One good example—I applied to a company in Stirling for a position as a driller, just outside Beauly and handy for home. I got the job and was told to report on site on such and such a date, and when I arrived on site there was only one chap there. He was an elderly Polish gentleman and was getting ready to start drilling with a machine I was already familiar with. He was very hard to understand as his English was very poor when he started the machine—it was almost impossible to make sense of him. I noticed right away that one of the tyres on the Rig was punctured: it was like a tricycle with three wheels! I had very little input as I awaited instructions as to what I was there for. When we stopped for our first tea break I asked the Pole when the puncture would be fixed. He shrugged his shoulders and looked away from me. My next question was how do you move the rig to the next hole? He replied, "With crowbar." I put him in the picture right away that there was no way I would be heaving any machine about with a crowbar just because it had a puncture! My new mate said it was a pest taking the wheels off to be repaired and we would also lose time. I told him that was tough but not to count on me when he was due to move! I could see he was squirming with embarrassment. He was due to move after dinner break; it would be impossible for him to move it himself as it was up a slope. He was very silent for quite a while before replying that we would be moving the machine after our lunch. I shook my head and said there was no way I was getting involved until the tyres were mended! I again got the silent treatment before he said to me that he preferred working alone, but couldn't there since he needed help. I granted him his wish and walked off! He called after me—what would he tell the boss in Stirling? I said just tell him I am a professional and don't lower myself to work with scrap. Do you blame me for not staying? That was one of half-a-dozen similar jobs I omitted from the form I had to fill in for McDermott's personnel department.

It had been nearly twenty years since I left school, was nearly fully employed, and the only training I had ever received was how to kill people during my eighteen months army training! The only certificate I held apart from my driving licence was a SHOT FIRERS licence so that I could handle explosives when employed in the construction industry. To get this licence was a bit of a fiasco! A big fat bobby called at the house and asked me a few questions, which were mainly my name and address. He was in the house all of about ten minutes and after he left I had approval to handle lethal substances that could blow things to kingdom come. With my driving licence I had to sit a simple test for the explosives thing—the mind boggles!

When I left the interview I had no idea if I had been successful or not, but word got round that there was a problem with the access road and the start would be delayed. Then we heard that the first seven trainees had started in the middle of December. It was a bit unclear as we entered the holiday period at the end of the year 1972. Around the second week of the New Year I received notification that my interview had been successful and they were offering me a position as a trainee welder, commencing on the 29th January 1973. I was over the moon! I was getting the chance of a lifetime to learn a trade midway through my working life. I had just passed my thirty-fifth birthday and this was a whole new ball game.

THE RESSURECTION

A few weeks before my interview with McDermott's our shift foreman at the H.H. had left. I was offered his job but the permanent night shift was getting me down. Shifting parcels from one lorry to another was not very exciting work, so I declined the offer, determined to get started at the new Arderseir Oil Rig Construction Yard. My start date was perfect and allowed me time to give two weeks notice. The Highland Haulage had been a good enough job, but I still had demons inside me wanting a job where I could use my brain instead of the usual brawn. My knowledge of Oil Rigs amounted to having watched the movie called *Giant* starring Elisabeth Taylor, Rock Hudson and the young James Dean. I later found out they were called nodding donkeys, not oil rigs.

At precisely 6 a.m. on Monday 29th January 1973 in a snowstorm I made my first of many journeys to the new facility at the Carse Of Arderseir to begin training as a welder. As I entered the site I had a rush of adrenaline—this was something completely alien to what I normally did for a living. There were a few guys waiting for instructions so we kind of formed groups appertaining to the trade we would be following. At 7 a.m. we were each allocated a clock-in number—mine was 0041. We were then handed over to a big American guy wearing dark glasses. He showed us to the store where we were kitted out with the relevant equipment needed for welding. Every piece of gear was brand new. Now dressed like brand-new welders, we were told to find a vacant welding booth and wait there till further instructed. The American was very vague about what was required of us—he was only standing in for our regular instructor who was on a course for a week. The one thing that stands out about the American was his dark glasses! I like to see people's eyes when talking to them, but this fellow was pretty faceless and I am afraid not very helpful. We were lucky that there were half-a-dozen local lads who had been training for about a month, so they kept us new guys right. Everyone was issued with dark glasses—this was to avoid being flashed by other welders. "Flashed—what was that?" Well, it's when the U.V. rays hit your eyes and split's the top layer of skin. It is painless though for the first few hours it feels like sand in your eyes; the pain doesn't start until the middle of the night—just when it's impossible to get any drops to ease the pain as everywhere is closed (a stopgap

120

is cold tea bags); one lesson learned is that after the first flash you make sure it never happens again if at all possible.

We were working a two-shift system, 7 a.m. till 5.30 p.m., and 5.30 p.m. till 3 a.m. It was continual practice for the whole shift, welding rod after rod until you got the swing of things. It took me four weeks to graduate to welding pieces of pipe together. After six weeks our foreman asked if I felt confident enough to sit my welding test. If I passed I would be moved onto production work. Every welder of the calibre we were being trained to had to sit a test every time he started on a new job or changed the type of welding rod he was using, so it turned out to be a costly operation. I decided to give it a go. I had nothing to lose if I failed the test—I would receive further training, so I took the plunge. McDermott's were testing about thirty welders every shift; that would be around sixty per day. They were hiring men from all over the country, many of them from shipyards and construction sites. We were not too popular, as we had learned in six weeks what these experts learned in five years, so there was animosity.

My nerves were taunt as I prepared for my test. Indeed, I was quite nervous about it. Suddenly this guy from Methil in Fife approached me and asked if I was one of McDermott's six-week wonders! I told him no, I was a McDermott trained welder. He turned to me and said, "Ye're wasting your time—when we, the Boiler Makers, take over this yard, the only job you crowd will be doing is labouring for us tradesmen." I ignored him and carried on with my test piece. John McIntyre, our foreman, was brilliant and coached us through the test. After the nerves left it was plain sailing!

After welding the test piece is visually examined for any external defects, some of which you are allowed to rectify by light grinding. It can be failed at that point. If it passes it goes for an x-ray examination. Again, it can fail at that stage. Finally it is cut into strips and mechanically tested. If this passes you are accepted to weld to that standard. We had to wait a full shift before the results were announced. It was agony! There were a couple of trainees that had already been passed the previous week, so it *was* possible! We were allowed to hang about waiting for our results, usually announced about ten-o-clock in the morning. The list went up and, *there*—I had passed along with another three trainees! Just great! I went looking for my Fife friends just to gloat a little bit, but when I enquired about them I was told they (Dippers) had failed the test. They didn't hang around and were long gone when they got their results; but they were not alone—the failure rate was high. We waited for further instructions as to where we had to report. My rate would also increase by five pence per hour to the princely sum of seventy-five pence per hour. My welder identification stamp was

E7 and every bit of welding I carried out had to be stamped with this number so that they could trace it back to the welder should a failure occur. The gaffer approached us with clipboard in his hand. He called out two welder indents and instructed that two guys where to report to start work. He looked at the two of us remaining guys and shook his head. "I have bad news for you two," he said—and my heart sank about a foot! What was wrong—they said we had all passed? It turned out that somebody had made an error and had cut up our test pieces incorrectly, so the insuring authority Norsk Veritas insisted we be retested. What a disaster! Anyhow, it had to be done so we started to set up two new test pieces. Tomorrow would be another ordeal. Another sleepless night, partly praying I would be able to hold my nerve for another three hours while I was retested. The guy in the next welding booth to me that morning was a little obese—German Harry; he was a welder so after a couple of days practice he was testing. In each booth there was one air line connection and we needed a power grinder. Harry decided it would be handy if we fixed up a grinder in my booth and a power brush in his booth; then we could share without having to change tools every so often. We were ready to start. This was the nerve-wracking bit! Normally you would weld about four inches on the initial pass; then you would have to grind the ends (feather them for easy start).

Harry was ready to grind first so he caught the grinder and yanked it out of my booth. The cable was round my leg one minute; I was carefully welding the next minute; the following minute I was more or less flat on my back screaming obscenities at the little fat German idiot! It was nearly the start of WW3! Poor Harry—he was beside himself with apologies! We shook hands and carried on.

I passed my retest with flying colours. Next morning Harry and I were sent out on site to work on the New Pipe Mill that was under construction. It was all secondary work but valuable experience and Harry was a grand fellow to work with. He had been all over the world working from welding to being a chef.

For the first time in my working life I came across discrimination. Our American foreman came round on the Friday and asked if we would be available for overtime on Sunday. Harry was in the toilet but I put his name forward as he was funding his digs out of his own pocket and I knew he would be glad of the extra cash. The reply from the foreman kind of shocked me when he said if he had his way there would be no bloody Germans working on the site, so he had no intentions of giving him extra cash. As he left he mumbled something about not forgetting the war. Harry never got any overtime and left a few weeks later. I grasped every opportunity I could get to further my knowledge of welding; once you were involved it was a huge subject, all alien to me but I was enjoying every minute of it the work. At that time it was probably fourth-class work reinforcing the pipemill machinery; but it was much needed practice for us guys who had very limited experience.

McDermott had a yard full of work with major contracts from Phillip's Petroleum and Occidental; they had many sub-contractors working to try and get the contracts complete on time. A month after leaving the Training School I was moved to a part of the Phillips contract. It was one of three one hundred metre long bridges, a perfect little contract for us to start off on. Two of us were welding the deck plate—a single pass fillet weld; it was sheer magic as we burned rod after rod and felt we were doing a grand job. Into our second day and we were approached by one of the sub-contract welders who seemed to be in a very unfriendly mood; he was most unpleasant as he told us we were doing too much work! We asked how he figured this out; he then started a spiel about how their union had fought for their rights and that they didn't want a bunch of hicks undermining these rights—and if we didn't slow down the Yanks would look for every welder on site to produce as much as we were producing. I paid no heed to this guy and tried to go even harder than before—there was no way I would be pressurised by a bunch of no-hopers. To achieve top rate of ninety pence per hour we had to successfully complete four welding tests using different techniques.

I kept pestering my boss to get a crack at the remaining three tests I had to perform. He finally gave in and I was one of the first trainees to achieve top rate on site. This welding lark was the best move of my life! I was now doing a job where you got satisfaction at the end of the day and when your work was tested and passed it was quite a feeling! At last I felt as though I was getting somewhere.

Three months after passing my test as a welder I was working away one afternoon when the Welding Superintendent pulled up in his Landrover and called me over. My little American Supervisor was sitting beside him grinning from ear to ear. The boss asked how I felt about the welding—was I happy in what I was doing? I told him I was. He went on to explain that the Americans were here short term and they would be handing over to the Brits as soon as they were capable of running the show. They would also like as many Scots as possible in the top team, preferably local people. His next statement nearly knocked me on my back—when he offered me a job as Leaderman (charge hand). I was a bit gobsmacked, as I never dreamed of doing anything other than welding this early in my career. Charlie the boss must have had great faith in me as he produced a new shiny white hard hat with my name and new title on it! I am sure I looked like a snowdrop until it got dirty. He went on to tell me of the marvellous opportunities available to us Scots people because in the States you had to wait until some-one died before there were vacancies for promotion. The boss told me that my ability to pick up the welding in so short a time and the fact that I had supervised people before influenced their decision to offer me this heady post for which I was being paid another five pence per hour.

One sound piece of advice given to me many years ago was never turn down a promotion as you could end up working for the biggest idiot born; so, remembering that advice, I accepted—my first step on the promotion ladder. Every welder on my part of the job was a McDermott trainee; as soon as they tested out they would be sent to us to work on the bridge.

Working on site was a different kettle of fish to the confines of the training school, so the new lads needed nursing along for the first couple of weeks. I was still able to weld but a lot of my time was now taken up in training and organising my squad of ten men. I was really enjoying myself and the quality of men we were getting was great.

One funny incident occurred on our bridge. It was virtually an oblong box, which was great as it was easy to cover against the elements. We started to erect tarpaulins. This would allow us to work inside and in the dry. By lunchtime we had nearly completed the task of erecting the covers. During lunch break, listening to the weather forecast, the newscaster mentioned we were to get severe gale-force winds later that day. Our American Supervisor decided this would be like a Louisiana Hurricane and made us remove all the covers, as he feared a massive storm! He would not take no for an answer. When the wind arrived it was like a strong breeze—it caused a slight sandstorm and was soon back to calm. We had to set to and start re-sheeting the bridge! Our supervisor was now convinced that our gales and his hurricanes did not compare.

Late at the back end of the summer we completed our bridge contract and were moved to the new Deck assembly building. It was huge and had a floor area of approximately eighty acres—surly the biggest building on the Moray Firth coast. Our new contract was for sub-assemblies for the ill-fated Piper Alpha Jacket owned by Occidental. I was soon into my second year and really absorbed in my work. It was hard going at times, not physical work but taxing on account of the length of hours worked; and, of course, you were working to schedules against the clock all the time. Early that spring the sub-contract workers started to cause labour problems so the company decided to get rid of them and hire a complete direct labour force.

I was called into my boss's office and asked if I would be interested in becoming a Supervisor, which would be a staff position on a salary—quite an attractive deal. I would be given a bigger work area and a bigger squad of men to look after. I would also get involved in the planning, which meant dealing with prints and drawings. This was all new to me but it would further my education and broaden my horizons. With my new position I was working alongside my American Supervisor who was supposed to pass his skills on to me. We got on very well together but the company had just hired a new British Welding Superintendent who was a mountain of a man from the Hartlepool area of England. Tom Flounders was over six-foot tall and weighed about twenty stone! He was one of the finest bosses I ever worked for—never panicked or got excited about things. He didn't need to, as his knowledge of welding was second to none. He made sure he passed on his knowledge to his understudies. Working for Tom was an education in itself. He had a way about him that made learning easy. With the help of his trusty blackboard in the office, he would draw sketches and diagrams that left you in no doubt how things should work. I had six wonderful years working for the Big Man.

Just before the Christmas break we had a dinner-dance in Auldearn. The Americans were invited and as usual they were mad keen on all the heavy Scottish dances! During a hectic Eightsome Reel I began to have difficulty with my breathing. I sat down and after a few minutes felt back to normal. I didn't say anything, just continued downing a few whiskies and got on with the dancing. We broke up for Christmas and the New Year. It was a very quiet time, as I don't recall any outstanding memories from that particular year. It was certainly changed days from when we finished work early afternoon on Hogmanay day, had New Year's day off and back to work on the second day of the year; now we had nearly three weeks, depending on when the holiday landed.

My social life was going well. I was able to follow my favourite football team most Saturdays. Inverness Thistle were going well—they had a good team and had won the league the past couple of seasons. We had a great home support and had decent crowds every home game. A crowd of us would gather in the Corriegarth before the game, nip back at halftime for a top up, and at full time it was the Heathmount to catch the full time results from around the country. There was always plenty banter as the results were relayed over the television. The Rangers and Celtic crowd would have a go at each other but it was all in good spirit. As soon as the scores were over it was home, supper, dressed and off to either the British Legion or the Thistle Club where we had many happy evenings organised by Helen, the Club stewardess. Our end of year break over, it was back to the grind—but it was easy for me as I enjoyed every day I worked in the Oil Industry.

I was doing meaningful, interesting work, and every day was an education for me. I was also dealing with people who realised I had a good working brain.

DON'T BECOME
COMPLACENT

I was flying high with a well-paid job and enjoying life to the full—but how quickly it can be de-railed! For me it happened in an instant.

It all became unstuck on a Friday morning around the 10th of January 1974. I got out of bed as the alarm clock burst into life, grabbed my clothes and headed for the kitchen. It was normal routine—I filled the kettle, switched it on and made my way to the bathroom where I continued getting ready to face another day at work. Back at the kitchen sink, I leaned over to get the boiling kettle when suddenly I felt an excruciating pain in my left side. It felt as though someone had stuck a knife in my ribs! I was struggling to breathe and ended up slumped on the floor. Our bedroom was upstairs at the front of the house; the kitchen was at the back—but I didn't have the strength to shout to get help. Gradually, my breathing returned to near normal and I managed to get upstairs where Jess got up and went to phone a doctor. We had no phone in the house so she had to go to Farraline Park where our nearest box was. This one was vandalised so she had to hike on to the post office on a cold winter's morning (they bred us hardy then). The doctor eventually arrived around 7 a.m., had a look at me he asked if I had banged myself at work, which I had. He told me to stay at home till Monday by which time I should be okay.

Around 5 p.m. my own doctor called to see how I was. He examined me again and detected a murmuring sound coming from my lung, though he could not pinpoint the cause. He called back at 11 p.m. and again examined me. At that point he said he wanted me to go to hospital and have an x-ray carried out. We arranged transport to Raigmore and arrived there just before midnight. The duty staff at the A&E started to examine me and wired me up to an ECG machine. The young lady doctor had just arrived at my bedside and was asking me questions when the door of the ward burst open and a drunk guy with blood pouring from his head staggered into the room. The doctor had a quick look at this fellow and told me she would need to get rid of him first in order to restore peace to work on me.

The doctor was a young lady, possibly under thirty, doing a grand job healing the sick. Midnight Friday most young people would be out dancing the night away! This lovely person dedicated to her profession had to put up with the most awful abuse and bad language imaginable. It was disgraceful—the wound on the drunk's head needed stitches and she was unable to give him any anaesthetic because of the amount of alcohol in his system—so she had to insert the stitches as he was. This brought a further torrent of abuse and foul language! The stitching compete, she asked if he had ever had a tetanus injection. Again, she was subjected to abuse, so she rammed the needle in his rear end through the trousers. It was good enough for the ungrateful pig! This was my first visit to a hospital late on a Friday evening—it was a real eye-opener. To treat this guy had taken fifty minutes; under normal circumstances it would be a ten-minute job. At that point the doctor had been working for ten straight hours and she would possibly be there all night. I knew this guy very well—he worked on the same site as me at Arderseir, but I kept my head well down as I had no wish to get involved with the man.

The rest of my time there passed without incident. Eventually they had carried out all the necessary tests on me and I was allowed home as they could find nothing untoward wrong with me. I had felt nothing since the initial pain in the morning so it was home and bed very late at night, thanks to a drunken ungrateful idiot. Next morning, Saturday, my wife went shopping. I decided to be useful and started to do some hoovering until she got back. As soon as I started to push the Hoover I felt a funny sensation in my chest, causing me to run to the toilet where I threw up masses of blood. Just at that point our family doctor appeared at the door. He took one look at me and started making arrangements to get me to hospital. This was difficult as there were no beds available except at Culduthel.

I eventually managed to get a bed in the old hospital at Culduthel. The bed I had been allocated had been vacated the night before. The occupant, whom I knew fairly well, had passed away—not the best of situations for a person in my position. The staff in Culduthel were just pure dedicated professionals. I could not have wished for better, and the two doctors—Mr Murray and Dr Franklin—soon diagnosed my problem. I had suffered a Pulmonary Thrombosis, which is where a blood clot either bursts in your lung or travels to the heart with possibly fatal conclusions. The first two or three days I was fairly ill and the medical team were pumping so much blood-thinning injections into me I was like a pincushion! Within a couple of days I had a hole in my lung, which caused breathing difficulties. To further complicate matters, I had a touch of pleurisy; which added to my breathing difficulties. But with the excellent care and dedicated medical people I soon began to feel better. One of the downsides of my stay in Culduthel, which catered for a lot of terminally ill people, was that my bed looked right onto the morgue and there were very few mornings that we were free of hearses picking up the overnight casualties!

It was amazing, the different reasons people had for having chest diseases. One old guy had been a butler all his working life and his cause of chest infection was the material used to clean the silver cutlery; once it dried and he started to polish it, there was a dust which over the years he had been breathing in. It eventually contributed to his death. Another elderly guy had worked in quarries all his life, and he was a victim of the quarry dust; yet another had been a traffic warden—his problem was being on point duty for hours on end, breathing in the carbon monoxide fumes of the passing traffic. These three men were all dead within days of being admitted to Culduthel. Whatever the reason for being in Culduthel, they received pristine care. For many of these poor people it was their last few days on this earth.

My release day arrived twenty-one days after I had been admitted. I was not sorry to be going home. I know I am the most impatient person on earth and my time in hospital didn't alter that. I was on the mend and rearing to get going again—though it did worry me a little that McDermott might just ask me to take another medical.

My first stop on the Monday after my release from hospital was my family doctor's surgery. He told me in no uncertain terms I would be off work for at least twelve weeks. This had me worried as I was unsure how safe my job would be; but at that stage I had no grounds to argue with the doctor so I accepted his decision. A month later I was on top of the world feeling just fine, so I went back to my doctor and he reluctantly agreed to let me return to work after my six weeks were up, but advised me to ask for part-time for a few weeks so I could ease myself back into working a full day. But Bert being Bert, he knew better than the medical people—and so I returned to work, going straight back into full-time working. In this way I made one of the biggest mistakes of my life, and consequently never recovered to one hundred percent fitness.

My first day back and I felt so tired it was unbelievable. The second day back one of my understudies had a problem on a flare stack sixty feet off the ground, the only access being by ladder. I started to climb the ladder and halfway up I nearly passed out with fatigue. By the time I reached the top I was totally done in! I realised why the doctor wanted me off for twelve weeks! I kept my problems to myself, nevertheless, and managed to struggle through by choosing where I went and what I did. Eventually things got better. My boss arranged an interview with me—it was an informal cup of coffee and a fag (yes I was still stupid enough to be smoking!). He asked how I was feeling and told me the Medical Staff had said I had been very lucky to have survived the thrombosis I had just suffered. He then dropped a real bombshell by offering me a further promotion—I would now be on the bottom rung of the senior management team as a Section Manager. I was flabbergasted!

FLYING HIGH

The new promotion meant I would be in control of half the welding in the huge shed we worked in. Having sixty men under my control, I would have two supervisors and four charge hands reporting to me and keeping the workforce going on the shop floor. My new position was taken up with a lot of planning and administration. We were using at least six different weld systems. Big Tom was very up-to-date with modern technology and we were forever experimenting with new ideas. It was very busy but interesting and not nearly as hard as what I had been doing. I soon got the hang of it and I had my Big mentor keeping me right.

The union were starting to take a grip. The guys who were appointed shop stewards were about the least loyal members of the McDermott workforce and seemed to think the company owed them a living. They made life difficult and were more of a handful than the actual work. Their continual faultfinding was time consuming, but as long as they were talking they didn't have to work. When speaking to certain shop stewards you had to be alert all the time and be careful what you said as they would twist your words so that the sentence would suit their needs when there were problems. Unfortunately we as staff had no training on how to deal with the union. The time wasted arguing with union reps was unbelievable. They had the advantage, as they were more or less fulltime fault-finding, whereas we had to fit them in-between our work schedules, trying to complete multi-million pound contracts—the thing that paid the wages. When I was unhappy with my previous jobs I just upped sticks and moved. The workforce we were dealing with were often pathetic with some of the trivial complaints we had to listen to. In many cases it was just a downright lazy character who didn't want to work, but our union brothers insisted their members be treated equally regardless of how bloody useless they were. When things were running smoothly McDermotts had a knack of disrupting the whole show by appointing a new Vice President. Our third in six years had just been appointed. It was all-change every time, even down to renewing the office furniture—it must have cost a fortune!

1978 was a year of major change. We had our new vice-president who was immediately named the Smiling Assassin. Things were not going to plan in the industry and our new VP's first job was to make one thousand men redundant. He kept smiling and denying there would be redundancies, but there were. In the end they asked for volunteers with the carrot being a fairly substantial pay-off—they had plenty takers. McDermotts then decided to alter the shift pattern, going from a two-shifts to a three-shift system; this led to a major strike. This was a sad time in my life, seeing hard working local lads being led astray by the laziest, most stupid people imaginable. Hundreds of the lads who I am sure never wanted to go on strike ended up in debt because they were afraid to speak up for themselves. The outcome after twelve weeks of being idle was that nothing had changed, and they returned to work under the exact same conditions. The ring-leaders had a great time as they partied on the picket line, then hurled abuse at people like myself who were only interested in earning an honest living. On many occasions the picket line guys would be lying drunk at the side of the road; staff guys were flagged down and asked to give certain people a lift home, as they were incapable of looking after themselves.

There were wholesale changes on the yard. One of the victims of the new-look set-up was my wonderful boss, Tom. His face didn't fit in with the new regime so he was transferred to Aberdeen—a huge loss to Arderseir as far as I am concerned. Soon after his transfer he was in a road accident from which he never recovered and died soon after, aged forty—what a waste!

I received a further promotion to cope with the three eight-hour shifts now being worked. I don't know if it was a wise decision as my health was never the same after my thrombosis. The work was hard going and the men were restless and uncooperative after the strike. My health started to let me down and eventually I was signed off work.

BACK TO SQUARE ONE

After a couple of weeks on the most horrendous medication, a Vallium-type drug, I wanted to get back to work. I was feeling much better—my doctor called my problem depression but I would have said work-related stress was nearer the truth, as I had no need to be depressed. I decided to take the bull by the horns and if my health continued to let me down I would have to resign—more stress as we were paying a mortgage.

Within a week I knew within myself I would have to quit. There were major problems with one part of the job and nobody really had any idea how to fix it, so I was back to where I started a month ago, being pressurised to sort out problems that are difficult to explain. My doctor had pointed out that the danger of working under the strain I was constantly under was the possibility of a stroke or heart attack, as my blood pressure would continually be high. After a twenty-year struggle to get to the top, regretfully I had to admit defeat and quit my present position. I asked for an interview with my then boss and laid my cards on the table. I could no longer work as a Group Manager due to my continuing health problems. Reluctantly he accepted my resignation and said he would talk to the personnel department and see if they could put me in a job with less stress. At this point I must praise McDermott's for their compassion—they offered me jobs abroad and various other jobs on the site; one was with my old sparring partner, Big Ron Bisset. Ron was now manager of the Quality Assurance Department and he offered me a job as an inspector in the Quality Control Department of his little empire. I would have to start on the lowest salary available but I couldn't care less—I was still employed and my service was still continuing.

Quality Control Inspectors were like the traffic wardens of the Oil Industry and we were treated like traffic wardens, more or less a thorn in the flesh of the Production people. From the lowest paid supervisor to the highest manager we were treated like the scum of the earth! After all, we were only trying to get our production people to work to the rules agreed with our clients when they agreed that our company had won the contract. Before we started production everybody involved was given a set of rules; the main one was more or less the same for every contract, so eventually everybody should have known the important parts of the

Specification we had to work to; but I am afraid it was not that easy and when we pointed out that they were doing the job wrong we were at fault, never the ones doing wrong—one of the big problems being that in Quality Control, if the client had a weak inspection team, it made our job a lot harder because our production colleagues would take full advantage of this situation. One example of this happening was a contract part built in Holland and shipped to Arderseir for completion; one of the client's inspectors was an alcoholic Dutchman who was drunk most of the day and even worse, when he was on the night-shift, this guy was murder to work with as half the time he couldn't remember what he had done the shift before. Most of our work required documentation verifying that it had been cleared by the inspection teams; sometimes our Dutch colleague would sign for parts of the job he had never been near and then he would refuse to sign for parts he had looked at so he was not easy to work with. On the whole I was enjoying my new field of employment, nevertheless—there were plenty of new things I had to learn about and I also had to start sitting exams to get my C.S.W.I.P. inspector's certificate, so life was again interesting and my health was getting back to normal or as near normal as possible. I had more time on my hands to learn how to read technical drawings and learn all about non-destructive testing, so my head was buzzing and my brain being used to full capacity. I also had the knowledge of production and was able to help the guys out, as I was well aware of the difficulties they encountered over the course of a day.

Big Ron Bisset was a lovely big guy to work for. He could be a bit volatile at times but he had a heart of gold at the same time. He would bend over backwards to help any of his people who were in trouble, but if you got the call to report to his office it could be for any number of reasons. I got the call one particular day. As I made my way to his office I was wracking my brain trying to remember what I had done that might have upset him. He was quite calm when I entered the office. I was offered a cup of coffee and told to be seated, so right away I knew I had done no wrong. He was not his usual forthcoming self and seemed to be hedging a bit; after going round the block a couple of times and some small talk he laid his cards on the table: as it happened, he was desperately short of experienced Senior inspectors and would I take a promotion and help him out? This meant that I would be responsible for the running of a complete contract. I would be allocated a squad of inspectors and a couple of technical clerks and left to get on with the job. Financially it was worth another couple of thousand per year.

I had vowed never to take responsibility again but the lure of the extra cash and the fact I revelled in responsibility was too much to resist: I thought what the hell and jumped in with both feet! I had already been on a course at the Welding Institute in Cambridge and had successfully passed my welding Inspector's exam. As soon as I accepted the Senior Welding Inspector's post I had to return to Cambridge and sit the S.I. Exam. I failed one section of this exam and had to do a re-sit, which I passed easily.

My first contract as a Senior Inspector was a small contract for the Danish Offshore sector, three small Jackets—just ideal to get started on. This contract was completed on time with very little hassle. In the meantime McDermott had been awarded a huge contract for Conoco. This was the Tension Leg Platform, the first of its kind in the British Sector. It was unique inasmuch as it was tethered to the seabed, opposed to being piled, so it actually floated.

There were a lot of political problems within the McDermott yard; bosses were not agreeing and there was tension. The guy in charge of the Quality Control on the T.L.P. had asked for me to go and work for him. My present boss said no, so there was trouble at mill. The guys given the task of running the Q.C. were newly promoted; they had no experience of handling men so they soon ran into difficulties. But it was a massive, difficult job and I don't think there was enough preparation put into the planning before the job started, and it needed the best, most experienced men McDermott had on their books to tackle this monster.

The T.L.P. had been running about twelve weeks when I got the call to report to my gaffer's office one Friday afternoon. He looked at me and said I would have to take over the running of the T.L.P. as of Monday morning; he was not happy but had been ordered to let me go so I would be reporting to a new boss on Monday morning. One consolation was I knew this fellow very well and knew we could work together. It took me all of about an hour on the Monday morning to suss out that this new job was a shambles, an utter nightmare, but above all it was a real challenge so sleeves rolled up and get on with it.

There were all sorts of snags on this contract. Firstly, the drawings were always behind and to add further problems the job was being altered on an hourly basis. It took nearly six weeks for me to get the thing back on course. One of my old Danbor colleagues was promoted to the same level as me and we worked the two shifts between us. So with hard work and perseverance we finally managed to get things shipshape and felt rather proud to have taken part in such a huge part of modern technology. The T.L.P. was a huge box divided into nine modules; each box was more or less identical so it would have been the most logical and possibly economical sense to number each box the same, i.e. weld number one on box one should have been the same weld as number one on box nine but each draughtsman numbered his drawing to suit himself, resulting in nine different numbering systems on that part of the job instead of one numbering system. The early planning was non-existent. To make life easier I got a lot of drawings changed but it must have cost a fortune.

We were still having major problems with drawings and this was a real headache. To make our department work properly we needed the drawings ahead of the job being worked. This was not happening! Sitting and thinking the problem over, I struck on an idea which I hurriedly contacted my boss about—what if we had a draughtsman of our own? We could get him to clear up the minor backlog that was giving us the most hassle; we would set up a board in our office and he would be on hand when required; it also cut out a lot of running back and forth to the main drawing office which was half-a-mile away only to be told when you got there you were in a queue—most frustrating. The boss thought this was a wonderful idea and got the ball rolling right away. The difference was tremendous—the only problem was one guy couldn't cope with our work so we got a second and within a couple of weeks we had *seventeen* draughtsmen working for us! They were costly as they were at a premium—hard to get and their rate was eighteen pounds per hour. We were working them seventy hours plus per week so you can imagine the bill for these guys! One of my main problems with 'draffies' was that I had no idea what their day consisted of and to look after eight on each shift was difficult, so I promoted one to charge hand and he controlled the rest. Things began to move a bit better.

It is marvellous how things transpire. The Boss of the McDermott drawing office more or less washed his hands of our operation; he was possibly over the moon to be rid of me, as I was always harassing him to get my work done now it was my own responsibility—the buck would stop at me.

One day my 'draffies' ran out of the special lead they used for drawing with. I approached the McDermott Drafting boss to see if he would give me some lead to keep us going. He refused, saying it would come off his budget. I wondered how a small quantity of lead required by my seventeen draughtsmen might jeopardise his precious budget—the mind boggles, but this was the kind of people we were up against.

We had a progress meeting every week. The progress was measured off the drawings, i.e. if there were one hundred welds on the drawing and we had completed twenty five, they would record that drawing as 25% complete; but the drawings were being updated every day so they may add another fifty welds to the drawing—so now we have one hundred and fifty instead of a hundred, the percentage completed would go down. Big Ken the boss would blow a fuse and rant and rave about the progress going backwards instead of forwards! They would all have their sarcastic remarks about it but none of them came up with a better way of doing it.

The Conoco T.L.P. was the Rolls Royce of the North Sea. Every detail was closely monitored, checked and recorded. It was a massive structure. The part completed in Arderseir was possibly one third of the project. We had three thousand, four hundred primary drawings to work with as well as one thousand, eight hundred secondary drawings; on top of that there was piping, electrical and painting, so if I were to say in the region of ten thousand drawings to be worked on I doubt if I would be far wrong. At its peak T.L.P employed worldwide in excess of twenty thousand people. Regardless of what anyone else thought, it was a marvellous structure to work on and I was proud of the fact that at 2 a.m. one morning I signed the release note to allow the tugs to pull out from the quayside heading for the area where our part would be mated to the part done at Nigg.

My Boss, Big Ron, decided to apply for a vacant position on the yard. It would be a step up for him. He got the job, leaving a vacancy as leader of the quality control department. The head of our Department asked if I was interested in taking over. There was a new title to the post—it would now be Chief Inspector. I had no choice but give it a try. There was more money and also a company car. My health was holding up so in with both feet once again and back at the top of the tree. McDermott's had just been awarded the Brit Oil Clyde jacket. Their site team turned out to be the worst I ever encountered! They were backbiting among themselves and really difficult to work with. I had never encountered anything like them and to get them to make a decision was near impossible.

The year was 1982 and guess what we were in the throes of? Another war! This time against Argentina. It was really brilliant—television was so far advanced that we could watch the guys getting maimed and even killed. Whoever sanctioned live television during conflicts was nothing better than sick. Two hundred and fifty seven young men in their prime gunned down defending a piece of rock in the wastes of Antarctica—that was the British! How many Argies suffered the same fate I don't really know; then there were the maimed and wounded, both physically and mentally. Then we get back to the kids left behind as orphans of another senseless conflict. I am sure the rank and file of either side never wanted to go to war—it was the wishes of the politicians once again.

In my new role as Chief Inspector I had plenty grief. My position meant that I was responsible for the Quality Control for the McDermott Organisation based at Arderseir. We also had a lot of work, both at the yard and at various subcontract sites throughout the United Kingdom. It was not unusual to get a call midafternoon to go and visit one of our subcontractors somewhere in the south. It was a case of shooting off home, grabbing an overnight bag and heading for the airport, arriving at the site at all hours of the night. We would visit the site next morning and catch the flight back north later that day—all hectic stuff! It was quite enjoyable as it gave me an insight into how other people operated. Of course none of them appreciated us carrying out audits on them as they felt we were snooping, but it was part of the job.

Life was chugging along nicely. The yard was still fairly busy. I had set a work record for myself, having been with McDermott's for Fifteen Years—a Guinness Book of records entry for me. In 1988 things began to slacken. We missed out on quite a lot of work being outbid by continental yards. A lot our work would be completed by the end of this year. Suddenly there were rumours of redundancies; then the rumours became real and people were being paid off—really severe cuts. As usual, we had a lot of work to be completed documentation wise, but they had no mercy. What I couldn't understand was why it was always the poorer paid guys who went first. Our department was looking like a tree with all the branches at the top still intact but with the roots being chopped away. Eventually it would topple over.

As I have said, we still had a lot of work to complete and the cutbacks were beginning to bite. With the threat of redundancy hanging over their heads, the men were not performing as they should. It was difficult, and could you blame people for not giving their all if their head was next on the chopping block? Our whole department was called to meeting and the future was explained. There would be no more redundancies but there would be people demoted and things were going to be tight, so everybody was expected to go that extra mile and do a little bit more to tide us over the present crisis. I could see the conscientious workers would be heavily leaned on and the not-so-conscientious would dodge along, doing only enough to get by.

I had a think about my health and could see the future being under continual pressure, so I decided to find out what I could expect in the way of a pay off package. My next port of call was at the personnel office asking what to expect in the way of money. The sum quoted was fifteen thousand plus a few pounds. Another long ponder and I decided with that amount of money I could clear all my outstanding debts, not that I had a lot. I tucked this information into the back of my mind and carried on in my new capacity of Senior Inspector. Once again I was beginning to feel like a Yo-Yo. One morning arriving at work, I had a nightmare to contend with—more work than I had men. I allocated the jobs and still had two barges to cover so I had to roll the sleeves up and cover them myself. We started at 7 a.m.; my bosses started to arrive any time after 8 a.m.—so much for doing that little bit extra. My boss had done a circuit of the worksites when he arrived at work. One of the client's reps had lodged a complaint about the inadequate cover we had on his job and the boss sent for me to report to his office.

As soon as I entered the office my boss started to harangue me about the complaint he had received. The other three bosses were sitting listening as I was torn to shreds. I had never ever been so criticised in my working life! I left that office totally humiliated as well as being ready to floor the first guy that got in my way. I had been bursting my gut while these guys sat drinking coffee, possibly discussing the latest game of golf! My mind was made up—I could no longer work with these people. I headed for my office and drafted a letter requesting my redundancy package.

My boss had a change of tune when the letter landed on his desk. He did his best to get me to change my mind but I'm afraid that after the slagging I took from him I had just about had enough—it was time for pastures new. His biggest worry would be the fact that I would not be replaced, but hell mend them—they should have appreciated what they had!

On the 18th December 1988 I received my final cheque from McDermott's—it was worth around eighteen thousand. My first stop was the Mortgage people to clear my mortgage—this was not too bad, as I only owed them seven thousand, which left me with eleven to bank. All I needed was to get a job as soon as the New Year arrived. It was nearing Christmas so no need to hold my breath until after the festivities. I had spent a few pounds on postage stamps as I posted my C.V. to every agency I had an address for. This again was all new to me. I felt a bit institutionalised—fifteen years with McDermott's was similar to having been in the forces! Everything was done for you—all you did was phone some faceless female and everything was taken care of. Getting a job might be difficult until I had broken the ice. By the end of January I was starting to get a bit restless as I had not received any offers or replies to my application C.V.s. Then out of the blue Friday afternoon I got a phone call from the pipe fabrication yard at Evanton—was I interested in a job? Of course I was interested in a job! When would you like me to start? Monday morning 7 a.m. if that's possible. Okay, see you Monday! About an hour later another phone call: was I available and would I be interested in going to South Africa? Sorry mate, I just committed myself to somebody else—thanks all the same.

I was over the moon with my new job. I had never worked with Pipe before so it was another string to my bow and the money was always better at the Pipe Fabrication yards. It would be short term but it was a start. Initially I had been offered ten weeks work, but the fabricators were having major problems with the material. I had learned all about the problems when I did my Inspection exams; now they were no longer theory but very much practical. The fabricator was pulling his hair out as the job started to run over the contract time. I was asked if I would go on the nightshift, as things were so bad they had to double shift the job. I didn't mind, as it was an enhanced rate.

I had been there eight weeks and there was no sign of them solving the problems so it looked like I would get at least another six weeks. The weather was getting better so the chances of getting work would improve. All the guys on the nightshift were from the North—Wick and Thurso area; they were all excellent tradesmen, having worked on jobs for Douneray. They were a fine bunch of guys to work with and no messing about—they just got on with the job. Eventually the problems with the steel were sorted out and the job was starting to show progress; it was estimated that we would be complete in four weeks' time but still working day and nightshifts—six shifts per week, twelve hours per day: it was hard going! I had the offer of a job going offshore with the pipe-laying barge but I never fancied being a sailor so I had to turn it down but it was encouraging to get an offer.

We entered our last week. I would be finished when the contract was complete sometime over the weekend. My supervisor, Bob Craig, said he was trying to find work for us and would let us know as soon as possible. In the meantime it was carry on with what we were doing. I was delighted to get the fifteen weeks work—it had earned me nearly fifteen thousand pounds.

A DIRTY SUBBIE

On the Thursday morning, as I finished my shift, the supervisor called me into his office and asked if I had a job to go to. When I told him no, he asked if I was interested in carrying on working for O'Neill. I was interested but where was the job? West Germany! I nearly collapsed—I had never been abroad in my life before, never mind work there. Nevertheless, it was an exciting prospect. As usual Jess left the decision about where I would work to me, so I had no hesitation in accepting the offer to go to Mulheim, a steel town in the Ruhr valley. I asked if I could finish there and then so that I could prepare to fly to Germany on the Sunday. I was told I was required to work until Saturday morning as they were short staffed. Great, finish Saturday morning, sleep all day Saturday, fly out of Dalcross Sunday forenoon! Jess would really be chuffed!

It turned out a bit better than that. I reported for work on the Friday night an hour into my shift, and I was told to clear off home and I would be paid for the shift. As I left Evanton that night I was quite happy with myself. I had survived my first job as a Dirty Subbie, the name given to sub-contractors on the Oil sites. The icing on the cake was that I had earned just under fifteen thousand for my effort.

Sunday morning, my case packed ready to leave, I was feeling a bit apprehensive. The one good thing was I had company as one of the other lads from Evanton had taken a job as well. I hadn't a clue what was in front of me. I had flown to London a few times before, but after that I had no idea. Our flight was at seven-o-clock in the evening. I never bothered to find out how long it took to get to Dusseldorf, but remembering back to the war films, the bombers seemed to take hours—so it was most surprising to find ourselves coming in to land fifty-five minutes after leaving Heathrow! The first sign I saw in German made me realise we were out of Britain—it was telling us the way out of the Airport: *Ausgang*! It was totally fascinating for me.

Our gaffer in Germany was waiting to pick us up. There were now three of us; another fellow from Edinburgh had joined us on the plane. I already knew him so it was fine. I dread to think how I would have got on by myself. We were twenty minutes from the Airport to the town of Mulheim. We had a hotel room booked for one night only but we were given a day to get sorted out. Three of us managed to get a suite in a hotel in the centre of the town. It was thirteen pounds per night for bed and breakfast. It was okay—we could do our washing in the bathroom and cook a bit of food so we were well off, really, as we could eat in the works canteen where you got a three-course meal for around a pound per day. Our landlord at the Hotel Fredericka was a smashing fellow and looked after us well. The hotel catered for a lot of opera singers and actors. It was funny when the Poles were staying there as they used to steal all the small packets of sugar, butter and the small jars of preserves! Hans knew all about it but said they were so poor that what they were taking were luxury items in Poland so he turned a blind eye. The breakfast was the same every morning—the usual array of cold meat, cheese and fresh rolls. He also dished out a hard-boiled egg to everybody in the dining room—he carried them in his blazer pockets! Now we were there for thirteen weeks and after a few days the hard-boiled eggs lost their attraction and we would leave them on the plate. When our host started to clear the tables he put the eggs back in his pocket so you could never be sure how old they were when you got them next morning!

HOW THE GERMANS DO IT

I drew the short straw and had to start work on the early shift. We were about thirty minutes walk from the steel mill but the weather was good and it was easier walking than trying to explain where you wanted to get off the tram if the driver could only speak German. The entrance used was gate No. 48—can you imagine the sheer size of the place! I was overawed—Arderseir would have fitted into one corner. It was a Manniesmann Pipe Rolling Mill producing over one million metric tonnes of pipe every year, built alongside the main railway line; they had a spur built through the site so that they could export all their goods by rail. The wagons were loaded in the yard for dispatch to Rotterdam or Hamburg ready to ship all over the world. I had never seen a set-up like it. Everybody used bicycles to get around the place as you could spend your day just walking.

My first job was patrolling the rolling mill. I had no idea what was going on—most of the workers could speak a little English but sometimes it was difficult. I shared an office with a German foreman but we could not communicate as he had no English and I had no German. The whole set-up was fascinating! First there was no overtime worked. The German workforce worked a thirty-eight hour week, no more, no less—it was brilliant. Unfortunately I had to work a twelve-hour day one week and the same on nightshift the following week. The nightshift was brilliant because the German production team finished at ten-o-clock at night. They had a few sub-contract testers who worked through the night. We were required to have a representative on duty as long as they were working, but we were never called upon so we would get the head down and sleep till the end of the shift. The first shift I worked I found out that after the lights were out the mosquitoes were active! I wakened up in the morning covered in bites, some of them like marbles under my skin! They itched for about six weeks until they disappeared.

The Germans could show us how to organise! The rolling operation was something to behold—they had to produce ten thousand pieces of pipe in twelve weeks. They really had everything running like clockwork—it was an art. At the end of the first week we were informed that the Germans had a week's holiday and the Mill would be shutting down. We were offered a week's dig money or expenses to get home for the week—and I chose to go home. We had to drive from Dussledorf to Darlington, after which I took the train to Inverness! It was a bit of an adventure for me as I was able to view the scenery. It took exactly twenty-four hours. Back in Germany we were in full swing as the mill spewed out lengths of pipe like it was a spaghetti factory. It was a joy to watch the efficient way the Germans went about their work—everybody in the Mill could do three or four different tasks; this was to avoid boredom as it was repetitive work: the workforce were moved around every so often. Another factor was that they only worked a basic week. Maintenance was carried out on the first shift on Monday morning. Production started about midday; then they worked two eight-hour shifts until 10 p.m. on a Friday. They had facilities for having a shower or a bath when their shift finished. I have never seen anything like it in Britain! Nothing stopped production—if they had a breakdown they had plenty spares. The only time lost was while the new parts were being fitted.

My part of the contract finished in six weeks, when I was shifted to the finishing bench. It was quite intriguing, like a big merry-go-round, and also quite an experience. As well as our contract, they were fitting in rush jobs in-between, so the machinery was never idle. The building was fairly old—many times I would sit on my own wondering how many tanks and other war hardware had been produced during the war years. I will never find out, as the Germans were not too keen to discuss the war.

The Germans made our group look inadequate—I have never come across a lazier bunch of people in my life! Our job didn't require us to overtax ourselves; in the first place, we were overseeing the people who were working for the German company, but there were Brits who arrived at work early so that they could grab the jobs that required them to do nothing! They were quite happy to sit around twiddling their thumbs all day while the local guys did the work. I was looked upon as an oddball because I always went to the finishing bench where all the work occurred; but the time flew past as I always had plenty to do.

Midway through the contract the Germans had a long weekend. It was not worth going home so I decided to visit friends who lived in Celle. Norman was a clerk of works attached to the forces. He and Heather, his wife, lived in married quarters with their two daughters. Their home area was Wishaw, but I had got to know them through Norman's sister who lived in Inverness. The train journey from Essen to Hanover was something else—it was Inter City; they charged five marks extra for this service but it was immaculate! Even the female ticket collector was so helpful it was unbelievable; she explained to me that I only had three minutes to get my connection from Hanover to Celle and that the platform was

No 1—all in German but I understood her perfectly. I had a brilliant weekend courtesy of Norman and Heather. A lot of people think I am a bit weird because I am interested in modern history, if there is such a thing, but by that I mean history that happened in my lifetime. The highlight of my visit to Celle was that I was able to visit the museum at Belsen. It was a pretty tame affair—all the literature was in German—and it was really low key. What got me was the shear size of the place! It was estimated that the area on show was only a fifth of the original place. If this is fact, the original place must have been enormous! It was really shocking. The cemetery in Celle was interesting in as much as there were three hundred and fifty graves—all British; they all died about the same time—August 1945. There were no reasons given. Two of the graves contained nurses. I had to return to work on the Monday afternoon but I will always be grateful to Norman and Heather for such an enjoyable weekend.

Our contract in Germany was just about to end. I had spent an enjoyable thirteen weeks and visited many places. I had a go at finding my father's grave in France but failed due to a multitude of reasons, one being that I didn't have the proper address and we never changed any money into Francs; this meant we couldn't use the motorways or fill up with petrol, so the whole visit to France was a disaster as far as I was concerned. The lad who was driving the car could speak fluent French, which was a great help, but try as we may we could not find the cemetery we were looking for. We started to run out of fuel and had to abandon the whole episode. We eventually headed for Belgium, to a place called Du Panne. My friend Maurice had a married daughter there. We booked into a hotel for the night—my only visit to Belgium.

We were sure our contract would finish on the Friday and we could head home, but on the Friday we were ten pipes short of the contractual number; our bosses asked the Germans to work on the Saturday to finish the contract but they refused as it would mean working overtime which was taboo in Germany. It was also a holiday on the Monday so the bosses had to plead with their workers to come in on the Monday to complete our work. At around midday we were complete and allowed to head for home. Maurice and I left Mulheim after midday and caught the ferry at Calais, after which we drove to Sheffield to where Maurice lived. He was kind enough to offer me a bed for the night, as there were no available trains till morning. I arrived in Inverness late on Tuesday evening.

I had been at home for two or three days when I got a phone call asking if I was interested in a job in North Wales working as an inspector on the Conwy Road Tunnel. I was a bit apprehensive, having already sampled life underground. I asked a lot of questions and was assured that there was no underground work—the job was a huge contract building a tunnel across the River Conwy. For anybody not acquainted with that part of the country, the town of Conwy was a walled town with an arch at the exit on the southern end of the town. There was no other way through North Wales except to pass through Conwy, which meant the cars were nose to tail twenty-four hours per day. The big vans had to negotiate the entrance and exit archways—it was a real nightmare of a place. The government decided to grant the money to build a tunnel. The system they used had been tried in Denmark and Singapore, where they built five huge sections of dual carriageway encased in steel. They then dug a trench across the river, and floated the tunnel sections out to the trench where they were sunk in position and joined together. Unfortunately I had left before the actual sections were removed from the Dry Dock, but you can imagine the size of this project, as each section of tunnel weighed thirty three thousand metric tonnes! The sections all had to be watertight so that they could float. This sounded like an interesting challenge so I agreed to take the job. I flew to Manchester and was picked up by the agency boss who drove me to the site at Conwy. As soon as I entered the office I recognised the site supervisor! I had a spent a week in Aberdeen on a paint inspection course and Dave Lockett had been the tutor.

Dave was now the Senior Inspector on this site so I had a headstart, as he was one of the best. As soon as the introductions were over I was given transport into the town to find digs. I was very fortunate to be given accommodation with an elderly Welsh lady and her husband. She had a self-contained summerhouse in the garden that suited me down to the ground. By the time I had the digs sorted out and returned to the site office, our agency boss had left for home. Dave called me into his office where we could have a private chat and he told me he had a problem with his back and could not get around the site very well—so would I be willing to cover for him if need be? Why not help a friend? That's what life is all about!

The Conwy Road tunnel was one of the biggest projects in Europe at that particular time, but sadly the job was a shambles; somebody had raised the money (£285 million) to build this project and awarded the contract to cowboys! I have never witnessed anything like it in my life—it was a disgrace; the first thing that caught your eye was the fact that the men, platers and welders, walked around the site wearing shorts, tee shirts and sunglasses! How they could work like that beats me, but I was only an inspector so what they did was no concern of mine; but if you are an honest person you can't help but notice: most of the guys were from the North East of England and they were all sleeping with local women; then they would have their wives or girlfriends down from Geordie Land for the weekend, when the local girl friends were turfed out until the Monday night, when the Geordie women would go home; then everything would be back to normal till the next visit! It was a home from home situation.

The tunnel was an eye-opener for me. Some of the practices carried out would make your hair stand on end. One of the worst things that got right up my back was the waste. Welding rods are a very expensive commodity, yet down there they would open a packet or tin of rods, use maybe two or three, then walk away and leave them. As soon as it rained the whole pack of rods was ruined and had to be scrapped. Getting guys to do an honest day's work was impossible; the sad part of it was it was good government money they were wasting. My job involved pressure testing the watertight bulkheads; this was done with a soapy water solution and air. I was given a squad of three helpers who did the physical work as required. It was well within our capabilities to do four tests per day, but they worked it in such a way that they did three and let me know that was all they were doing. I had no jurisdiction over them so I just had to be content with three tests.

Around the fourth week I received a bit of a blow when I had word from home that my stepfather had had a stroke—he was seventy-eight. He was a tough old nut so I fully expected him to be on his feet and getting home in a couple of days, but sadly, at 6 a.m. the next morning, I received the dreaded call that told me he had passed away overnight.

The next three days of my life were a bit of a nightmare. Within minutes of receiving the phone call I was on my way to the railway station at Llandudno Junction where I boarded a train for Crewe. I arrived in Crewe around eight-o-clock; from then on it was utter chaos.

During my lifetime I have on many occasions travelled by rail. I have read in the press of people having nightmare journeys. I was about to experience my first one and, to make matters worse, it continued into the return journey. Leaving the train at Crewe, I headed for the information board only to discover it was blank. I had a look around and found a guy in authority and asked what was going on. He informed me they had experienced a train crash the night before and it had knocked out all the signalling equipment, virtually paralysing the British Rail network systems. I explained my circumstances and that I needed to get home as quickly as possible. His advice was to use the local trains, which were still able to function; but it meant that you would maybe have to change at every station. That didn't bother me as long as I was heading north. Eventually I arrived in Edinburgh at the back of 2 p.m. The next train north would be after 4 p.m. so I booked my luggage into the left-luggage kiosk and went for some food. Just before departure time I withdrew my luggage and paid the three-pound fee before heading for the north platform. According to the information board the train was due at approximately twenty past four. Parading up and down the platform was a Norman Wisdom look-alike in a BR uniform and on his hat it said "Platform Supervisor". A middle-aged lady arrived with her luggage and asked this clown if this was the platform for Inverness. He looked at her and said, "Aye, but the train is rinnin twa hoors late." He near caused a riot! There was no mention anywhere that the train was late. A few of the passengers were like me and had withdrawn their luggage presuming the train was on time. He was called a few fancy names but I don't think there was a very active brain so it was like water off a duck's back. I eventually arrived home around eleven-o-clock, shattered.

My next day was an ordeal, as I had to go and look at the old man's remains. He had lived a tough life, having had to work physically all his life for very little in return. I doubt if he ever earned over thirty pounds a week during his working life, but once the family had grown up and flown the nest, I would say he enjoyed himself.

We buried the old man on the Monday. He got quite a good turnout with many of his old friends in attendance. I had to return to Wales on the Tuesday morning, leaving Inverness at ten to eight. I had given my landlady the time—I would arrive back just as it was given to me courtesy of British Rail. We were jogging along nicely through the Badenoch area, a quick stop at Newtonmore, and we were on our way—it is lovely moorland on the outskirts of the village, but only if you view it in the passing. Our train decided to stop in the middle of the moor and two hours after stopping we were *still* viewing the barren hillside with not one bit of information as to why we had stopped! People were starting to get irritated as some of them had appointments in Edinburgh and Glasgow. The train was getting unbearably hot—there was little evidence of air conditioning, and the only way you could get a drink was to pay the inflated prices charged by the trolley operator. The situation was getting grim.

Suddenly we had life among the British Rail employees in the way of an announcement that told us that the reason for the delay was that a goods train had broken down between us and the station at Blair Athol; they had removed our engine and sent it down the line to move the goods train into a siding. It's like something you would watch on Thomas The Tank Engine! The announcer seemed to think he was doing us a favour by letting us know that the engine was on its way back and we should be mobile again within half-an-hour—big deal! We arrived in Edinburgh approximately three hours late. The knock-on effect was that all the connections were missed. Instead of leaving Edinburgh at two-o-clock I managed to get away around four-o-clock. It must have been one of the hottest days in living memory; the air conditioning was not the best and the carriages were stifling hot. We were about an hour out of Edinburgh and had just passed through Carstairs when, low and behold, we ground to a halt! One hour and twenty minutes later we started off again. To this day I have no idea why we were stopped—all I know was that while the train was not moving it was even hotter than before; the sweat was running down people's faces and we had to buy drinks from the expensive trolley. Not one member of British Rail showed face or made an announcement during that delay. I was now seething with rage—it was a total disgrace! By the time I got to Conwy it was near midnight; everywhere was closed and it was impossible to get any food. I was so mad I got my writing pad out and wrote a thirty-eight page letter to British Rail and, believe me, I didn't mince my words! During that year I had used the train a few times and had the tickets in my wallet, so in my letter I enclosed tickets to the value of one hundred and thirty eight pounds. Everybody, especially my wife, told me I would never hear a word from them, but my letter must have had an effect on somebody as I received an apology plus a cheque for the full amount my tickets had cost for that year—very decent of them.

Back at work and we were progressing through the pressure testing. Suddenly one Friday my boss asked me if I would be working on the Sunday. I usually did the seven days, so I asked why he wanted to know. He told me I would be the only man on site as the locals were having a day off and most of the other guys were taking it off as well. I made enquiries why nobody wanted to work and was told there was a christening in Caernarfon on the Sunday and they usually had a big party after the bairn was christened; all the lads were invited and did I want to come along? I declined the invitation and opted to work instead. The site was unusually quiet on that Sunday but I had peace to do my job.

On Monday morning the site seemed unusually quiet. There were one or two more than there were on the Sunday, but something was amiss. The first guy I met was reeking of booze and he had two of the blackest eyes I ever saw on any human being. I asked what had happened and he told me about the christening, saying that afterwards they had a barbeque and everybody got pissed, then fell out. The police had to be called to stop the fighting. He said a good few of the lads wouldn't be at work that day. In fact, it was about Wednesday before we had a full complement back at work, nearly everyone of them sporting black eyes or having areas bandaged. The Caernarfon Christening was some event!

We had now entered the last phase of the pressure testing. A different, more severe test had to be carried out on the watertight bulkheads. Each unit had to float under its own steam. Basically they fitted a pressure gauge to the bulkhead and then pumped compressed air into the chamber until it registered 100 psi. It was then put on hold for a designated period of time; if it remained steady the test was successful. Unfortunately if the pressure dropped they had a leak, which had to be repaired, and the test had to be repeated. As this was the first test of its kind on this project all the top brass were there. The site foreman who was not the most pleasant of people was taking a keen interest; his surname was House—an appropriate Christian name would have been "Shit" because I am afraid that was what he was. Everything was connected up, ready to apply the pressure. Mr House was taking centre stage, the air pressure was applied and nothing happened. Hurrah—we had a leak! It was announced that we had a slight problem and would have to abandon the test, as some adjustments were required. They would let the people know when they were ready to restart.

The following account of what was about to take place was unreal! The project was way over budget by millions. One quote I heard was that it had doubled in price since it was awarded to the contractor. This didn't really surprise me, as the practices that took place were shocking. One other thing I would like to highlight was that when this tunnel was operational it was below the sea, underwater, with thousands of vehicles driving through it twenty-four hours per day, all carrying human beings. The test had failed and they splashed soapy water round the weld seams in the hope that they would find the leak. I knew it was a waste of time, as the pressure was not holding at all; if it had been surface you would have seen or heard it, but the bad news was that it was internal. Mr House called me to one side and, believe this or not, he asked me to turn a blind eye to his next piece of magic: he wanted to fix another gauge on the bulkhead next to the one that was leaking, then pump them up; if they held everything would be okay as the leak would be on the internal plate separating the two boxes. Right away you would have a weak point plus a possible crack, which could propagate causing the whole thing to collapse, maybe not immediately, but with stress and strain it was a real possibility at some time. Anybody with any knowledge of fabrication should have been aware of this. I took a deep breath and gave my answer: "No, you will have to open the box and carry out a repair." I knew there would be ructions—they didn't like to be contradicted. Our man got quite menacing as he threatened to get me run off. I asked him why, reiterating that I wouldn't help him to cheat. I then told him I couldn't care less whether I was run off or not since I could work anywhere in the country since I knew what I was doing; I had been trained on spotting the kind of mistakes he knew very little about. My parting words on my way out were: "I will call in at the resident engineer's office and let him know what's going on; maybe we will both be looking for a job after that."

As I made my way up the side of the dry dock I glanced back to see what was happening. I could see they were getting rigged up to do the job properly. Mr House came over and apologised for his behaviour and asked me to forget everything that had been said; he even asked if I would stay on and witness what they were doing so that they could get the test under way again. I took great pleasure in telling him there was a forty-eight hour delay before we could close off the bulkhead again—just to show him who was boss at the end of the day.

The job was coming to an end and I didn't know how much longer I would get. My mind was made up when I received a phone call from home telling me a local agency had a job for me at home. I phoned that night and was offered a job at Cromarty Firth, twenty minutes from home. I wanted to stay in Wales for two weeks to complete the test programme, but the agency offering me the job put a gun to my head and told me if I couldn't start the following Monday the job would go to somebody else. I had to take this job to get back home; no matter how much I enjoyed the Conwy tunnel job, I needed to be at home, so I managed to give my gaffer nearly a week's notice leaving on the Friday afternoon. They were not exactly happy at my leaving when the contract was nearly finished; in fact, it was a few years before that Agency offered me work again.

Back home my job was oil related work. It was pretty humdrum compared to the huge site in Wales, but at least I was in my own bed every night. The Agent I was now working for had pressurised me to come home right away or I would lose this job. He also promised me at least two years work. It is ironic therefore that the first week I sat around doing nothing, for the job hadn't started; eight weeks later I was called into the contractor's office and told I was surplus to requirements and would be paid off the following week!

What annoyed me about that Agency was that I could have completed the work in Wales before I had terminated my contract—but that's life in the industry I chose to work in. It worked out okay for me in the end, since the Agent I was working for asked if I was interested in Wytch Farm. Scratching my head, I repeated, "Wytch Farm? Where the hell and what's that?" He explained it was a big Gas Gathering station on the south coast of England near Bournemouth. He didn't exactly sound enthusiastic about the place or the job, but advised me to give it a try. First thing about Wytch Farm was the difficulty getting there from Inverness. One had to start off with transport to the airport, then fly to Heathrow, run to the bus station, jump on a coach for Bournemouth, then travel by train to Wareham, and taxi or walk to the village where one could hitch a lift to the site—which was five miles away after all that. Leaving Inverness at 7 a.m., we would be in the office at work around midday.

Wytch Farm was a unique place in many different aspects. It was a gas gathering station, picking up the gas from the field just offshore from Poole harbour. It was a huge site. Normally these sort of places are three or four stories high, but the only reason Wytch Farm was allowed to proceed was if all the structure was kept at tree-top level—environmental rules; so instead of a huge plant reaching up to the sky it was spread out over many acres. That was the first unusual feature about the place. The second thing that you noticed or at least I did was the amount of people wandering about aimlessly. My old boss at Arderseir used to call them "sand dancers"—I am sure they could have got by with half the squad they paid wages to, but that's life.

Wytch Farm was one of the most corrupt places I have ever worked in. There were so many fiddles going on it was unbelievable!

STALAG WYTCH FARM

I had been brought up to believe in honesty. I am married to a lady who hates dishonesty. Indeed, dishonesty was never one of my policies. If you told the truth you could repeat it over and over without any worries! Shortly after arriving at Wytch Farm I was introduced to my supervisor, whose name was Graham. He was a lovely person, possibly highly qualified in his profession, but he didn't impress me as being capable of handling a squad of men. He was too gentle, polite and soft. The animals he was supposed to control had sussed this out and immediately christened him "Granny". I was indebted to him till the day I retired, as he gave me the opportunity to learn a new phase in the oil industry that was to enable me to read drawings relating to pipe work within two weeks of being there.

I had it sussed—the client was B.P. and they were accepting my work without it being checked, even after two weeks after I started on the site. We worked on site for ten hours per day. My rate of pay was £120 a day. If we were behind with paperwork we could carry on and work another three hours a day and we were paid overtime. I worked all the hours going—it was just as well doing that as sitting in the pub every night. We had to submit a time sheet every Monday morning. The first scam at Wytch Farm was explained to me on the Monday morning at the end of my first week: we were to submit a timesheet recording the hours we worked the previous week; they were collected by one of the clerks. When I handed him my timesheet he asked if it was one or two; he had lost me and I asked him to explain. "Well, it's like this—we fill in our timesheet with the correct hours we worked, we hand them to Granny (Graham), he checks them but doesn't sign them; he hands them back to me. If any of the lads missed a shift or any overtime they fill in a second timesheet showing the extra hours. I scrap the one Granny has looked at, then take them to the main office for the manager to sign." I thought to myself, bloody marvellous! I work all the hours going and end up with the same amount of money as these cheating, conniving, lazy buggers! They were screwing the company for hundreds of pounds every week and getting away with it!

The next scam was rather degrading as far as I was concerned. Our contract was for ten days working and four off; to get your time off we had to sneak off early on the Thursday in order to get the Inverness flight at twenty to eight from Heathrow. We were supposed to work the full shift on the Thursday. At lunchtime we would jump over the perimeter fence and, bent double, we would run down the side of the wood where a pre-arranged Mini Bus would be waiting for us. Lying almost flat in the bus, we would speed past the offices on the first leg of the journey home. I dreaded it as at any moment I expected a security man to step out and apprehend us. If you watched the film *The Great Escape* and remember the prisoners running across the open ground crouched double until they were under cover ...—well, that was a similar situation to what we had to face every ten days.

Apart from the scams it was a wonderful job for me. I was more or less my own boss left to do my own thing. I was well respected by the BP site team and, above all, when I finally left Wytch Farm I could work on any type of oil-related job. The main thing was I could work off any kind of drawing, be it Piping or Structural. I had five wonderful months at Wytch Farm, having survived the horrible gales they had that winter 1989/1990. Luckily we were home for our long weekend, so we missed the worst of it.

My job at Wytch Farm was coming to an end. There was word that I was being shifted to another part as the guy on that job couldn't cope—he had a severe laziness problem and just did enough to get by. In the meantime I called home and my wife gave me a Glasgow phone number—an agency required me to contact them A.S.A.P. I called that evening—it was around ten-o-clock; the guy who answered said we knew each other though I hadn't a clue who he was. He wanted me to work for his company at home back in Arderseir and asked if I could come to Glasgow for an Interview. Not possible, as I was attending a wedding my next weekend at home.

My next weekend at home was going to be hectic. I was flying home on the Thursday evening, arriving in Inverness possibly after ten-o-clock; I would need to catch up with any outstanding items on Friday, then go by rail on Saturday to Edinburgh to attend a wedding. I also had another little matter to attend to when I got to Waverly Station in Edinburgh. I had agreed to be interviewed for the job I had been offered over the phone. I thought why not and agreed to meet Bill Rennie, one of the directors of a company called Petrology. I vaguely remembered meeting him a few years previously in Arderseir. He was keen for me to go and work for them. He told me the deal and was quite happy for me to work my notice in Wytch Farm, then start with them in ten days' time. We agreed the deal and I went on to enjoy a lovely day at the wedding, the bride being from Lewis and the groom from Edinburgh. Back to Inverness on the Sunday. I had to catch the flight back to London Monday morning and work my week's notice at Wytch Farm. My present agent was none too happy with me but I had to look after my interests because as soon as they were finished with me I would be dumped. I was pushing myself to the limit—home on the Thursday late, then catch the flight south to Glasgow. Friday morning it was hectic stuff.

Enter into the world of the employment agency! I still try to figure out if I was manager or mother to these guys! It was another eye-opener, but I wouldn't have missed it for the world. I was employed for exactly two years. At the peak I had five hundred men under my wing. Altogether over the two years there were exactly one thousand men that had passed through our office. There were various reason for that. Consider that our client would require a couple of hundred men for a few weeks; then they would pay them off. Sometimes they requested men; we recruited them, sent them to the site, then were told they were no longer required. The men in turn blamed the sub-contractor, usually with the comment that the left hand didn't know what the right hand was doing. At times it appeared that way. During that period the client introduced a drug testing programme where everybody new coming on the site had to be tested during their induction, usually on a Monday morning or afternoon for the nightshift workers. The failure rate was about one in five, but some of them failed themselves as they were under the impression that the test would detect alcohol; so if they had a pint before reporting for work they would go into the toilet cubicle and dip the plastic cup into the toilet pan so their sample was pure water! The nurse knew as soon as it was handed over because the real thing was warm whereas the ordinary water was cold! This also happened with the guys who were genuinely using dope. A couple of amusing incidents regarding the drug thing happened about then. Our client was requiring a supervisor and I was sent a bundle of C.V.s from head office. One of the names was of a guy who had worked at Wytch Farm. I had come across him down there so we put him forward for an interview. He was accepted for the job and told to report for his induction on the Monday morning. Before he left site on the Friday after his interview I called him into the site office and laid it on the line about the drug test and explained that if he took drugs not to bother turning up on Monday. He assured me he was clean and I would have no problem with him and off he went. On the Monday when I arrived at work my first job was to confirm everybody had turned up and get them drug tested; then the client took over and went through the safety induction. This normally lasted for the first half of the shift. Every last detail of how they were supposed to go about the job at the McDermott site was thoroughly explained; they were then kitted out and ready for action after the lunch break. My new supervisor was there in all his glory, even getting the guys who were employed by our agency organised for me as they arrived.

In the early days of the drug testing the samples were sent to Raigmore for analysis. We didn't receive the results until the following day. You could always tell if there were any failures as the client would send for me and the guilty party to tell them they had failed the test and their contract would be terminated immediately. To get back to my new supervisor—when I arrived on site I had about a dozen new starts that morning; my new supervisor had them all lined up as though it were a military operation; he was in full charge! I did my part of the induction and handed my squad over to the client's safety people. I would not see them again unless they had any queries. Tuesday was execution day, normally around eleven-o-clock. Right on cue the phone burst into life—it was one of our client's personnel guys: would I get myself and my new supervisor up to their office? I asked what's up only to be told I must have a good idea what's up—"just appear here shortly!" I had to go on site to find my man. I advised him to take all his belongings with him, as I was certain he wouldn't be back. He looked alarmed as he got in my car, asking me anxiously what the problem was. On explaining his drug test was positive, he started to protest his innocence, querying the methods used for testing the samples—really just squirming and lying his way out of the mess he was in. Our client's representative had no mercy—our man was guilty, end of story! He was not required to carry on working and had to hand in all the equipment. As I transported the guy to the main warehouse I had a chat with him and explained that the drug tests were more or less foolproof and were carried out in the medical laboratory at the local hospital, so to be found guilty he must have smoked cannabis in the past forty-eight hours. He gave me a great spiel that he didn't touch alcohol but got his buzz from having a wee puff at a joint! He said he was so over the moon getting the job with us on Friday that he went home and had a few puffs to celebrate his good luck. At that point I did highlight that I had warned him not to touch drugs over the weekend. He shook his head, muttering to himself, "A ken, a ken!"

The second humorous incident concerning the drug culture happened one afternoon. It was a Thursday, the busiest day of my week, around four-o-clock. I got a phone call to report to the client's personnel office, urgent! As I entered the office everybody had a phone to their ear and it looked like there had been a death. My first thoughts were that there had been a road accident and one of my guys had been seriously hurt or even killed. I asked what was up and eventually was told "Drugs!" It was then explained to me that one of the landladies from a boarding house in the town had called in to say her grandchild had picked up a piece of cannabis in her sitting room and if the company were not prepared to do something about it she was calling the police. I asked what involvement I had in the affair, only to be told that the guilty party worked for the company I represented. My first reaction was to ask the guy's name. I was told it was McLennan. I checked my notebook and told them the guy didn't work for me—I had no McLennans on my books—only to be told we must have as the guy told his landlady he worked for us. Under severe duress I was made to go to the town of Nairn and confront the woman who raised the complaint. I was accompanied by one of our client's personnel people. He knew all about the drug scene so he took charge. I took a step to the rear and let him get on with it. We rang the doorbell of the house bearing the street number we were given, and through the glass door we could see movement. The door was opened by a huge woman with a small child in her arms. She got down to business right away and told us of her dilemma. She explained that the bairn had "picked up this," and produced a piece of toilet paper wrapped round a small round brown object. (I would describe it as looking like a deposit left either by a sheep or a rabbit.) She had picked it up, she said, in the living room first thing that morning, saying that the only person who could have left it was her lodger, McLennan. My colleague took control and sniffed the round object. He looked at it and then confirmed it *was* cannabis. He then showed it to me. I had never seen anything like it before, so I took his word for it. His next comment was that it would be worth about seventy-five quid on the street. He then asked if he could use the phone so he could contact the police. At this point I reneged as I had no intentions of getting involved with any police; furthermore I was certain the guy McLennan had nothing to do with me or the company I worked for. I was shown into the living room while my man phoned the police. Sitting on the couch was the woman's husband; she spoke to him and when he answered I could see he was foreign, either Polish or Czech; he spoke with an eastern European accent. Sitting in the living room with Stan was rather boring as he never acknowledged I was there, but I could see something was troubling him as he was fidgeting about. His wife reappeared and asked if he was all right; he said "no" rather abruptly! She asked him what was wrong and he looked at her and said, "Is it okay if I turn on the telly because we are missing 'Home And Away'?" (The Australian Soap). I thought to myself, here we are in the middle of a drugs heist and he is worried about missing 'Home and Away'—what's the world coming to, I ask you! My mate had now contacted the cops and was in full flight on the phone, telling them the gory details. The next moment he was in the room beside Stan and me, telling me we had to report to the Police Station. I was *not* amused! At the police station I recognised the cop as soon as we stepped in the office: his mother used to be our neighbour! My man handed the cop the piece of Cannabis, and the cop looked at it and said it would be worth about ten quid on the street—clearly it was losing value by the minute! When the police had finished taking the particulars we headed back to the site. As I stepped through the door at least two people shouted, "Bert! That guy McLennan doesn't work for your company—he is with Corries!" I just shrugged and said, "I told you that before we left the site."

Petrology was a smashing company to work for. I enjoyed looking after their employees up to a point, but I was more suited to a more technical type of job. However, I made quite a lot of friends—and a few enemies, of course—but on the whole I didn't have a lot of hassle. One of the guys, Tommy from the Gorbals in Glasgow—Queens Street, I think, was where he stayed with his "Burd"—was a lovely guy as far as I was concerned. He never gave me any hassle. One payday he arrived in the office and told me he was taking the Burd to Turkey for two weeks holiday but he had a problem—he needed to get two hundred Bar out of the bank. It would clean out his account but he would have seven hundred on his hip for the holiday. He asked me if I would go to the hole in the wall and use his card—he would give me his pin number. I was not too keen but, anyway, him being Tommy, I agreed. When I got to the bank the hole in the wall was not in use but they would give you the money at the counter. I had a dilemma—what if they asked my name? I could be in trouble. Anyhow, so as not to let my man down I went ahead. The sweat was off when they handed me a portable machine to enter my pin number. I got the money, no bother, and handed it to the owner. He was over the moon and told me he was going for a few pints with the boys and heading down the road in the morning. Tommy finished up having too many pints. He got very drunk in Nairn. The next day some of Tommy's mates called at the office to let me know he had been mugged on his way home from the pub. They had cleaned him out! He had never felt a thing. He managed to borrow enough money to get away on his holiday, nevertheless, but he had a huge debt to face up to when he returned.

Exactly two years to the day I started, my job with Petrology ended. There was a bit of a downturn in the work situation. I was lucky and managed to get started back at my own trade as an Inspector. For the first time I was going to work at Nigg. It was okay—I knew a lot of the boys working there, so I had no problems work wise.

Unfortunately my health was playing up. I had developed high blood pressure and I was not aware of the problem until I had to undergo a medical at Nigg. My B.P. was through the roof—they were not going to allow me to start. Eventually the charge nurse told me to lie down on the couch in the small ward in the medical centre; she would re-test me in half-an-hour and if there was no improvement I had no job. There is always a funny side to most crises—one of the nurses was exceptionally good looking. After about ten minutes she came into the room and asked me how I was feeling; then she started to take my pulse! So there I am, trying to get my B.P. down to an acceptable level with this gorgeous nurse more or less holding hands with me as she checked my pulse—you canna win! Nevertheless the treatment was successful and the next B.P. check was acceptable with the proviso that I made an appointment to see my G.P. I fought a battle with high B.P. for the next eight years, changing medication many times with no success. I finally asked to see a specialist. Later on I will give the final outcome of this problem. My contract at Nigg lasted nine months. It was okay except for the hour each way when the roads were very demanding; we had to travel in the height of the tourist season—it was murder going on the night shift! Over the years there were numerous fatal accidents.

The oil industry was going through a bad patch. Work was not so plentiful unless you were prepared to go abroad to places like Brazil, or even Russia; they were too far away for me. My high blood pressure also caused me a problem inasmuch as I developed a fear of heights, which included flying. The next couple of years of my working career were a bit unsteady as the work was really starting to dry up. I was managing to tick over but had spells where there were no offers. Then one day we were visiting a friend on the Black Isle. She asked if I would be interested in working for a contractor who carried out all sorts of jobs, i.e. fencing, draining, building sheds, and he wintered hundreds of sheep. He offered me casual work. We also had an agreement that if I were offered a job with an oil company I was free to go.

So started a friendship that lasted until my friend's untimely death six years later. Working with Davie McKenzie was an experience—there was nothing he couldn't turn his hand to. Once he found out I was fairly handy he used me as his welder, joiner and any other jobs he could make some money from. His main source of work was fencing: he had his own sawmill and produced all his own material. Unfortunately Davie had fallen victim to the saw miller's disease and allowed his hand to get too close to the lethal saw, which resulted in his hand being nearly totally disabled; but he was hardy and very few chores proved too much for him. Being totally obsessed with the Highlands, I was in my element working for Davie as we roamed all over, working in places like Torridon. Tourists pay a fortune to visit that part of the world. We went there every day for weeks removing redundant telegraph poles. The rain was sometimes horrendous but the wonderful views compensated for the rain. I could have spent the rest of my working career doing the type of work Davie did. As well as Torridon, we were in Lochcarron, The Great Glen and all over Ross-shire; then in the summer we had the harvest at his croft so the work was varied as well as far-flung.

During my spells with old Davie I had some wonderful times. The variety of jobs he carried out and some of the marvellous places we worked in made it a pleasure to be associated with the man. He was jack-of-all-trades and was highly depended on by people from all over the Highland area. We had some great laughs! The only thing that wiped the smile off your face was the wages—I had got so used to earning high wages and what I earned with a contractor would barely pay my income tax in the oil industry; but it was lovely to get away from the rat race. That summed up the oil game: with my friend Davie I only worked forty hours a week; in the oil contracts it was often double that amount of hours. I was still picking up work in the oil industry. As long as I could get at least twenty weeks a year I could make reasonable wages. Some of the jobs were different and a new challenge.

The year was 1994 and the spring of that year changed my life forever. From the first day I arrived in Inverness I had been a keen supporter of Inverness Thistle Football team; for over thirty-five years I seldom missed a home game if I could at all manage. Suddenly the talk of the town was amalgamation with our greatest rivals, Caledonian, and entry into the Scottish League. To the majority it was the only way forward. I never really agreed with the decision but when you are in the minority you might as well keep your trap shut. Before the final game arrived I decided to write a lament/poem. There were all sorts of meetings and arguments for and against the union of the two Inverness teams. I never really got involved but some of the dirt that was cast up caused a rift between rival supporters that never really healed. Quite a few were like myself and actually gave up supporting the local team, which was a shame, really, as I enjoyed my football. I still watch the game but it stopped giving the buzz I used to get years ago—hence the reason I am now an armchair supporter, often reading a book and only looking at the television when I hear them shouting a goal has been scored! You see it that often re-played, they are never missed; maybe this is the reason why I can read at the same time as the football is on!

Inverness Thistle had a small social club in the centre of town. The lady steward, Helen, was a great organiser, doing all sorts of social evenings. We had many good nights there, at Burn's Suppers and various fund raising evenings. One of Helen's social evenings did nothing for your head; the next morning there were very few who attended that didn't waken without a severe hangover! The social club is also gone and recently I saw an application in the local paper for permission to build flats in the old social club premises. Suddenly the last game to be played at Kingsmills Park was upon us—it happened on Saturday 14th May 1994, and our opponents were Lossiemouth. I have a feeling the score was 3-1 in our favour, but I am not really certain. I have the final programme giving all the statistics, everything except the last score. I can even chart the first game I watched the Jags play; it was against Peebles Rovers in the Scottish Cup season 1955/56. We drew at Kingsmills Park and got beaten in the re-play; that was the start of a long and enjoyable association with the now defunct Inverness Thistle Football Club. Over the years I made many friends through my attending the matches. We had great success during the season 1971/2/3, winning the league two seasons on the trot, but we had great players. One of the outstanding players I ever watched was Charlie Duncan, still involved in the game as manager of Fraserburgh. Ian Cummings had a football brain second to none; there were others in that team who were exceptional and a joy to watch. Our wingers, Tichy Black and Tony Fraser, stars of pure magic. Our forwards, Ian Stephen and Jonnie Cowie, possibly still hold the goal-scoring record for a season; then there's my old mate Dave Milroy, as good a centre half that ever graced the Highland League.

AS THE END DRAW'S NEAR

THE END OF THE SEASON IS DRAWING NEAR,
EXTINCTION FOR THE JAG'S HAS BEEN ACCEPTED I FEAR.
AS THE FLOODLIGHTS GO OUT AT KINGSMILLS PARK,
INVERNESS THISTLE WILL FADE INTO THE DARK.

THE END OF AN ERA, SOME FOLKS SAY,
IN THE PRESENT DAY CLIMATE THEY HAVE HAD THEIR
DAY.
FOR THIRTY-FIVE YEARS I HAVE WATCHED THEM PLAY,
FOR ME THE FINAL GAME WILL BE A SAD DAY.

I'D SIT IN THE STAND, OR STAND ON THE TERRACING,
AS OFTEN AS NOT IT WAS BLOODY WELL PERSHING.
THROUGH SUN, RAIN, HAIL AND OFTEN THICK SNOW,
AT HALF TIME TO THE HEATHMOUNT WE'D GO,
A FEW HEFTY DRAMS WOULD HELP YOU TO THAW.

NEWLY RECHARGED AND BURTSING WITH POWER,
"COME ON JAG'S, GET INTO THIS SHOWER!"
OVER THE YEARS I WATCHED SOME GREAT GAMES,
SO MANY PLAYERS I HAVE FORGOTTEN THEIR NAMES.

TO GO TO KINGSMILLS WAS ONE OF MY HOBBIES,
WE ALWAYS HAD BANTER WITH THE PATROLLING BOB-
BIES.
THERE WAS ALWAYS SLAGGING WITH THE RIVAL FANS,
ARGUMENTS OFTEN GOT OUT OF HAND.

WHAT OF RENATO WITH HIS BRIDIES AND PIES,
TALK OF A MERGER BROUGHT TEARS TO HIS EYES.
WHAT OF OUR PARK, PAINTED BLACK AND RED,
AND THE HARDY SUPPORTERS WHO STOOD IN THE
SHED?

THE GROUND WILL BE SOLD TO WEALTY FAT CAT'S
WHO WILL BUILD PRIVATE HOUSES OR PENSIONERS
FLATS.
ALL I HAVE LEFT IS MY CLUB BADGE AND TIE,
AS I STAND BY AND WATCH THE JAGS DIE.

OVER THE YEAR'S THEY CAUSED ME SOME STRIFE,
WHEN I PREFERRED KINGSMILLS TO SHOPPING WITH
THE WIFE
MY SATURDAYS WILL NEVER, EVER BE THE SAME,
MY MATE WON'T CALL, "IT'S SETTERDAY—THE JAGS ARE
AT HAME!
"ARE YEA GAN UP THE HILL TO WATCH THE GAME?"

One of my main sources of entertainment ceased to exist the day the Thistle played their last game. It was as though something had died. I could no longer generate interest in the new set-up. We are on the verge of entering the Scottish League but it is very doubtful if I will become a supporter ever again.

I was bobbing and weaving on the job's front that year (1994). I picked up a rather interesting contract that only lasted a couple of months; but, again, it was different. I had submitted my C.V. to a small local agency and had more or less forgotten about it when out of the blue I received a call asking if I were available to go to the Isle of Lewis to work for the Hydro Board. Their Power Station in Stornoway was fuelled by diesel and they needed to renew the pipelines under the Quay at the harbour. This was where the tanker docked and pumped the fuel to the station. There were other small bits and pieces to be done, but the stainless steel pipelines were my main job. I ended up doing everything, including my own discipline, which was welding; then there was painting, and safety, such as checking the scaffold was safe to make sure there was no fuel spillage when we removed the redundant pipe; then they added the environment which included the harbour. It was a brilliant job for me. I was flown over on Monday morning, then home on Friday evening. One fascinating aspect about Stornoway was the fact that all the big airliners pass over a radio beacon on the island; so middle of the afternoon they would start appearing over the horizon in their hundreds! On a clear day the amount of air traffic was unbelievable! After passing the beacon they headed off to their intended destination—quite a sight. My time in Stornoway was short and sweet, eight weeks to be exact, but I made a few pounds to keep me going to my next job.

The next couple of years saw me in steady employment as a Senior Inspector, mostly on Pipeline work. It was long hours but we had most weekends off and I was home every night. McDermott, now known as Barmac due to the amalgamation with Brown and Root at Nigg, had opened up a new Pipeline facility and they had over a year's work. They were carrying out a training exercise as well as trying to carry on production, so it was pretty hectic. Pipeline work can be pretty monotonous as it is pretty repetitive, but we had some wonderful times at Arderseir. The client's inspectors on one of the contracts were, to say the least, more suited to being gangsters than working for an upmarket Oil Company! Every weekend, when they arrived back at work, they had some sort of loot to sell—watches, tee shirts and other items most likely off the back of a lorry. One of the guys who would be middle-aged seemed to be the ringleader. One Wednesday he called in to my office and said he was off home as he had a court appearance on the Friday and he didn't expect to be back for a few months. Thinking it was a road traffic offence, I asked what he had done. When he told me I could hardly believe my ears! He had been involved with the theft of a fifty thousand pound lorry load of whisky! Frank had been the driver. He was sentenced to nine months in jail. On the Monday morning he phoned from the jail to remind us to fill in his timesheet so that he would get his last weeks' wages. He had no shame!

That same year I managed to land another interesting job working for my friends at Petrology. My job was recruiting welders to work on offshore contracts in Norway. Every different aspect of work I carried out made my C.V. look rather good, so I was keen to try as many different disciplines as was possible. The fact that I was quite well known was also a factor that helped to land work. I was based in the Petrology office block in Clydebank. I travelled down from Inverness on Monday and home on Friday. Half my day would be spent in the office contacting welders on the phone. This could be quite frustrating, as they would agree to travel to the test centre, which had a limited number of places available, and then fail to appear. This often meant that there were spaces at the test centre idle. They were usually at a premium so it did try your patience at times.

The second part of my day would be attending the test centre, which was situated at the opposite end of the city. By the time you sat in traffic jams, a good part of the day would be wasted. I enjoyed my stint in Clydebank and sadly had to leave due to circumstances outwith my control.

As was the norm in the oil industry, every six months or so you would update your C.V. and circulate it round the various companies in the hope they would offer you work. At that time the work was fairly scarce. I had thoughts of getting out of the oil game but none of the local employers were interested in you if you had worked within the oil industry: too many of them had been let down by people whom they had employed, possibly trained in a new skill and as soon as there was a new contract awarded to one of the construction yards they upped sticks and were away. My luck held out on the employment front and over the next two years I had more or less steady employment working on various Spool bases at Evanton, Arderseir and Leith.

Around this time the big topic within the Oil Industry was the fact that Lord Cullen was conducting an inquiry into the fatal accident that caused the Piper Alpha to explode, causing one hundred and sixty-eight men to perish. One of them was well known to me and I had talked to him in Inverness on the Sunday before it happened. The Cullen report cost millions of pounds and he made various safety recommendations. All the new rules were implemented relating to safety, costing the industry millions. The Alexander Keilland was another avoidable disaster, caused through people who had never been properly trained to work on steel. Every accident can more or less be traced back to carelessness, lack of knowledge/training, and often ignorance.

Shortly after I posted out my most up-to-date C.V. I received a phone call from one of the Barmac guys who had received a copy. We were well known to each other but the news he gave me just about caused me to collapse! I could not believe what he was saying, especially the fact that the government had just spent a fortune on the Lord Cullen report: this guy was telling me that Barmac were closing down their Quality Control Department as such, and they would no longer be employing Inspectors. The production Supervisors would be responsible for their own quality. I was unsure whether to laugh or cry; more than half the people supervising had very little idea of what quality meant. They had never been trained for it and their knowledge of drawings was limited; again, they were never trained, so how this was ever allowed to happen I will never understand. I am sure this will not go down well with the people I worked with. But if there were still an oil construction business in Scotland I am almost certain there would soon be another major tragedy in the North Sea—because I witnessed things on the last rig I worked on that were downright dangerous. Accidents only happened because the guys in charge had not received enough training. I had no problem with the closure of the Quality Control division since I was qualified to do all disciplines and was more highly qualified than some of the people I worked for.

My wife and I had been married forty years. We had a bit of a celebration, and then decided to have a big holiday. As neither of us are keen flyers or sun worshippers, we decided on a coach tour round Eastern Europe. It lasted fifteen days.

Our geographical location proved yet again to be a bit of a drawback, since we had to be in Perth for 3 a.m. to start the first leg of the journey that ended in Portsmouth some fifteen hours later—for our ferry crossed to Le Havre.

Our first day on the Continent we drove through France and Germany till we reached the town of Mannheim for our first overnight stay. In the evening we went to Heidelberg, a beautiful old city. Unfortunately it was getting dark so we never managed to see the full beauty of the place. Next morning early we left to drive to Austria. Our hotel was seven miles from Vienna. The night we arrived at the hotel we were supposed to visit the Prater Wheel, but it was so wet we stayed in the hotel. There were two Dutch Coaches in the same hotel, so we had a party. There was a local accordionist playing music, and one of our party from Glasgow (where else?) asked if he could play *"Yea canna shove yir Granny affa bus!"* The man couldn't understand him so our Glaswegian sung it unaccompanied! The Dutch gave him a standing ovation!

The next day we spent an enjoyable time visiting the city of Vienna. We had an early night, as our next day was a long haul through Austria and Hungary to Lake Ballaton, which is a holiday resort. Hungary was quite a fascinating place with a lot of medieval castles; they were trying to promote the tourist industry so there were lots of modern buildings like the place in which we were staying. We had three memorable days before we were due to drive through Slovakia to our next destination, which was Krakow in Poland. For some reason that was never explained to me we were not allowed to buy food in Slovakia. It was the only country where our passports were stamped. We had to buy a pack lunch in Hungary and were allowed one stop so that we could eat. Our scheduled stop was at the top of the Tartra Mountains, an area that was being developed into a ski resort. Slovakia was the most beautiful country I have ever had the good fortune to travel through: the mountains started just beyond the grass verge at the roadside and sloped upwards into the sky with lovely green foliage. As we reached the brow of the mountain, where we were to stop and eat, the first sign to greet us was a Big Mac establishment. We were allowed to buy refreshments at the restaurant beside the car park, but the woman would only accept Deuchmarks or Sterling; they didn't want any of their own worthless muck! I bought three glasses of lager and a white wine and it was less than £1.25. When we finished eating and drinking our refreshments we all toddled off to the toilet. Standing at the door was the lady who had served our drinks, waiting to charge an entrance fee for the toilet!

Our next destination—Poland—was a cultural shock! It was like being in Scotland around the time the war finished. Everywhere there were horses and carts and a few very old beat up cars. It was fifty years behind the times—very poor people and lots of children and adults begging in the main cities. One of my interests in life is the war—in fact, both world wars. Part of our tour in Poland, if we wished, was to visit the site of the Concentration Camp at Auschwitz. This was one of the most awesome places I have ever visited—it is so grim and gruesome, a lot of the people on our coach could not continue round the place. For the Polish tourist board it is one of their biggest earners—the day we were there I counted over thirty coaches. Less than three miles away there is another camp where the female prisoners were taken; you don't hear a lot about it but I can assure people this place is just as gruesome as Auschwitz: this one is called Birkenau. Both places are preserved just as they were the day the inmates were liberated.

We left Poland with its rather ancient culture and headed for The Czech republic. It was more into the twentieth century, but still a lot of poverty was in evidence. We toured some wonderful old palaces and castles and of course viewed the Bohemian crystal. We left the Czech republic early in the morning as we had a long drive across Germany to our overnight stop at Metz in France. We were on the road for at least twelve hours with a stop for half-an-hour at Nurnbergring where the motor racing circuit is in Germany. One night in Metz and we were off early morning. The next stop was rather special for me as I always wanted to visit Paris and finally I had achieved my goal. We were only there for five hours but we managed to sail along the Seine passing the beautiful bridges and buildings that form along either bank of the river. We had enjoyed fourteen wonderful days that included scenery and marvellous weather. We never experienced rain except one evening in Austria; from when we left home nothing but brilliant sunshine! As we headed for the ferry at Le Havre we were brought back to reality when we witnessed a horrific motorway pile-up. Thankfully it had occurred earlier in the day and on the opposite carriageway from where we were travelling. It happened near Dunkirk in the early morning fog. We never found out how many casualties there were but somebody mentioned that there were thirty-three vehicles burned out. We could see the skeletons of lorries, cars and buses being cleared away as we passed—not a pleasant ending to a wonderful holiday.

Back in Portsmouth and reality—rain, muggy weather at 6 a.m.! We had another full day travelling before we reached home. On the Monday it was back to work. The next couple of years I picked up work mostly at the spool bases, but it was getting harder all the time. I decided to apply for a position as a welding supervisor with Barmac. I needed to work and I wanted to be at home. I sent in my C.V. and the most of the guys in charge had worked alongside me for the best part of twenty years, but they didn't have the guts to reply to my application for work. Through the grapevine I got the message that I had been blacklisted for some obscure reason. It made me think that nobody really knew what I had done for McDermott's over the years; even though I say this myself, I was probably one of the most conscientious, loyal workers ever employed by that company.

As luck would have it, I was in Inverness one morning and happened to bump into the site Superintendent. He asked me where I was working, and on telling him I was unemployed at the minute he asked why I was not working for them, as they needed all the experienced supervisors they could get. I explained that for some reason I was blacklisted and nobody would talk to me! As he said goodbye he said he would have a word with his understudy and for me to give him a phone and he was sure they would have a job for me. When I returned home that day there was a phone call waiting for me with a job so I didn't need to depend on Barmac at the moment.

My latest job was on the Arderseir site on the spool base. This would last for about three months. I made enquiries about why I was being ignored for a job but even guys who I classed as mates would not tell me anything. Some of them had been given a start on the managerial ladder by myself but that seemed to be forgotten. One thing about me—I never let anything get me down! I knew I could work if Barmac didn't want me; there were plenty others who did. Near the end of my spell at the spool base a couple of the younger guys who had got themselves into management positions asked me if I would be interested in working as a Supervisor. I explained that I was willing but that somebody (I have a good idea who) had blacklisted me, but if they could get me a job I would make sure I didn't let them down. The younger lad, Jimmy, was dead keen to get me in his squad so he started the ball rolling and before I knew it I had been given an interview. (I was, after all, one of their best-known ex-employees.)

The interview I felt was a bit of a fiasco but in the end I must have satisfied someone as I was accepted for a job. I had actually dropped a few rungs down the ladder but that didn't bother me a lot. I had work and was getting home every night. As well as supervising a squad of welders I was still called upon to carry out inspection on riser lines; this is an important part of most oil contracts. I had quite a wide experience of riser lines and pipelines, but I was appalled at some of the antics that were used on that particular job. For a start I don't think the people supervising or managing the job realised that the Department of Industry had a big input into the manufacture of riser lines; after all, these was the high pressure pipes used to draw the oil from the well to the production platform, so special rules applied to that part of the job. I was not a popular person when I rejected the first part of the job. I was asked to pass and sign my name, verifying that the job had been done in accordance with the specification required. It was even more shocking when the manager was overheard telling his men not to pay any heed to me—he would soon overrule my decision. Thankfully somebody with a bit of knowledge told them to start from scratch and get it right this time round.

My initial contract was for six months, but that soon passed and before long I had been working for a year; then I was transferred to the Nigg operation working on the huge Elf Elgin Platform. It was a bit of a challenge but I knew all the guys working there so that made all the difference. I was due a summer vacation. One of my ambitions was to visit the French Riviera, so we made enquiries about a coach tour and booked for a ten-day holiday.

The French Riviera was all that I had read about it. We were not too enamoured with the town of Monte Carlo, but the rest was worth going to see. The views were brilliant. The motorway that runs the complete length of the coast from Marseille to the Alps is a piece of engineering worth seeing on its own. They just tunnelled through the rock, sometimes only for a few yards, and the next stretch would be over a mile. We have nothing like it in Britain. Then there was the railway! This also ran along the magnificent coastline at fairly reasonable rates. We were staying in a small town between Monte Carlo and Nice called Beaulieu-Sur-Mar, right on the beach surrounded by millions of pounds worth of Yachts. In the evening we would go to a small pub on the main street where we got friendly with a huge Dutchman and his wife, who were retired. He had been head of the Dutch fire service, a lovely down-to-earth big man who enjoyed a joke and a laugh. The day we left to come home he was standing at the end of the street so that he could wave us good-bye.

Back at work and soon it was Christmas, and we were still employed. That was eighteen months and no definite word of being paid off. But the rumour-mill was working overtime, and by March the rumours were beginning to come true. The main body of workers were being placed on thirty days notice as per the agreement of the yards; it was a very unstable way of working as you ended up with a different squad of men every week: just as you were getting used to one squad some of them would be on the list to go; some of the guys played on this and it was difficult to get an honest day's work out of them. I was on my final thirty days' notice and would definitely be getting paid off on the 29th June 2000. I received a pay off cheque of around two thousand pounds and out of the blue I got word of a job at the spool base at Arderseir, starting a week after I was paid off—so I was all geared up to get some work done at home before starting my new job.

IT'S ONLY A THIN LINE

I had an appointment at Raigmore Hospital about my Blood Pressure where I was examined by a Specialist and given yet another pill. At work Barmac also gave me a medical a couple of weeks before I was paid off. Neither of these people found me to have any life-threatening problems. The week before I was made redundant I had wakened at 3 a.m. with pains in my chest but put it down to indigestion. I had a couple of Aspirin and a cup of tea and felt fine. I was ready to go to work, leaving home at 5.45 a.m, my last Sunday morning before I got paid off.

As I walked the gangplank to get on the Rig I experienced the same pain again. This time I had a glass of very cold water and felt fine again. Because of what I was to experience that weekend or early the following week, I can't more or less remember exactly what happened on the Sunday, which was the 3rd July 2000. It was the final of the European Cup featuring France against Italy. I remember watching it and because of what was to follow it is very clear in my mind. Italy was winning 1-0 and I remember saying if they won the cup it would be sin because they were the most defensive team in the tournament. Suddenly, with very little time left, France scored the equaliser. I am sure everybody in Inverness must have heard the shout I let out! We now had a game on our hands! The Italians could no longer sit and defend. France scored again, possibly in extra time—I can't remember but from a personal point of view I felt justice had been done. After the game was over I headed for bed, feeling okay. I fell asleep and as far as I can remember slept soundly. I awoke at approximately 3 a.m.—and lo and behold, my old friend the pain in my chest and down my arms was back! I tried my past remedy—a couple of Aspirins and a cup of tea. This time my cure was not working. The pain was getting worse by the minute, until I could no longer bear it—especially down my arms was agony! At around 5 a.m. I roused my wife who immediately called my daughter who lives ten minutes away. She was at our place in minutes and called a doctor and an ambulance. (The ambulance arrived in minutes, but four years later we are still waiting for the doctor to appear!) Before five thirty I was being hooked up to all sorts of monitors and drips. Once I was settled the little Indian doctor came to my bed and asked if I

171

knew what had happened to me. I answered no, as it never entered my head that I had suffered a heart attack. He pointed to the monitor and said it was still happening—he could tell by the trace on the screen.

It didn't really sink in until the head surgeon arrived later that morning. He explained that I had suffered a myocardial infraction, which meant my heart would more than likely have sustained some damage; but they would have to carry out a scan to assess how much damage had occurred. I still didn't realise that my working days were over; in fact, a good amount of my life came to a sudden halt that fateful morning. I had all sorts of medicine pumped into me to try and clear the blockage that had caused my heart attack. It was deemed to have been caused by cholesterol. I spent four days in the high dependency unit before I was able to go to a mainstream ward. I had a chat with the consultant and he more or less told me that my fitness for my age probably saved my life. It's funny that dying never crossed my mind—all I could think about was to get better and carry on living as best as I could! Of course, lying in bed you don't really realise just how unable you are to carry on as before; once the medication kicks in and causes all sorts of dizzy spells, the truth starts to sink in. My spell in hospital lasted eleven days, but I had the best of care and attention. I had an ultrasonic scan and the man who did this assured me that the damage to my heart didn't look too bad.

MY HEART ATTACK

I'll never forget the excruciating pain,
Hope never to experience the same again.
In Raigmore flat on my back,
Having suffered a heart attack.

A Myocardial Infarction, the surgeon said,
"Pretty severe, you could have been dead.
We will try and prevent further ills,
Just follow the instructions on the boxes of pills."

In my ward a monitor with green flashing light,
As I lay and pondered my latest plight.

The doctor came in and soon revealed all,
My blood level showed too much cholesterol.

You get the best attention in the I.C.U.
Waited on, hand and foot by the angels in Blue.
Then the fight begins to get back on your feet,
Plenty exercise, plenty sleep,"Oh watch what you eat!"

It fairly plays havoc with your former lifestyle,
I now spend my time walking mile upon mile.
Instead of heading to the pub for a game of darts,
I go exercising and walking trying to keep a healthy heart.

On my third day in the I.C.U. ward I was transferred to a single room in the main hospital. I was feeling okay. I had argued with the nurses in the intensive care over the use of the bottle when bursting for a pee: I could not use the bloody thing when lying down or sitting up! I had to be standing up which the nurses frowned upon, as you were supposed to do as you were told. I realised how weak I was the first time I was allowed out of bed. One of the side effects of my medication was dizziness, which was horrible. Unfortunately, four years on, and I still have dizzy turns when I bend down and get up too quickly. But be thankful—I had escaped a major illness without any major damage, like being paralysed or any of the other horrors that are associated with heart attacks and strokes.

When on my own I could try and sort my life out. Thinking back, I had been working for forty-seven years and in all that time I only ever remember being late twice, and both times were drink related, such as, on one occasion, wetting the baby's head. I had never been reprimanded for my work or conduct, and most of my employers would have rehired me, as quite a few did over the years. The vital statistics were that I had been in fifty-three different jobs during my career; one I stayed in for sixteen years. The truth is, my tally was nearer sixty, as a few of the jobs I only stayed about a day—I didn't count them as being employed. I never really claimed dole money unless it was in my own interests; sometimes it was convenient and it made sure your card was franked.

Eleven days after being admitted to hospital I was released with instructions to take things easy. Being a person who had to do everything at sixty miles an hour, it was difficult to toe the line and follow the instructions. Within ten days my grass needed to be cut so I got my daughter to ask the surgeon if it would be okay to do so. His reply was to do what I felt. I was capable of doing it, but cut half one day and finished it off the next. I was also walking much further than was recommended before I should have, but I felt good and never overtaxed myself.

My returning to work was never discussed, but I knew in myself that I would probably never be fit enough to do what I had done in pre-heart attack days. My biggest enemy was and still is tiredness; sometimes it gets so bad I have to sit down and have a sleep—but again it is a small price to pay for being alive. A few weeks afterwards, you start getting your act together again, which means strict food, watching your weight, plus miles of walking—then rest. You are asked back to hospital to have a session on the treadmill; you start off at a fairly slow speed; then it's increased until you more or less beg them to stop! I did well on it—I can't remember how long, but the medical people seemed surprised at the time I recorded.

I was still two and a half years from retiring. Jess was retired but my income had dropped from five hundred a week to seventy-two—not exactly an amount that would lend itself to living in luxury! I had a private pension but to take it early could incur a penalty when I reached sixty-five; but I have a brilliant adviser who managed to pull some strings and I received my pension without penalty. We were now on a more solvent plane once again, so to cheer myself up I went out and bought a new car, the second such purchase I had made in my lifetime, my first being a Hillman Imp in the early nineteen seventies. My latest model was a Skoda, bought for less than five thousand pounds. Four year on I still have it and it runs magnificently. Shortly after buying the Skoda, I gave my middle granddaughter a lift into town. She shut the door and walked away. I said to her she would need to push down the door lock. Making a gesture with her thumb, she said, "Have you not got central locking? Looking at her, I replied, "My dear, it's a Skoda—you're lucky to get four seats in it, never mind central locking!" The two of us had a good laugh about it.

During the first eight weeks after being released from hospital you are invited to attend a physiotherapy class at the hospital one afternoon weekly; when this is finished it is left up to yourself to keep up the exercise. I still did some stretching exercises and walked for miles, but it was not the same as doing it under supervision, so I was delighted when a group of the people with heart problems decided to form a club, calling themselves Inverness Bravehearts! We are still active and meet weekly for an hour's exercise and, of course, you get friendly with other people the longer you are together.

Our lifestyle had completely been turned on its head. I tried to carry on as normal as possible. My heart is damaged—the percentage of damage is a mystery. It is about the only question the surgeon could not answer. I now am aware of just how far I can go and also the tasks that put a strain on my heart—two of the worst being raking the lawn with the wire rake and brushing the slabs with the deck scrubbing broom; so those are two jobs I avoid like the plague. The rest of my year was spent taking it relatively easy. I made a few bird nesting boxes, tiled the bathroom and decorated my bedroom—jobs that I found to be within my capabilities. I also joined the gym and most mornings in the winter I spent on the exercise machines.

Having plenty time on my hands, I had time to think over the things I should have done but never got round to doing. One of the most important to me was that I had never visited the cemetery that held my father's remains. I had tried ten years previously, but due to unforeseen circumstances I had been unable to find the place. One thing that I find frustrating when abroad is that we Scots can't speak any other language than English! How I wish I could speak French and German, but can't, and am now probably too old to learn—but you never know.

It was six months since my heart attack. I was feeling fairly good although I could tell that I was not in the same state of health that I had been in pre-heart attack days; but I was lucky—I am sure I had used up my nine lives and two of them had been life threatening. I decided before it was too late that I would get to France and visit the cemetery where my father is buried. But whom do I contact? I wrote to the War Graves Commission and they sent me brochures of companies who did tours of the war cemeteries; but they were very expensive and all started from the Midlands of England, which meant that, being resident in Inverness, we would have an overnight stay involving more expense.

I had been a member of the British Legion for many years so I decided to write to them and ask if they knew of any organisation leaving locally that visited the war cemeteries. I posted the letter and forgot about it. It was still fairly early in the year, possibly the end of February, while sitting watching the television when, one afternoon, I was aware of a gentleman approaching the front door. I recognised him as being a prominent member of the British Legion committee. When I opened the door he said, in true Invernessian dialect, "Oh! It's yersel—did you write this letter?" The man on our doorstep was Jackie McLennan. Jackie was fairly well known to me as he did a lot of work for the British Legion social club selling tickets and generally helping to run the bingo etc.

I invited Jackie in and, as is customary and in accordance with Highland Hospitality, offered him a dram! In my house you get a choice—Malt or cooking! We got down to the business of my letter to the Legion; it had been handed over to Jackie at a committee meeting. To explain the situation: there is a sadly depleted Association that makes a yearly pilgrimage to France and Holland to visit historical sites of interest. A lot of the places are to do with the first and second world wars. This is the N.V.A.—Normandy Veterans' Association. I have to confess that I had never heard of them until my friend Jackie appeared at my door. To be accepted as a fully-fledged member you had to have taken part in the Normandy offensive during the battles in June 1944. Jackie explained to me that they were going to North West France that particular year—2002. He was aware that there were empty seats on the coach. If I got in touch with the Chairman he would be able to say if they could visit the area my father is buried in. Jackie phoned the chairman there and then and told him my story. I also spoke to the man and told him I had all the maps and information I needed to get to Longueval cemetery. We agreed that I would send the bumph that I had received from the War Graves Commission; he would then confirm if they were going anywhere near where I wanted to visit. Within days I had a reply stating that it would be no problem stopping at the cemetery, which is in the Arras/Albert area of France; all I had to do was pay a deposit to make sure of my seat on the coach and everything else would be taken care of. We were going for eight days, staying in a hotel in a small village near Epernay, which is in the heartland of the champagne country—places I had never heard of. When it comes down to the nitty-gritty of life we don't really know an awful lot.

The weekend before leaving for France I had an invitation to attend a school reunion in a small school near Banff. It was over fifty years ago that I attended that school, but the whole of my family were attending so it was like a small family reunion as well as the school. I knew one or two of the people there but not many; there were two sisters, both well over eighty years old, so the age groups were well represented. I enjoyed the evening—it had been well organised.

The following Thursday we left for France. After an uneventful crossing as far as I was concerned we docked at Zebrugge. Looking at my watch, I said to Jackie we must be running late. He had already been along to the shop, so he had the up-to-date news: "Oh aye, we're late—the boat broke down in the middle of the channel and we were stopped for a couple of hours." Just as well I am a heavy sleeper—I never heard a thing!

Our first stop of the day was at Vimy Ridge. Luckily our highly efficient chairman, Bill Loggie, gave us a rundown on the places we visited. If he hadn't, many of us would have been clueless. I was beginning to realise how little I knew about our modern history. Vimy Ridge was awe-inspiring. It is the monument dedicated to the Canadian Forces killed in the battle for Vimy Ridge—altogether sixty thousand lost their lives! After gazing at the monument, which is a work of art and paid for by the Canadian government, you can visit the battlefield, which is preserved more or less as it was when in use. We spent a very interesting couple of hours before we left, heading for the Cemetery at Longueval. As we got nearer to the place I was feeling a little apprehensive. The cemetery is from the First World War with three thousand graves in it. They built an extension to bury the Second World War casualties—there are only one hundred and twenty graves in the new part. I have visited the war memorial where my father's name appears in the cemetery at Fordyce Banffshire; it is on the outskirts of the village and surrounded by rural landscape. Of course, there you are in the farming heartland of the northeast of Scotland.

As we pulled up at the cemetery gate I was surprised to see how similar the surroundings were to the surroundings of my father's home village of Fordyce. Both are situated in rural areas with the main activity being farming. The only thing I noticed profoundly different was that the memorials were at different ends of the cemetery. I had no difficulty finding what I was looking for as I had the map courtesy of the people from the War Graves Commission. The thing that bothered me was that I had no feelings whatsoever—slightly emotional, perhaps, but otherwise I could have been looking at anybody's headstone; but then, of course, I had been fifty-nine years without a father so I had no idea what it should feel like. I was content within myself that finally I had made the pilgrimage and saw for myself the peaceful surroundings where my father was at rest; and yes, I did feel better about it—I no longer feel that there is something missing in my life. I had my video camera with me and recorded all the highlights of the holiday as I have done for years.

We left Longueval and headed for our hotel, which was in a small village near the town of Epernay. This turned out to be a bit of a laugh—the hotel owner was just starting to deal with touring buses and you could tell they had very little idea of how the meals should be served; the food was excellent but our evening meal would last for hours due to poor service. One of our party referred to it as Fawlty Towers and the man who was in charge had a good resemblance to Basil! On the Saturday it was a big day for the veterans—they were taking part in a parade at Compienge. Again my lack of knowledge of both wars shone through as I had never heard of the place. I did know what events took place there; whenever I heard them talk of the railway carriage, this was another piece of thrilling history for anybody like me who doesn't know the story. Briefly, what happened was in 1918: after the Germans were defeated the Allies delegated a place for them to sign the surrender, and they picked Compienge in the middle of Rethondes Forest outside the town. They used a railway carriage as a sort of office. In 1940, when the Germans overran the French, Hitler (to rub their noses in it!) ordered the French to surrender in the same place and in the railway carriage! Now the place is a sacred shrine and is only opened for heads of state and other important dignitaries. We were highly honoured as they opened it especially for the Normandy Veterans. Inside the building is the railway carriage, as well as an eternal flame and a tomb for the Unknown Soldier. Only six veterans were allowed inside the carriage to sign the visitor's book and no photographs were allowed. We had a very moving ceremony inside the building. When this was over we were invited to the Hotel de Ville (town house) for a reception. I have never seen so much champagne consumed in my life! I well and truly put my foot in it that day—one of the ladies who were doing the translation happened to stop to speak to me. I congratulated her on her grasp of the English language and she replied in her best Yorkshire accent that she should have as she belonged to Leeds! She just happened to be married to a Frenchman. Have you ever wished you had kept your trap shut?!

At the end of another lovely day and my head crammed full of history, we headed back to see Basil in Fawlty Towers. This was the worst evening of our stay as he had no staff to serve the meal—it was near eleven-o-clock when we left the table, although the food was excellent as was the wine. The next day we were bound for Verdun. Again, my ignorance of what happened during the First World War was evident and I was about to receive another marvellous history lesson, though if it is something you enjoy it's not a problem!

MORE HISTORY LESSONS

For our visit to Verdun we had a tour guide. They were usually brilliant and explained points that we would never have known about. Our guide that morning was a German woman who was married to a Frenchman. One thing that was prominent in that area was the wild poppies—they were everywhere. There are poems and songs about the war and the dancing red poppies are often mentioned. We were given a fascinating tour of the battle area and given all the statistics. It was mind-boggling! There were millions of men killed and wounded; they really never kept a proper tally. It was so horrendous; our guide told us that even today, if they have gales and trees are uprooted, they often find human remains under the base of a tree.

Our coach ended up at a kind of monastery, a huge structure. The cellar level is used to store the remains found on the battlefield. It was the brainchild of a priest. The building was funded by selling building blocks to the relatives of sons, husbands and any male relatives who were killed or missing during the battles. The name of the deceased was sculpted onto the block; in this way the walls were covered with the names of young men. Round the cellar were windows through which you could view the human remains if you so wished—mostly body parts; it was estimated there were parts of a million bodies stored in that awful place. There was a large steeple on the building, built in the shape of a bomb—it has a strong resemblance to the space shuttle that the Americans use in modern times, though the monastery was built long before the shuttle was designed. In front of the monastery there is a huge military cemetery with at least three thousand graves in it. One unique feature is that there are quite a few Muslims buried there; their headstones all face Mecca.

Leaving the monastery at Verdun with our heads throbbing with statistics, we were driven to the bottom of the mountain—and again we were totally overwhelmed with what we were about to witness. We arrived at a small entrance going into the side of the hill. It was level with the main road. We had to walk about twenty yards inside the mountain until we arrived at an area where there was a souvenir shop and various vending machines, possibly a small café. We were then handed a ticket, which allowed us entry to a small waiting area. In this area we boarded a small electric train, a two-carriage affair; then we took off through a curtain and for the next forty minutes we were absolutely overwhelmed with what we were seeing. The mountain was a labyrinth of tunnels, possibly twenty feet high and just as wide! We were driving through a self-contained city with every possible commodity needed to survive from day to day; once they had all the supplies inside you could close the outside door and nobody would know you were there. This place was used during the battle at Verdun to treat the wounded; it was also a rest and recreational area for the troops before they returned to battle. It was truly remarkable. The French have again preserved this place and it is now a major tourist attraction. We headed back to Fawlty Towers for our evening meal and straight to bed as we had another full day sightseeing in the morning.

Our next day was another adventure but much more pleasurable. This time we were visiting a distillery where they made champagne. There are hundreds, similar to our own whisky distilleries. The one we visited was called Mercier; this was one of the few cellars the Nazis never found, so its contents were more of less intact after the war. This was another fascinating place. You entered a lift and dropped down nine meters; after exiting the lift we boarded a small train and for the next forty minutes we drove along tunnels with crates of bottles stacked from the floor to the ceiling! All the time we had a guide telling us the history of the place. At intervals along the way there were statues and murals painted on the walls. At the end of our tour the guide told us the statistics; the most mind-boggling was the fact that there were ninety-six million bottles stored in that cellar! He was French so I asked him to repeat the figure, just to make sure I was hearing properly.

Another fascinating detail about the place was that it was the only cellar the Nazis never found during the war. As far as I could understand, the contents of the cellar were more or less intact when the war finished. After we were given the customary sample bait to encourage you to buy a bottle, we moved on.

Next stop was a smallholding, like one of our crofts. It was like a cottage industry with these smallholdings producing champagne on a much smaller scale. The one we visited produced less than five thousand bottles, but it was quite interesting to see. We were again given a sample but I was not persuaded to purchase a bottle. Moving on, we finished our day with a cruise along the River Meuse; it was quite nice with a couple of French Chateaux up on the hillside. On the way back to the hotel we did a detour to the city of Rheims, so that we could visit the place where the Germans surrendered at the end of World War Two on the 7th May 1945. I was totally disappointed with the place after the pomp and ceremony at Compienge. This place looked like a hostel for the homeless tucked away behind the railway station; not very impressive, but the history was there—another piece of education as far as I was concerned.

As we left our hotel the next day we were on our way home, but our excellent Chairman never wasted a minute of our holiday time and on the way back to the ferry boat we had another important place of interest to visit—La Coppelle. I think that is the proper way to spell the name. In my ignorance I had to ask what that meant, and one of the more knowledgeable of our party explained it meant The Rocket, or words to that effect. We were going to visit the site where Hitler launched his V2 doodlebugs. I was overwhelmed since I had never heard of the place, but believe me it lived up to all my expectations. As seemed to be the norm in that part of France, everything was underground. The Tunnel leading into the main chamber was driven by slave labourers; it was fascinating for me as I had worked underground, and seeing the drill marks on the tunnel walls was quite mind-boggling; to people who had no idea I suppose it meant nothing. We were given a headset and radio so that we had a running commentary as you walked through the place. I was totally fascinated. In the main chamber they had models of the rockets suspended from the roof! The roof was another statistic worth noting—it was a huge dome shaped structure with a fifteen-foot thick layer of reinforced concrete. There would have been a lot of blood, sweat and tears associated with that place before it was completed. I had experienced the lot and worked for German bosses; we were free but they still wanted their pound of flesh every shift.

After such a marvellous holiday, which was interesting from the minute we landed in France, we headed for a huge Hypermarket near Dunkirk so that we could stock up with cheap booze before we headed for home. What a way to end such a wonderful experience!

◆   ◆   ◆

When I started this account of my life it was a sort of protest against war and the fact that people lose their lives fighting wars; wives loose their husbands and children lose their fathers. Sadly, as I continue with this tale, once again two British soldiers have been killed in Iraq this past week; one was a twenty-year-old boy, single, with no family, which, as far as I am concerned, is a blessing; the other chap's particulars have not been released yet so we don't know what his status was. Another thing that strikes me is that all the countries in which these types of events take place are near the centre of where the bible was founded; you would hope these people would be so well brought up that war would be the furthest thing from their minds! But instead of peace and gentleness, some of the worst atrocities known to mankind are being committed in that very place; then people try and get you to believe in the bible—yet they can't explain why these things are allowed to happen.

Last week, in one of the weekend supplement magazines, was an article that jumped out at me; but then this was one of my pet hates—the fact that war deprived me of my father and even to this day I often wish I at least knew what he was like. My interpretation of the article was that it was written by a young lady in her middle twenties; her mother was an actress from the swinging sixties who had the girl and brought her up as a single parent. The following statement was what she told the magazine reporter: "It's not easy if a child wants a dad and he's not there. Mum grew up with a perfect family. She doesn't know what it's like." Unfortunately I didn't keep the whole article so I have no names, but my point is that the trend nowadays is for single girls to bring up their offspring single-handed. I often wonder how many of the kids will eventually miss the fact that they have no father; it's not the first time I have been told not to be silly when I tried to explain how much I missed my real father during my lifetime—but it's like the young lady said: "She doesn't know what it's like."

Anyhow, that whinge over, it's back to the wonderful holiday I had just experienced! I had made a few friends with the lads from the Normandy Veterans Association and due to my efforts to help I was made an honorary member; now, four years later, I am still involved and still enjoy their company.

To keep myself fit I still walked a few miles daily. I had joined the gym but found that I could do with something else to keep my mind active. Jigsaw puzzles are okay now and again, but I needed something more challenging. I was visiting my brother one day; he had an ancient computer lying unused, so I asked if he wanted to sell it. We made a deal and I loaded it into the boot of my car. This was great! I now had something else to keep me occupied.

My daughter arrived at the house one day and asked if I would be interested in looking after a garden for an elderly lady. It was just a postage-stamp size, so I agreed to take it on. It got me out of the house every second week. The garden took about an hour, but by the time I had tea and a blether, it lasted two and a half hours. A lot of elderly people living on their own can be very lonely. I never realised there were so many until I got involved with gardening. The next person to offer me a job was our minister. Again, it was a postage-stamp sized garden, so I now had two as well as my own to tend. Before long I was doing six gardens and turning down as many! I could be employed fulltime if I cared, but six is plenty. My heart is damaged so I have to be careful, my main enemy being tiredness. But every new day is a bonus! I have been present when three people suffered a heart attack—they were less fortunate than me and didn't survive.

We had a very quiet life. The rest of that year I attended one or two parades with the N.V.A lads—the chairman and I along with our ladies visited St Valery-en-Caux, a place often spoken about in the Highland region due to the fact that the Highland division was captured there during the war. Many young Highlanders are buried there, so it was one of my ambitions to pay a visit, courtesy of the Inverness Town Twinning committee. We travelled on their coach and enjoyed a wonderful six days in that lovely little town. The hospitality shown by the Magnan family was just as you would receive in the Scottish Highlands, but then again their town is very like the little fishing towns situated around the Scottish coast. Thierry and Annick and their two lovely boys made us feel as though we were at home and nothing was too much trouble for them. We will be indebted to them for the rest of our lives. We visited our eldest granddaughter in Edinburgh a couple of times; otherwise we had very little excitement.

Our next big adventure was the N.V.A. trip to Holland the first week in May to attend the Fifty Eighth Liberation parade in a place called Wanganen. The salute was taken by Prince Bernhard of the Netherlands, a very frail old man aged around eighty. He was involved in the war. As usual we were treated with the greatest of respect, but then the Dutch and French seemed to appreciate the fact that they are free and show more patriotism than we Brits do. I get the feeling we take it for granted. The poor turnout on Remembrance Sunday reflects my statement. As usual, we had a wonderful holiday with the Normandy Veterans. Bill Loggie had organised a full programme of places of interest.

My heart attack was now two years old and I felt as though I was back to peak fitness, although I was still prone to having the odd bout of angina—nothing serious but it was still evident. Around this time I was in contact with my younger sister Irene. She and her husband Jess run their own business supplying agricultural plant and the spares that go with them. She was having difficulty getting people to work in their stores department and had a vacancy at that time. She asked if I would be interested in the job and, more to the point, would I be fit enough for it? I was over the moon with the offer since I had not considered ever working again. I had no idea what the job consisted of but I was willing to give it a go. My sister was really looking for me to do a lot of the paperwork, but that was not really my scene; if there was work to be done I had to get stuck in! I had not anticipated the weight of the boxes of bolts and spares that were a big part of their daily throughput of stock. Within three days I realised I had made a mistake—I was not fit to work an eight-hour day and I started getting angina pains, so there was no point in trying to carry on. I had to admit defeat and finish my short time as a storeman. Clearly my working career was well and truly over. I still do a bit of gardening for some elderly ladies around town, but only if the job lasts about two hours. I quite enjoy it and it gets me out and about. I usually finish up about the end of November until the end of March; during the dead of winter months I get stuck into a bit of DIY and tidy up around the house. I also do a fair amount of walking to keep my fitness up. It is fine when the weather is favourable, but I have great difficulty with the cold, especially around my legs.

We are nearing the end of 2003 and there is a great adventure ahead of us. Next year, if there is a seat for us on the N.V.A. coach, we are heading for Normandy to take part in the sixtieth anniversary of the Normandy Offensive. The rules are that the Veterans get the first option of the seats on the coach; then, if there are any left over, we are invited to join them. So I am keeping my fingers crossed that Jess and I are allowed to go. What an honour that will be, especially for me; but it will be into the New Year before anything is confirmed. There will be a lot of work for the Chairman to plan this very special pilgrimage.

NORMANDY

Our family were dealt a horrific blow when my sister's husband was diagnosed with a severe illness. He put up a wonderful fight against it but sadly passed away. He was a lovely big man loved by all our family and he is sadly missed by us all.

Before the end of January 2004 we had been given conformation that we had been lucky enough to obtain seats on the Veterans Coach bound for Normandy on 2nd June. It was a good way off but I still found it quite exciting, and quite a mystery, as I had no idea what lay ahead of us although I had been involved with the Veterans for the past couple of years and had been made an Honorary Member at the last dinner dance we attended. I had also taken part in a few parades with them, so I thought I was aware of the format. In the meantime the War in Iraq was going full tilt. The invasion to topple Saddam Hussein was over, but the Americans were now engaged in a battle against terrorists; every day there were reports of American casualties. This was not what had been planned as it was supposed to be a quick sweep through Iraq, topple Saddam, elect an Iraqi government, and then withdraw all foreign troops and they would live happily ever after; but I am afraid not all fairy stories have a nice ending.

The 2nd of June was soon upon us and we were gathering in Church Street in Inverness. It was an early start as we had a long haul to get to Hull in time to catch the overnight Ferry to Belgium. Bill, the chairman, had his hands full right up until we departed. One or two of the old boys who had wanted so much to be in Normandy for the pilgrimage were unable to travel at the last minute due to various reasons, mainly health, so their places had to be allocated to others who were on the waiting list. We had a full complement of fifty when we left our starting point—twenty-five veterans and twenty-five carers and helpers as well as one or two partners.

The journey south passed without incident. There was the usual banter; we had our usual comfort stops, and also stops to pick up one or two couples on the way. We had our annual stop at Lockerbie where we had lunch at the local ex-servicemen's club and possibly some refreshment if you were so inclined.

We arrived in Hull with plenty time to spare, and then boarded the ship at our leisure. This was our holiday started, as far as we were concerned; part of our package was that we had a five-course meal and a breakfast on board the boat. The food is usually excellent and you are spoiled for choice. As we don't often meet the other members of the party, we usually have a few drinks before heading for bed. Again, the crossing was smooth and without any hitches. We arrived on time and were soon on our coach again, heading for our first place of interest. Our chairman used every minute available; we were heading for the Belgian town of Poperinge to visit the original headquarters of the Toc-H organisation at Talbot House. This was a rest centre for the troops of the First World War, opened in 1915 by a couple of Army Chaplains; it had recreational facilities and places of worship. One outstanding feature was that the minute you entered the door your army rank ceased to exist and everyone was treated as equals. We spent over an hour in the magnificent old building and received the customary cup of tea before boarding our coach and heading for our hotel in a little seaside town called Blonville-sur-mar, facing the English Channel and not far from the beaches where the battle for Normandy took place. The hotel was an old French building, but they have much more character than the modern Nova Type buildings. We were early to bed the first night as we had early starts for the first couple of days, and possibly long days; we were entering unknown territory and didn't know what to expect.

Bright and early next morning, we had breakfast and started boarding the coach bound for a place I had never heard of. My knowledge of the Normandy area of France was practically zilch. The reason for this was possibly the fact that none of my relatives had been involved in the invasion. We had very little communication facilities at the time of the invasion and the school never mentioned the Second World War so the place names being bandied about were totally alien to us. That first morning our destination was Colville/Montgomery; the latter part of the name was in honour of our great leader Field Marshall Montgomery. I didn't know such a place existed! Dead on time we set off and soon came up against our modern way of life and the fear of terrorism—every road junction was manned by armed police/soldiers and there were restrictions on which road we were allowed to travel. It was busy as quite a few places were holding ceremonies and parades to mark the 60th anniversary of the D-Day invasions, although the next day was the official day.

We arrived at our destination in plenty time. Colville/Montgomery was a small seaside town with a statue of Montgomery in the square looking out towards the English channel where so many of his men gave their precious lives as they started the defeat of Hitler and his army of thugs. It was quite a small parade that morning and was over in about an hour. The bit that fascinated me was the beach—it was dead flat with not one inch of cover for an invading army to take advantage of! As you stepped off the beach onto the road, it is doubtful if you would have stepped up more than eight to ten inches.

From C.M. our next destination was Caen where there was a British garden of remembrance. This was due to be inaugurated by HRH Prince Charles. This turned out to be the worst couple of hours of our whole visit. We were all seated in a sort of arena where there was a military band playing. The Royal party were on a platform but it was below the level of where we were sitting so we were unable to see anything! It was a searing hot day with temperatures touching thirty-five degrees. Our instructions were to be seated around two-o-clock, which we did, but the heat soon became rather unbearable and the older men in our party began to burn. Luckily the French people realised there was a problem and started to supply bottles of water and they also had students with water sprays, spraying people's heads and faces; their quick action saved a rather nasty situation as a lot of our party were rather severely burned, even to the extent of being blistered. At least seventy percent of the audience were aged around eighty; it was rather inconsiderate of the organisers to allow the whole ceremony to be nearly two hours late in starting and keep people sitting in the most awful heat imaginable—something we native Highlanders are not altogether used to. To crown it all there were very few people who could see what was going on so it was a complete waste of time for everybody concerned. Another whinge on my behalf: the toilet conditions were atrocious—Porta-loos! As usual, they soon get blocked and you can imagine the stench as the sun got hotter and hotter. It was totally disgusting.

But we survived the ordeal. We never saw the Gardens of the Prince of Wales, but we all ended up with a lovely suntan! It was getting near eight-o-clock when we arrived back at Blonville, but they had a lovely dinner waiting for us. The starter was a huge plate of prawns. Quite a few at our table didn't like shellfish so I was able to have a feast fit for royalty! Then a few glasses of wine and we were off to bed. The next day was to be the big one—another adventure, and it promised to be another exciting day for me. We were going to make history as the parade at Arromanches was to be the final time the Normandy veterans would be on parade on this famous battle arena. I was looking forward to being there but first we had a huge parade at Bayaux.

Wednesday 6th June 2004 will be a day etched in my memory for ever. I was about to embark on a trip that proved to be one of the outstanding features of my life—being present at the final celebration of the battle that was to end the Second World War! It was a privilege to find ourselves in the company of such exalted people as the Queen, the Prime Minister, Chirac the French President and many other dignitaries—such an experience was way beyond my wildest dreams.

Our first pilgrimage that morning was to the cemetery at Bayaux. There was a huge parade and memorial service. It is hard to put a figure on how many people were there, but it would have been well over twenty thousand. The place was heaving with Veterans from all regiments of the British Army, Air Force and Navy, all men near the age of eighty. Every major battlefield along the Normandy Coast was holding parades and services that morning, so it was very busy; the sun was shining in Bayaux but there was mist in some areas, causing programmes to be disrupted. Our parade and service was delayed for over an hour as we waited for the arrival of the French President who was with President Bush at the American Cemetery at Omaha. By the time the service started it was difficult to say how many people were present, but the place was jam-packed. By mid-morning the heat was tremendous. One piece of luck we had was that there were plenty trees around so they did offer a bit of shade. By twelve-o-clock the ceremonies were complete at Bayaux and we were ready to move on; but the congestion outside the cemetery was utter chaos! It was stated that there were one hundred and sixty-one coaches from the U.K. alone. If each carried fifty people, that accounted for over eight thousand bodies along with coaches from Holland, Germany and Scandinavia, not to mention people who had made the journey by car. Can you imagine the headache trying to get some semblance of order with well in excess of possibly twenty-thousand bodies milling about, many of them disabled and in wheelchairs? We had no other option but to find a space under the trees and sit it out till our coach arrived to take us to our next destination, Arromanches.

We boarded our coach about 4 p.m. and made the short journey to the little seaside town, which was about to take on an air of importance for that evening as the final episode of the Sixtieth Anniversary Of the Normandy Invasion took place in the presence of Her Majesty the Queen. Arromanches looked like the setting for a war movie—it was the perfect arena for the drama that was about to unfold: firstly, the dignitaries arrived and proceeded to their seats on the raised platform; out in the bay was the Mulberry Harbour remains; behind that was a Royal Navy Frigate which fired a twenty-one gun salute during the proceedings. Along the beach were various landing craft of the type used sixty years ago. As the curtain went up the veterans started to enter the square and march past the raised dais where her Majesty the Queen watched them file past. They did this twice as it was a very short distance. They then halted and the Queen, Prince Phillip and President Chirac carried out a walkabout between the ranks of veterans. We then had a twenty-one-gun salute carried out by the Frigates anchored just beyond the remains of the Mulberry Harbour. The setting for this historic occasion could not have been manufactured by a television or movie studio—it was just perfect. Finally, after much emotion and the singing of Auld Lang Syne, the final curtain was brought down and we started to disperse and head back up the narrow streets to where our coaches were waiting to pick us up. This was the start of another logistical nightmare—can you imagine between fifteen and twenty thousand people, many of them disabled, trying to get on board coaches that could only enter the village in single file? In our case we waited till well after ten-o-clock before we were able to get on board. By the time we arrived back at our hotel it was nearing midnight. But it had been a wonderful day—one of my lifetime highlights! It was no problem going to sleep that night, as we were totally exhausted.

All the pressure was off us now. The important parades were passed. We could now enjoy a more leisurely break and visit places of interest. The 7th of June saw us driving along the coast, passing our day visiting memorials and cemeteries that had been requested by the members. That day was another historical adventure for me as I would be visiting places I had never really heard of, the first being Ranville Cemetery, Ranville being the first place to be liberated in 1944. There was a huge cemetery there, beautifully kept, and also a lovely old church with a window dedicated to the Airborne Division. We were following the footsteps of the German Chancellor, Gerhard Schroeder, who had paid his homage the previous day. From there we drove on, passing the famous Pegasus Bridge, complete with the famous little Café. The area was swarming with Americans so we kept going until we reached the magnificent memorial at Sword Beach. It was fascinating, as was the flat beach where the battles took place. I was overawed that a beach with no cover whatsoever had been chosen to mount an attack. Leaving Sword Beach, we headed for Bayeux once again where we had lunch and visited the famous Caen Bayeux Tapestries. Early afternoon we were searching for a very interesting place; again, I had never heard of it. The only sign that anything ever happened there is a couple of plaques cemented into a wall and telling the brief story of Le-Fresne-Camilly. This was the site of the first landing strip built under enemy fire from the 10th to 17th June 1944. This was to allow Allied aircraft to land. Stopping long enough to take some photos, we were soon on our way again to yet another magnificent piece of architecture. This was the tribute to the American servicemen who gave their lives at Omaha Beach. It is something to behold with around ten thousand Crosses and Stars of David. From a viewing platform you can view the actual beach. It was the complete opposite to the others as it was quite a steep slope from the beach to the higher ground level. We were again following in the footsteps of a famous world leader as president George Bush had been there a couple of days earlier. Our next stop was a complete contrast to the other places we had visited—the German Military Cemetery at La Cambe—yet another fascinating place but so dull and drab looking. Whereas the Americans had sparkling white granite-like headstones, the Germans had grey and brown colours and most of the headstones were lying flat, completely different but nonetheless worth the effort of going to see it.

The day was wearing on and we still had quite a long drive back to our hotel. We had one more request to fulfil that day—one of our members was an Aircrew member during the war and he had friends from a crashed bomber buried in Cheux Cemetery. We soon found all six lads' graves; they were buried side by side. Our friend was happy he had found what he had come for, so we boarded our coach and headed back to our hotel for a late dinner once again.

One of our days we dedicated to visiting St Valery en Caux, the small town where the 51st Highland Division were overwhelmed in 1940. They have strong links with the Highland Region so we were made very welcome. I had already visited St Valery so I knew some of the people there. It is a lovely little place and they have not forgotten the sacrifice given by the Scottish Soldiers of the Highland Division. From St Valery we had a leisurely drive back to our hotel. An early night was on the cards as we were heading for home next morning. We still had business to attend to on the way home with another Cemetery in Le Harve. One of our members had mates buried there so his request was granted before we made for the port and the ship that took us back to the U.K.

That year it was Branch 60 Highland and Islands' turn to host the yearly parade of remembrance. It was held in Dingwall where a march past was held along the main street led by the young people of the local Pipe Band. There was a good turnout from all over Scotland. After the parade we had a good Celeidh in the British Legion Social Club. We started off 20.05 in much the same way as our previous years, taking life easy until the weather got better.

We had one weekend in Edinburgh with our eldest granddaughter. During that time we visited East Fortune to see the wonderful Concorde. It was well worth the effort. On the Sunday the granddaughter trailed us for about the tenth time to Edinburgh Zoo. I am beginning to get to know the animals by their names, but it is always an interesting day and a beautiful walk. Back home I was doing my good deeds by gardening for elderly ladies in Inverness. It keeps me amused and the old dears are delighted to get the grass cut and the borders tidied up.

The Normandy Veterans were going to Holland again. This year they were invited to take part in a couple of parades marking the 60th anniversary of the Liberation of Europe. We would be staying in the little town of Zeddam near the German border. As usual our chairman had a full programme for us to enjoy. We left Inverness on the 2nd of May and had the usual haul to Hull where we boarded the Ferry for Rotterdam. After a short drive through Holland we arrived at our first destination, the huge flower mart at Aalsmeer where we were in time to see part of the auction taking place. People from all over the world buy flowers on-line; it is a fully automated system and quite fascinating to watch. The weather was poor but everything took place under cover. An hour or so later we were on our way to another magnificent display of flowers at Kukenhof. This is reputed to be the biggest flower show in the world. It would certainly take first prize for the display of tulips.

We spent quite a while there before moving towards our hotel. Some of our members have been there for at least three times before, so they know the family that run the Familiehotel Englebarts. It is a lovely place—the people are nice and the food is first class. Day two and we had a very lax programme. At midday we got ready to visit a local castle for a guided tour. This was the Huis Berg Castle in nearby Herringberg. Later in the evening we had been invited to take part in the local Zeddam Remberance Service. This turned out to be a bit of a disaster as the heavens opened and the rain just about washed us out! Next morning we were up and dressed in our best ceremonial gear as we were taking part in a big parade in the town of Wageningen. We were there at the request of the Organising Committee to be involved in their parade marking the 60th anniversary of the Liberation of that part of Europe. We had been there two years before; there had been a big parade but it was tiny compared to this one, which would probably be the last, especially for the veterans as age was taking its toll. There were Pipe Bands from Scotland, Canada and Holland, as well as representatives from all over, including old soldiers and men of the Modern Dutch Armed forces. The march past salute was normally taken by the old Prince Bernhard who was a veteran in his own right, but sadly he had passed away earlier in the year aged eighty so the honour fell to his twenty-year-old grandson. As this was the last parade we would attend I was determined to take part; normally I stayed out of the parades and filmed it for our veterans but this time I was in it for real. We were lined up five abreast quite some distance from the centre of the town. Our group were about six from the front. Suddenly the Pipe Bands burst into life and we were off marching! Pipe music does something for your spirit and you just seem to float. The march was about three miles long and there must have been enough people on parade to stretch the full length. As we moved nearer the town centre the crowd started to get bigger. Both sides of the street were jam-packed. We had to close ranks until at one point we were single file. There were thousands and thousands of people clapping and cheering, hugging and kissing people as we gloried on past the raised Dais where Prince Bernhard in full Military uniform took the salute. It was a day I will never forget—an experience I never ever dreamed of, but the Dutch know how to have a remembrance parade and they appreciate the fact they are free! Waganingen is a place that will be etched in my memory forever; that parade will not be forgotten along with other parts of Holland and the people are always so friendly.

Our next day on the agenda might not reach the peaks that our Anniversary Parade did but for me it was another one of my ambitions achieved. The 6th of May was dedicated to visiting memorials and cemeteries at the request of our members; some of them had relatives and also mates buried in Holland. Our first call was at Reichswald, just across the German Border—a huge burial ground with many Scottish young men buried there. Many of the graves contained Aircrew. The reason for this, as I was told, was that this was the route that the bombers were ordered to pass through after their bombing raids—something to do with saving fuel. The Germans soon cottoned on and it was just a slaughter.

Our next visit was to the town of Uden. Again the cemetery was near the town centre and had quite a few Scottish soldiers buried there. Then on to the town of Arnhem, where we visited the Airborne Museum—a very interesting place. From there we travelled the short distance to Osterbeck Cemetery where many of the Airborne troops are buried. Again, it is a huge place. One of our members had a cousin buried there. On the move again and we were about to fulfil one of my life ambitions by being able to walk across the Arnhem Bridge, famous for the movie A BRIDGE TOO FAR! It is quite a large structure and crosses the Rhine, a very busy waterway. Another two important bridges were crossed that day, one being Nijmegen and the other the Grave.

Our holiday was getting near an end; one more day to go and it was to be a leisurely sort of day with a visit to the Netherlands Open Air museum. We could hear what kind of day it was with the rain battering against the bedroom window, so our visit to the museum was a complete washout although we did manage to see a wonderful three-dimensional display in a huge plastic bubble. Although it was wet we enjoyed our visit.

We took our leave of the Family Engelbarts and started our journey to the ferry. We had a couple of places to visit on the way, the first being the Royal Dutch Porcelain factory at Deft. It was well worth the visit. Onward to Rotterdam Harbour where we were booked for a 75-minute cruise of the biggest harbour in the world; it was an interesting tour and we passed huge container ships form every part of the world. After that breathtaking week it was back to the Ferry, a smooth sail across the Channel/North Sea and the long haul home by coach.

The veterans were not finished yet—we still had one more Parade! This year in Brechin, so early on the morning of 5th June we set off by coach to take part in Branch 85 Tayside and Mearns Veterans Re-union. It was a fine day out with the usual Parade marching to a Pipe Band. The local High School unveiled a Plaque that had been commissioned by a local artist. This was to commemorate the Second World War. We had very little planned until later on in July when we had an exciting few days planned. If you remember back to our ill-fated jaunt to Ullapool, you might recall the chap Frank who was the third member of our party; his wife was German and they had returned to her homeland thirty years previously. We had lost touch with them when out of the blue we had a letter asking if we were the same family they had been neighbours with all those years ago! We replied that we were and they replied that Hilda (the Mother) and Susan (the daughter) were coming to Inverness in July and they would like to visit us. We were delighted and looked forward to seeing them again. We had three wonderful visits from them and renewed an old friendship.

We hope to see them again in the near future. I continued with my gardening jobs; thankfully it was a good summer. We had a get-together with the Veterans at their yearly Dinner/Dance in Dingwall. A lovely evening was had by all. Jess and I decided to have a holiday later in October; my younger brother Geordie, another Ullapool adventurer who was married and lived in Penzance, was not keeping too well so we decided to have a week with him and his lovely wife Diane; then we would head for London where I would have an army reunion in Milton Keynes; so we decided to stay for a few days with my cousin Lydia and Steve before we came home.

On the 13th of October we left Inverness bound for Penzance. It must be the most difficult place in Britain to get to from our part of the world—it takes ages! As we are non-fliers we have to depend on the trains and the fastest we can get to Penzance is fourteen and a half hours; but we have done the journey quite a few times so we are well aware what it entails. We arrived dead on time, fair play to the rail companies! My brother Geordie and Diane were waiting for us. He didn't seem to be his usual self and when we reached their house he was really toiling; the walk from the street up the steps to their living room seemed to be too much for him. Both Jess and I were really worried about the condition he was in. Once

Geordie regained his composure we had a few drams before retiring to bed. We did our usual tour of the beauty spots with Geordie and Diane and I fulfilled yet another ambition by spending a day at the wonderful Eden Project. Soon it was time to take our leave and head for London where we were meeting up with my cousin Lydia and Steve who live in Watford; they had taken a few days holiday so that we could have time together. Steve is a Londoner so he knows the city like the back of his hand and he was prepared to take us anywhere we wished to go. Another of my ambitions was to visit the Imperial War Museum, so Steve took us there and we had a lovely few hours browsing around the wonderful old building with its artefacts of war.

On the Saturday I was attending an army reunion in Milton Keynes. Steve dropped me off at the T.A. Barracks where I was staying overnight and said he would pick me up in the morning at 10 a.m. I was waiting at the gates about five-to-ten but no sign of my transport; eventually he arrived when it had just gone twenty past. I looked in the car and noticed he was alone. On asking where the ladies were, Steve told me Jess had had a slight accident and was waiting at home. When I got to the flat in Watford I was in for a shock. Jess was pretty badly injured. She had stumbled whilst getting out of the car and landed full force on the street, causing severe bruising and a gash to her head. This mishap put a slight damper on our holiday; although she bravely carried on, she needed quite a bit of help.

It was getting near time to go home and I had a bit of a dilemma: how was I going to manage to get four pieces of luggage and an invalid wife on board a train? Thankfully we had no changes till we reached Inverness. Steve, born and bread in London, had all the answers at his fingertips! I am sure we have "Teauchter" stamped on our foreheads when we are far away from the High-lands. One quick phone call to Steve and everything was more or less arranged. It was after six-o-clock in the evening so we were too late to arrange things that night, but the railway people gave us a Reference Number. Next morning we had to contact the company we were travelling home with, giving them plenty time to make arrangements. Our travel company was G.N.E.R and within minutes of speaking to the gentleman at the desk we had a wheelchair arranged to get my wife from our car to the train and an attendant to push it. We had about twenty minutes to wait before we could board the train so the chap left us just off the platform and said he would be back in ten minutes; true to his word we were heading for our carriage with plenty time to spare when our attendant, a huge coloured chap, returned. He had also contacted Inverness to arrange a wheelchair to meet us when we arrived home. My praise for the G.N.E.R company couldn't be high enough. I know they can have problems that cause disruption to people's lives, but they did us proud that day and we both really appreciated it.

Home safely, we settled down for the winter with nothing really planned. My wife was still fairly immobile so I had to carry out some of the duties she normally did. I decided to do a bit of renovation that included quite a bit of DIY, but I had done this many times before so I paced myself and worked for about four hours per day.

On the 3rd of November I had an important engagement to keep. I had been invited to attend the opening of the new Heart and Stroke facility at the local hospital; five of us heart attack victims were to be presented to the Princess Royal, Princess Anne! I had never been close to any member of the royal family and was quite excited to meet the Princess, even though many bad stories had been written about her. But I can only give my opinion as I found her. As she walked into the room the first thing you notice is how tiny she is and with a figure that Twiggy would have been proud of! She chatted to quite a few of the people present before she reached us. After the formal introduction she chatted away, asking about our new lifestyle since the heart attack. She had obviously done a bit of homework on heart trouble as she was well clued up on this scourge of Scotland.

Life was back to normal. I hate the dark evenings although I always have things to do. I prefer it when it is bright till bedtime, but we have four seasons so we have to take the good with the bad. Near the end of November that brilliant Irish football genius, Georgie Best, was having severe health problems; poor George had been chastised in the press because his illness was self-inflicted, but his problem is a severe disease that is very difficult to shake free from. Alcoholism to some people is as deadly as Aids. Not only does it destroy the person drinking but also the family who have to put up with the weird behaviour of the alcoholic—the lies, deceit and all the other bad things that go along with that awful disease.

George Best could no longer fight his health problem and finally died. He was given what nearly amounted to a state funeral, televised from start to finish on the 3rd of December 2005. Both my wife and I are very keen football fans, mostly armchair now, but we settled down to watch the final journey of the great George Best. I found the service very moving and emotional. I had never seen George play live but had watched Dennis Law and Bobby Charlton when I worked in England. The service over, they started to move the coffin to the door when suddenly our phone rang and my sister-in-law from Cornwall was on the other end:

she was clearly distressed and it took a few seconds to realise she was telling me my brother Geordie had passed away that morning!

I can't really describe the feeling that ran through my body. I was totally devastated and found it hard to take in. My brother was popular with lots of people and that reflected on the crowd that turned up at his funeral. We made the journey to Penzance by car this time. It was the best option for us at that time but it is a long, tiring journey that I wouldn't like to make too often.

◆   ◆   ◆

Well folks, that's me right up to date. I am sixty-eight today and what you have just read is my life story, which I would dedicate as a protest against all war. We are still having to use guns in Iraq with ninety eight young British soldiers killed and the horrendous figure of young Americans rising almost daily—the mind boggles. The last casualty list from America was well over two thousand; add to that the thousands of Iraqi casualties—and for what? Will it achieve peace in our lifetime? I doubt it.

I am now settling down to have another Christmas and hopefully the next year may be the end of all wars and conflicts. Why can't we live in peace? After all, we are only passing through this world and our time is limited—very short for some and slightly longer for others; unfortunately there is no guarantee.

◆   ◆   ◆

Januaury 2006 and I have spent the month going over my book, correcting bits and pieces. The news has been bad from Iraq—another two Scottish Soldiers killed, young men in their prime. The total now stands at one hundred. One of the chaps has left three bairns orphaned, another three to face an ever-increasing difficult and dangerous world; their ordeal will be more difficult than what I had to face as we didn't have the horrors of drugs, terrorists, paedophiles and all the other nasties that are now an accepted part of life. One last joke, if you like to call it that, is that the Iraqi dictator Saddam Hussein who is the supposed reason for this war is now on trial for the atrocities he committed; but watching the report on the television you get the impression that he is still dictating how the trial should be conducted and walks out of the court when he feels like it. Next time he storms out of the place they should string him the way he did to so many other poor innocent people during his time in charge. Many of them never even had the offer of a fair trial.

◆   ◆   ◆

Well, folks, it is now March 2007—how time flies! I gave up on this writing lark, but have a new lease of life so I promise it will be finished and printed this year. I am into my 69th year, so I will do my best. Last year we spent ten lovely days cruising the Rhine with the Normandy Veterans; then our Granddaughter got married and we are also now four generations with the birth of our Great Granddaughter Chloe. In June I had the most heartbreaking decision to make—to have our wonderful little pal Kizzy put to sleep; she was our pet Shiz Tsu, a wonderful companion, but she was failing fast and there was no cure so the kindest thing was to end her misery. It is hard to get over even though people insist she was only a dog.

We had a trip to Cornwall to see my late brother Geordie's family. Apart from that the year passed without a lot of excitement. Saddam Hussein has gone but they are still fighting over Iraq. The death toll is mounting daily—more widows and more children left fatherless. It would be lovely if we could all live in harmony without conflict.

This year we celebrate 50 years of marriage. Here's hoping we have many years to come. My book of the next twenty years will be published in twenty years' time!

THE END

ABOUT THE AUTHOR

Bert Scorgie was born into a family with strong military connections. His Grandfather, Father, and both uncles were involved in both World Wars. His father was one of the B.E.F 51st Highland Division sacrificed at Dunkirk. "I look back and wonder what for," the author says, "but life for me had to go on."

The author spent 3/4 years of his prime employed as a Tunnel Miner working on the Hydro Schemes in the Highlands of Scotland. The tunnels were under peat and various different soils and clay. The miners went by the glamorous name of the Tunnel Tigers, hence the title *Tigers Under the Turf*—but tunnel mining was anything but glamorous!

More information at www.diadembooks.com/scorgie.htm

978-0-595-45544-7
0-595-45544-1

Printed in the United Kingdom
by Lightning Source UK Ltd.
124582UK00001B/181-183/A